France
FROM THE AIR
Yann Arthus-Bertrand

Introduction by Charles Osgood
Text by Patrick Poivre d'Arvor

Captions and interviews by Catherine Guigon

Translated from the French by Nicholas Elliott

All photographs by Yann Arthus-Bertrand, except those on pages 125 and 130–31 (Claudius Thiriet) and on pages 252–53, 262, 264–65, 296–97, and 310–11 (François Jourdan), Altitude Agency.

Abrams, New York

The Diversity of France

This is a book for all who love France and all that France stands for. A book for those whose spirits rise on the long, poplar-lined country roads into Picardy, or before the vast horizons of the wheat fields of the Beauce. For those who dream of the golden, incense-smoked interior of Notre-Dame on a Friday night, when the rush hour crowds on their way home stop to light candles and listen quietly to the plainsong.

Over the last few years, in a series of wonderful books, Yann Arthus-Bertrand has made us see the world in a different way, most memorably in his UNESCO-supported *Earth from the Air*. Now he has returned home to give us a France viewed with deep knowledge, curiosity, delight, and what one can only call tenderness. These days we are so often told that we are part of, and should aspire to, the one global culture of modernity; but this book is about difference, and as such, it is a rebuke to regularisation, uniformity, and monotony in thinking and being.

"France's name is diversity" said the great medievalist Lucien Febvre. Indeed, it has been axiomatic among writers that France is diverse to the point of absurdity, "varied to a degree met in few countries in the world." As any traveller knows, every part of the country obstinately betrays an extraordinary local character in food and drink, custom and dialect, field and building styles. Regional dialects still proliferate in a land where in the mid-nineteenth century, astonishingly, half of the communities were largely non-French speaking. Even the measurement of wine casks has a bewildering range of names and capacities between one *pays* and another. Every town, every region, and in some parts almost every valley (in Burgundy even every hillside!) has its own character, its own soil and custom of cultivation, all part of what Alexis de Tocqueville aptly calls "a way of life and a way of death."

And these differences inform every page of this book. Of course, the identity of a civilisation is rooted in many things, but landscape has a special place, and this is a portrait of French civilisation in its many landscapes. From the air, we can see those patterns of life all the more clearly, like the deep bone structure of the country, built up over more than four millennia. From the air, away from the beaten track, in places still mercifully unreachable by car, these images go beyond the manmade landscapes of the present, the surface ephemera of history, to reveal the older, deeper, patterns of the past.

Arthus-Bertrand has a fabulous eye for shape and colour. He relishes the almost surreal intensity of fields of apple trees, lavender, and cognac vines. He cannily juxtaposes the hand of nature and the hand of man. In his lens, the stark geometric beauty of the concrete and metal Millau viaduct over the Tarn Valley is fit to stand by the tenuous tracery of a Gothic cathedral, no less aspiring and ethereal. He makes delightful and unexpected parallels between a Renaissance garden and a modern housing estate, between a maize labyrinth and the glistening arabesques of tidal mudflats, between Disneyland Paris and the real-life fairy tale of Mont-Saint-Michel. But he never lets us relax our engagement simply to see a pretty picture, always reminding us with wit and clarity who we are—and who they were. Sometimes, as with the medieval towns of France (better preserved than anywhere in Europe) in Pelissane, Gruissan, or Ramatuelle, the continuing connection of past and present seems perfectly balanced. These lovely towns are practical, habitable, self-sufficient places where, in the twenty-first century, it is still possible to live on a human scale.

Then there is the south. "Correct me if I am wrong," Ernst Renan wrote in 1872, "but the similarity between England and northern France appears to me increasingly plain every day. Our craziness comes from the south, and if France had not drawn Languedoc and Provence into her sphere of activity, we should be a serious, active, Protestant and parliamentary people." One may laugh, but I'm a northerner, born in the cold industrial north of England, and I know what he meant. Looking at these pictures, I naturally identify with the rocky shores of Brittany: a bleak, sea-girt peninsula by Cape Finisterre, for example, where a swift bit of Anglo-Saxon DIY would soon turn a ruin into a snug home, secure from the northern blasts, where one would sip porridge by a peat fire happy as any Breton, our old Celtic kinsmen. Many places in Britain can be like this, but France has so much more—she is a continent in miniature and has other climates and cultures. In landscape and in sensibility, she is the bridge between northern Europe and the Mediterranean.

These images can conjure up our own ghosts as well. Turning the pages, I relived the journey that I first made as a teenager from the drizzle of the Pas de Calais to the scented hillsides of Languedoc and Provence, a land of thousand-year olive trees, mulberries, and figs. Stumbling upon sun-beaten Roman aqueducts and amphitheatres—still standing as if only recently fallen into disuse—and dazzled by the sheer intensity of pink pathways and cobalt skies. "I know I shall always love nature here," wrote Vincent Van Gogh (another northerner, of course). "Those who don't believe in the southern sun are true unbelievers!" Civilisation was never the same in the south. In the ports and coastlands here, one touches the Mediterranean world of France, where a common language and culture links France with the Maghreb, with Tunis, Alexandria, or Beirut. This is the world of authors such as Jean Giono, Carlo Levi, and Lawrence Durrel: an older world still discernible to the traveller—or the photographer.

Which I suppose is to say that, viewed with a historian's eye, the history of France is writ large in these pages. Over the Lot Valley, ink-black storm clouds mass in the spectacular double-page spread of an ancient Gaulish hilltop. Here a little village, founded in the seventh century to serve the nearby Romanesque monastery of Saint-Gery, still nestles today. This is a photograph of another time. Look too at the walled coastal village of Talmont sur Gironde whose ramparts, built in 1284 by Edward I, encircle the squat church of Saint Radegund. Only a parked car or two seems to stand between us and those long-forgotten battles. Even further back in time, here is an amazing image of the last burons. These stone houses-cum-barns were the homes of the transhumant herders who wandered the high pasturage of Aveyron with their great flocks right up to the threshold of the modern age. They are almost gone now—there are only two families left—but theirs is a way of life that has come down to us straight out of prehistory.

And what do these images tell us about the identity of France? Speaking as a student of history, I think they show us that she was not born in the fires of the revolution, in the constitutional struggles of 1848, or even in the grim battles with the English in the Middle Ages. Rather as France's greatest modern historian Fernand Braudel put it, her idea of herself was formed deep in the past, through the everyday existence of those long-forgotten human lives that created this landscape.

This book is far more than a book of photographs, and in fact it is more even than a book about France. Like all Arthus-Bertrand books, it is about ourselves, about the way we live on earth, and the way we exist in our landscapes. He tells us something about the quality of civilisation and shows us how, at its best, civilisation is grown organically and over time, conserving what makes life worth living. These pictures portray a creative balance between "local" and "global" knowledge (with more than a hint that the "local" is still preferable, a sentiment with which I wholeheartedly concur). Seen in that light, the best of these pictures are visionary landscapes, photographed, chosen, printed, and juxtaposed with painterly art—aware of the beauties of human interaction with the landscape over time. Of all the images, my mind keeps turning back to the haunting shots of the little towns. Vézelay is described in this book as "a high place of spirituality in France," but can we still talk of spirituality in our time? This book suggests that we can, and shows us that the core of this spirituality is to be found in the sum total of the lives lived by human beings over many centuries: their links to their landscape, their "local knowledge" in work and play, in life and death—what one might call the givenness of the past. That, in these pages, is the image of France.

—Michael Wood

Beloved Country of My Youth

Sky of France, French skies. Plural France, multiple France, wild as its coastline and rugged as its mountains. Seen from the air, France is a land of plenty, a land the large migratory birds cannot help breaking their journey in, for it provides the sweetest stopover. France is also the country the gods contemplate from their home above the clouds. It is said the gods are rather indulgent with France, and, despite its occasional uproars, history tends to prove the rumor right. Goethe said, "Happy as God in France." I can hardly disagree.

How can Yann Arthus-Bertrand's photographs of France give such a striking image of happiness, when France's inhabitants, if asked, will complain about anything and everything? The first answer, the most obvious one, has to do with the distance from which Yann looks at things. Seen from a distance, everything seems more beautiful. And seen from above, everything seems more harmonious. The secret of the charm and nobility in Yann's pictures is the loftiness of his photographic vision. Yet one does not reach these artistic heights simply by going up in a helicopter, a plane, or a glider, in a hot-air balloon or on the wings of a seagull. One must also have the grace and the talent to capture a country's soul with a single picture.

As it happens, France's soul is an anguished one. The dark waves crashing down on France's shores tell us as much about the country as its more luminous side. Which brings us to the second potential explanation for this apparent contradiction, the typically French combination of fascination and repulsion in the face of happiness.

The average Frenchman pretends not to like himself, or rather not to like his compatriots, though in truth he secretly worships himself. It is no coincidence that the rooster is France's athletic symbol. The rooster loves to preen his feathers and admire them. He likes to show off in the farmyard, surrounded by his hens, and, from time to time, to let out a cock-a-doodle-do, which aims to be the nation's pride and joy. But watch it: If you get near the rooster, he will bristle, and rudely be on his way. Many foreigners have justifiably criticized us for such behavior. Yet these very same foreigners will often add that once you've won the trust of this beautiful country's inhabitants, they prove to be friendly and devoted.

"Gentle France, beloved country of my youth," sang Charles Trenet. I'm not sure France is all that gentle, except, once again, when seen from the air. From the air, France is neither flat nor jagged, neither arid nor arduous, but incredibly gentle, even when you focus on its relief. The Gers might take the prize for the gentlest slopes. Take a ride in a hot-air balloon from Castet-Arrouy to Miradoux, about the time of day when the sunflowers lean in to salute you, and you will understand why Tony Blair, the gentleman from gentle Albion, the country that loves moderation in all things, used to spend his vacations here, before he was lured away by incomparable Tuscany . . .

Though the Gers claims a gold medal for its harmonious curves, and the Côte d'Azur deserves one for its climate, the Loire Valley leaves all the competition in the dust when it comes to quality of life. How sweet the Angevin life, cherished by the poets Ronsard and du Bellay, with its exquisite art of dazzling you with freshly bloomed roses, then letting them wither before you, in a perfect metaphor for a love gone stale. The Loire, the most French of rivers, provides the ideal border between the two Frances, the north and the south. It is called the most French river because it is the longest (may male pride take comfort in that), and the most unpredictable. It is the most French river because it is occasionally the laziest, despite the fact that its treacherous nature makes it the most dangerous. Like so many things French, it is as dry as a bloodless heart. And judging by the number of royal chateaux along its banks, it is rich with French history. But the Loire is also the most French river because it constantly wavers between north and south from the moment it springs from the Mont Gerbier-de-Jonc. It could choose to flow into the Channel, like the Seine, whose source is not so far from its own, or into the Mediterranean, like the Rhône, which briefly parallels its course, but in fact it comes to rest in the Atlantic. This looks like an easy, nearly horizontal line on paper, but in reality the Loire's course is very complicated. The surrounding relief is not very helpful in assisting the river to find its natural rate of incline; yet another reason why the Loire closely resembles the character of this rebellious country, which only has the appearance of being so closely policed.

The Loire is the dividing line between two Frances. Though about equally populated, the two sides couldn't be more different. The North has always turned to Germany and, more rarely, to England; it fought these two invasive but admired neighbors long and hard, for nearly a millennium. As for the South, its natural inclination is toward Spain and Italy. Whether by historical coincidence or demographic miracle, today these five countries are about equally populated. As the most heavily populated countries of the forty European nations, they also constitute the bedrock of Europe, which is patiently and painstakingly building itself up to eventually be able to compete economically with the United States and China.

So France finds itself torn by the four countries that exercise a magnetic attraction on it. Though it is separated from its neighbors by unmistakable barriers—the Pyrenees, the Alps, the Jura, the Rhine, the Channel—France has slowly let itself be drawn in by their influence, while filtering out those elements that don't fit in. We've built chalets in the Alps, half-timbered houses in Normandy and Alsace, ochre and pink roughcast houses in Provence, and blood-red houses in the

Basque Country. Seen from the air, where borders are abolished, the French territory seems far vaster than what we see on the map. Suddenly, the Val-d'Aoste, French-speaking Switzerland, the eastern plain of the Rhine, and the land beyond Quiévrain are ours.

But let's not bring up these old small-town squabbles. Our own squabbles are petty enough. And though they may be petty, they certainly account for the charm of what we refer to as "provincial life." We have life-or-death rugby and soccer matches between teams from towns barely a mile apart, village fairs we attend with the express goal of seducing a girl from the next village over, and every contest under the sun, from pétanque games to local beauty pageants, from the loudest drum majorettes to the largest municipal choir, the best-equipped firemen to the oldest church, the tastiest wine, the sweetest fruit, the rivalry between Reims and Épernay for the title of capital of Champagne. . . . All it takes is an athletic event or a village dance to convince us the world revolves around us. We yell and curse and make up dime-store tragedies and collective catharses for which we are pretentious enough to put everything on the line: our raisons d'être, our loves, our roots, our very lives. This is the unique alchemy of this intensely close-knit, muddled country, a country drawn to death and wed to life, a country overwhelmed by its own power.

I'm not referring to nuclear power, or to oil—we only draw a few barrels in the Southwest, in Alsace, and in the Paris Basin—or even to hydroelectric power, where France's assets are limited to the Rance hydroelectric-power station and a few dams on the major rivers. France's power is telluric, in the full sense of the word. When you look at France from the air, you get the sense that it is irrigated by billions of little veins coming from the bowels of the earth through its center in the Massif Central. Remember that the volcanoes of the Puys chain, which are more than one hundred thousand years old, have only been inactive for seven thousand years.

So lava continues to churn in our hearts, anxiously awaiting an opportunity to spill out. Maybe that's why we're so irritable, so stressed out and quick-tempered. Traces of this telluric power can be found in all granite soil, whether in Brittany, Corsica, or Alsace. In fact, the Massif Central belongs to the Hercynian platform, as do the Armorican Massif, the Ardennes, and the Vosges. The Massif Central is also responsible for perfectly dosing the flow of water to the country's four major rivers: the Seine in the north, the Loire in the northwest, the Garonne in the southwest, and the Rhône in the east.

What we learn from the sky, as we look down on France, is that four-fifths of France's surface area is taken up with hills, plains, plateaus, and mid-size mountains. We learn that it is perfectly defined by its natural borders, that it is deeply rooted in the European continent to the east, and as sturdy as a ship steeled to meet the battering of the ocean to the west.

Meteorological observations tell us that France, being halfway between the Equator and the North Pole, enjoys a temperate climate. Yet the clash of maritime and Continental air masses, as well as polar and tropical ones, gives rise to an array of local weather variations, which accounts for those famed microclimates proudly trumpeted by any tourist board worth its salt.

As for the atlas, it reveals that France is the largest country in Europe after Russia, but that demographically it only ranks fifth. France is home to only one in one hundred inhabitants of the earth (ranking seventeenth). Its population density is relatively low compared to the densities of neighboring countries such as the United Kingdom, Germany, Belgium, the Netherlands, and Italy. The major urban zones are primarily concentrated in the Rhône and the Loire Valleys; in the North; along the Mediterranean coast; and, of course, in the Paris Basin, the demographics of which ripple all the way to Rouen, Orléans, and Reims.

One night, inspired by a passionate correspondence about the vast bay of Mont Saint-Michel, Yann sent me a text message that simply read: "Franceisbeautiful." We had spent the whole day in a helicopter, being constantly dazzled by the seemingly endless wonders of the northern coast of Brittany.

One of the truly beautiful things about France seen from the air is what the geographers call its Euclidian harmony: three maritime flanks (1800 miles of coastline), three land borders (1300 miles), and not a single point in the nation farther than 250 miles from a coastline. West of the diagonal connecting Forbach to Biarritz, the vast majority of the country is less than 650 feet above sea level (with the exception of a few small Breton peaks). East of this line, mountains cover a quarter of the land, and the Mont Blanc, not satisfied with being the highest peak in France, reigns highest in all of Europe. This was reason enough to photograph it from every possible angle, in white and in rose, for inclusion in this volume.

Now let us turn to the geologists. They teach us that this diverse relief is the fruit of one of the richest histories in the world. You have to listen to the geologists to truly understand the beauty of this country when seen from the air. They tell us that the ancient relief (Massif Central, Brittany, Ardennes, Alsace-Lorraine) is due to a folding of the landmass over several tens of millions of years during the Carboniferous. Then came the natural phenomena of the Tertiary: fractures, distortions, collapses, and, of course, erosion. As for the sedimentary basins (Aquitaine and the Paris Basin), which also date back to the Paleozoic, they are formed of regular strata that shape our hills, plains, and plateaus. All of this has an impact on the coastlines, of course. The slopes of ancient solid rock chains such as the Armorican Massif run down into the water and create the jagged coastlines associated with Brittany and Corsica in a furious melding of land and water. On the other hand, the plains extend into the low, sandy coasts found in Aquitaine and Languedoc, or into the straight, chalky beaches of Normandy. The Mediterranean coast draws its high cliffs and narrow bays from the Alps. West of the Rhône, the lagoons and their offshore sandbars shape the coast's appearance. Hence the strange struggle between the land and the sea depicted in these pages, the struggle between what shifts and what is solid.

This is what statistics and satellites tell us. But if you get a little closer, you discover a country that is even more complex. To understand it, you must now turn to the history books. The first thing you discover is that the custom of referring to France as a hexagon would once have been quite inaccurate, for the country was short at least one side. . . . Let's start with the Romans, who came up with the name Gaul to describe an area including the land we now know as France, with Northern Italy, Belgium, Switzerland, and the left bank of the Rhine thrown in for good measure. In fact, if you consider the survival of certain customs and the sustained use of French in most of the above areas, the Romans may have been on to something.

To whom do we owe our civilization? What caused us to be what we are today? According to the answers given by Académie Française member Jacques Bainville in his monumental *History of France*, we owe it to the Roman conquest. "Civil war, the great Gallic flaw, delivered the country to the Romans. An undefined, unstable government and a primitive political structure hovering between democracy and oligarchy made Gaul's efforts to defend its independence in vain."

The same conclusion holds true throughout the centuries: divided, the French are sure losers. United, they are invincible. Unfortunately, the French have division in their blood, just like rebellion. It is striking to note that things haven't really evolved: France is still more or less divided between the right and the left, like the two ventricles of a heart. When the right splits, it loses power. When the left follows suit, it can't hold on to power. And though the country still has a taste for democracy, its rulers don't mind acting like monarchs, using their long mandates to re-create the system of courtesans and new aristocrats.

Jacques Bainville followed his line of thought through to its natural conclusion: According to him, the French have never turned their back on the Gallic lark, and the national uprising fervently led by Vercingétorix still fills us with pride. The Gauls had a military temperament. Their expeditions once took them across Europe, all the way to Asia Minor (it is only fitting that today Turkey should be knocking at Europe's door, but ungrateful France only wants to open it a crack). The Gauls even managed to terrify Rome, as they victoriously stormed into the city. Though a people will not survive without military skill, this alone is not enough to survive on. The Gauls passed this knowledge on to their descendants. The heroism of Vercingétorix and his allies was not lost: it was like a seed. Yet it was impossible for Vercingétorix to triumph, and it would have been a disaster for him to do so.

I'll let the academician take full responsibility for the following statement, though it is hard to deny that "We have force to thank for the fact that we became superior civilized beings, and that we have been considerably ahead of other peoples." The force he speaks of was the force of the Roman conquest and of an exceptionally assimilated colonization.

To this day, when I look at the map of Gaul two thousand years ago, I have the decisive impression that I am looking at today's France, seen from the air, a France without borders and without shame. The vast Gallic territory was initially populated with Celts and a multitude of tribes. This mosaic of peoples was given a semblance of unity by the Romans, but it exploded as soon as colonization ended. The barbarian invasions overcame whatever glue had held them together. All the history books agree that it wasn't until the fifth century and the emergence of the Frankish kingdom that Gaul became an authentic nation: France. Yet the Merovingian France united by Clovis soon fell back to its atavistic, divided ways. It took Charlemagne's dismembering of the empire, in the ninth century, for a first sketch of the kingdom of France to appear.

With their mustaches and flowing beards to the wind, Vercingétorix, Clovis, and Charlemagne stood on each others' shoulders to elevate this country to greatness. But their every attempt was doomed to failure, and the task of elevating France was passed on to the next generation. Finally, in A.D. 987, one thousand years after the Romans had arrived, an assembly of lords chose Hugues Capet, a duke of France and smalltime owner of a narrow stretch of land, as sovereign. Through conquests and annexations, his successors Philippe Auguste, Louis XI, François I, Henri IV, Louis XIV, and Louis XV patiently worked to re-create the France left to us by the Gallo-Romans. They were followed, of course, by Napoleon and a sudden swelling of our borders, but that swelling quickly subsided, and France was returned to the comfortable outline it had two millennia ago.

Whether seen from the air or in the pages of an atlas, there's no denying that France, which is sometimes reduced to the barbaric name of the Hexagon, seems solidly in place. I trust Perpignan and the Roussillon to serve as our central anchorage point. I also trust the Basque Country and the Var to ensure the equilibrium at our nether end. And the rest of the country is just as harmoniously balanced. Where our hourglass figure dips in around Lac Léman, the Atlantic coast matches it line for line, on the same parallel, between Vendée and Charentes. Where Brittany stretches out comfortably, seeming to reach out to breathe in the ocean and catch a distant whiff of the New World, Alsace follows suit, at the same latitude, remaining on guard, making sure that all is quiet on the Eastern front, for history has taught us to be on the look-out. From Strasbourg to Dunkirk and from Brest to Calais, the roof of France follows the same incline, the better to protect us. There is no doubt that today France is firmly secured. Yann's pictures speak for themselves: France is solid, from its most modest cabin to its most imposing monument.

Half a century after Bainville, Georges Duby, another academician with vast historical knowledge, reminds us that at a mere 620 miles from north to south and from west to east, this harmonious stretch of land occupies a very small portion of the world's surface: it comes in thirty-seventh in a ranking of the world's countries by size. So why does France continue to play a leading part in world affairs? This is Duby's answer: "It is an extraordinary territory due to its location in the heart of an area, Western Europe, which, over a period of two millennia, has twice been the cradle of important civilizations that expanded on a global scale. A territory at the crossroads of those lands which rose from the sea, open to every endeavor, to every adventure, thanks to its double identity as a terrestrial block jutting from the neighboring continent, immense Eurasia, and as a coastal land besieged by the flow of four seas, the pathways to every coast in the world. It is a touching territory, thanks to the variety of its landscapes and promises, a place where one can move from the soft grays of the Nordic polders to the chiseling light of the Mediterranean headlands, from the wheat-heavy plains to the biggest glaciers in Europe."

"A touching territory." This is what I think of every time I travel through France, whether by foot, on horseback, or in a car, in the air, on the sea, or on the railways.

Having made my way down every back road in the known universe and been around the world about a hundred times, I can attest to the fact that no country is more varied than France, that no other place has more astounding diversity. Because every acre has been worked and polished by man, in his image, every acre is different from the next. From one league to the next—for the league is a far more evocative, and exact, unit of measure than the mile—you discover the renewed singularity of the landscape. Nature, the great organizer, may have a lot to do with this, but Man has always left his mark. And since the French are quarrelsome, reluctant to listen to authority or to be followers, every single place cultivates its differences. You lose track of that when you leap from one city to the next on a plane, a high-speed train, or a highway. You have to travel by foot to marvel at the landscape and thank the millions of anonymous souls, largely farmers, who have bequeathed us this beauty and harmony.

Sublime France, down to its most obscure corner. Lavender France in Haute-Provence, golden yellow in the Breton spring thanks to the broom and the gorse bushes, off-white in the Baux-de-Provence or along the Durance, ocher in the Roussillon, fat with clay and brown furrows when fall comes, watery green in Sologne, apple green in Normandy, dark green in Alsace or the Limousin. Rainbow-colored France, because after the rain, the sun always comes out.

France of hope in Vézelay, of remembrance in Dunkirk, land of take-offs in Champagne, of suffering in Alsace, of gourmet eating in Périgord and Bourgogne, of resistance in the Cathar country, of marsh waters in Brière, in the Camargue, and in the Poitou. Here and there, this land has to hold its own: At Cap Gris-Nez, at the tip of La Hague, at Penmarch, or in the Raz de Sein, across from the only island named Companion of the Liberation (*Compagnon de la Libération*). At Cap-Ferret, this land fends off the furious assaults of currents that would like to submerge it. Sometimes the currents choke it with sand, as they do at the Mont-Saint-Michel and Aigues-Mortes, but Man fights back, builds dikes and dams or, as in Rochefort, offers himself the illusion that he still lives next to the sea by building the *Hermione*, an exact replica of La Fayette's frigate.

Bursting with pride, Man thinks he is stronger than the elements. He knows he will only be here for one hundred years, at the very most, but he insists on leaving his mark, on marking his territory the way the wolves do. At night, he howls to the moon. Hidden behind that luminous white sphere, Yann Arthus-Bertrand continues to photograph him.

Previous spread

● **Mont Blanc at sunrise.**
In 1865, Captain Mieulet, a specialist in geological survey maps, measured the tallest peak in Western Europe to stand at 15,771 feet. Today that figure is in doubt. In 2001, expert geometers with the National Geographic Institute (IGN) used a GPS system to come up with the revised height of 15,782.15 feet. Yet following the heat wave of 2003, readings taken at 500 different locations suggested the Mont Blanc had shrunk to 15,775.75 feet. This shrinking is probably due to the evolution of the glacial drift and the ever-increasing number of climbers venturing above 13,000 feet.

When we took off from Val-d'Isère, long before sunrise, it was -40° Fahrenheit. The driving wind made the cold bite twice as hard. As we reached the peaks, the helicopter's door was wide open, and my film was shattering as I loaded the cameras. Suddenly, the peak of the Mont Blanc came to life, as it was struck by the first rays of sunlight.—*YAB*

In this picture, Mont Blanc is as rose-colored as can be, enough to make the Mont Rose, on the Swiss-Italian border, jealous! It's nearly flesh-colored. It looks like a picture of some kind of open-heart surgery.—*PPDA*

Following spread

● **Stormy skies over the Lot valley.**
A storm has broken over the foothills of the Massif Central, clouding the sky around Saint-Géry, in the Lot. This village of 300 inhabitants, founded around a monastery in the seventh century, dominates the undulating landscape of the Lot valley. The nearby cliffside hamlet of Pasturac is home to a lovely Romanesque church.

Pages 16–17

● **The Place Charles-de-Gaulle, once known as the Étoile (the Star).**
The Place de l'Étoile has a diameter of 787 feet. This intersection of the contemporary 8th, 16th, and 17th Paris arrondissements was redesigned in 1854 by architect Jacques Hittorff, an assistant to Baron Haussmann, the prefect of the Seine responsible for radically altering the layout of the capital. Twelve rectilinear avenues were laid out to lead to the Place and form the celebrated star. Private mansions with direct views of the Arc de Triomphe, inaugurated in 1836, were built between courtyards and gardens around the Place. Shortly after General de Gaulle's death in November 1970, the Place de l'Étoile was renamed in honor of the first president of the Fifth Republic.

When you're in a car, stuck in a traffic jam, you can't possibly fathom why this Place is referred to as a star, because you can't see its avenues radiating out. But once you're in the air, it's as clear as day.—*YAB*

Two centuries ago, it was nothing but a wooded hill. Then Napoleon came along. A star for generals, for battle-weary soldiers, and for victories.—*PPDA*

Opposite

● **Skiing on the slag heaps of Nœux-les-Mines.**
The old mining country is going green. The industrial wastelands of Nœux-les-Mines, in the Pas-de-Calais, have recently undergone environmental redevelopment. In 1996, one of the slag heaps was converted into an artificial ski slope thanks to a huge plastic mat kept slippery by constant watering. Since the closing of its coal mines in 1988, after one hundred and fifty years of mining, the Nord-Pas-de-Calais has been coming up with these kinds of imaginative ideas to redefine its image. Some hundred and thirty slag heaps have been reforested and turned into green lungs where one can observe fauna and flora, go paragliding, or participate in orienteering races. This slag heap chain now draws over twenty thousand visitors a year.

Pages 14–15

● **Agricultural specialization, a regional phenomenon.**
According to a study published in 2002 by the Fédération nationale des syndicats d'exploitants agricoles (FNSEA—National Federation of Farmers' Unions), farms are more specialized today than ever before, and specific types of agricultural production are concentrated in specific regions. This trend was particularly marked between 1988 and 2000, and has accentuated the differences between regional landscapes. For instance, two-thirds of French wine production is concentrated in four regions (Champagne-Ardenne, Aquitaine, Languedoc-Roussillon, Provence-Alpes-Côte d'Azur), and half of what is known as "soil-free" growing in France takes place in Brittany and the Loire areas. As for large-scale farming, it is divided between the southwest and the north of the Paris Basin (shown here).

Bales of straw were once square, but today's farming machines produce round bales. This has totally transformed the landscape. And with the bales so randomly placed, the fields look like art installations. As for the bales themselves, once the hay is covered with a plastic tarp, they look like giant marshmallows.—*YAB*

You have to fly with Yann to understand how profoundly fascinated he is with fields. He hovers over them with his helicopter like a bumblebee over a patch of lavender.—*PPDA*

Pages 18–19

● **Port-Grimaud, a twentieth-century architectural success story.**
Sitting below the medieval village of Grimaud, the lakeside town of Port-Grimaud has imposed itself as a successful modern development here in the Gulf of Saint-Tropez (Var). Conceived in 1966 by architect François Spoerry, this ocher and pastel-colored village with Roman tiles on its roofs has been marvelously integrated into the Mediterranean landscape. The 160 acres of Port-Grimaud give water pride of place—water occupies 42 percent of the surface area, versus 33 percent for parks and gardens, and 25 percent for buildings. The town has 8.7 miles of quays, and houses can be accessed either by foot or by boat. The international renown of Port-Grimaud draws thousands of visitors per year.

There are no customs paths here. The village was built on a huge marsh, and the entire seafront belongs to the inhabitants of Port-Grimaud. Today, the law governing coastlines protects the coast from privatization and stipulates that beaches are part of the public domain. Port-Grimaud remains, in my opinion, an authentic success, particularly now that the passage of time has endowed it with a lovely patina.—*YAB*

A successful adaptation of architecture to its terrestrial and maritime surroundings. It's strange to see nearly as many boats as houses. Taken as a whole, it looks like the tentacles of an octopus, or of a big sea anemone.—*PPDA*

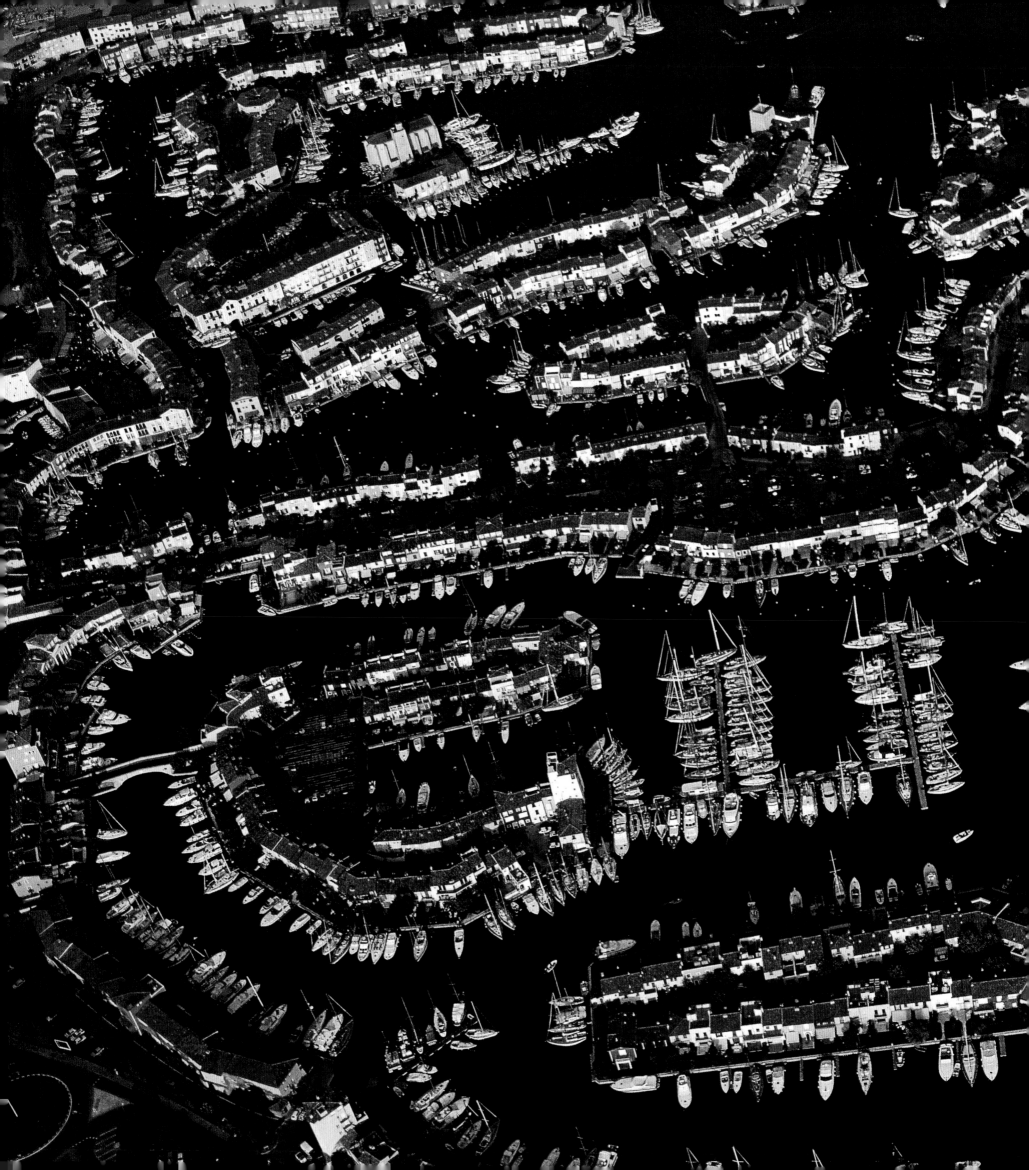

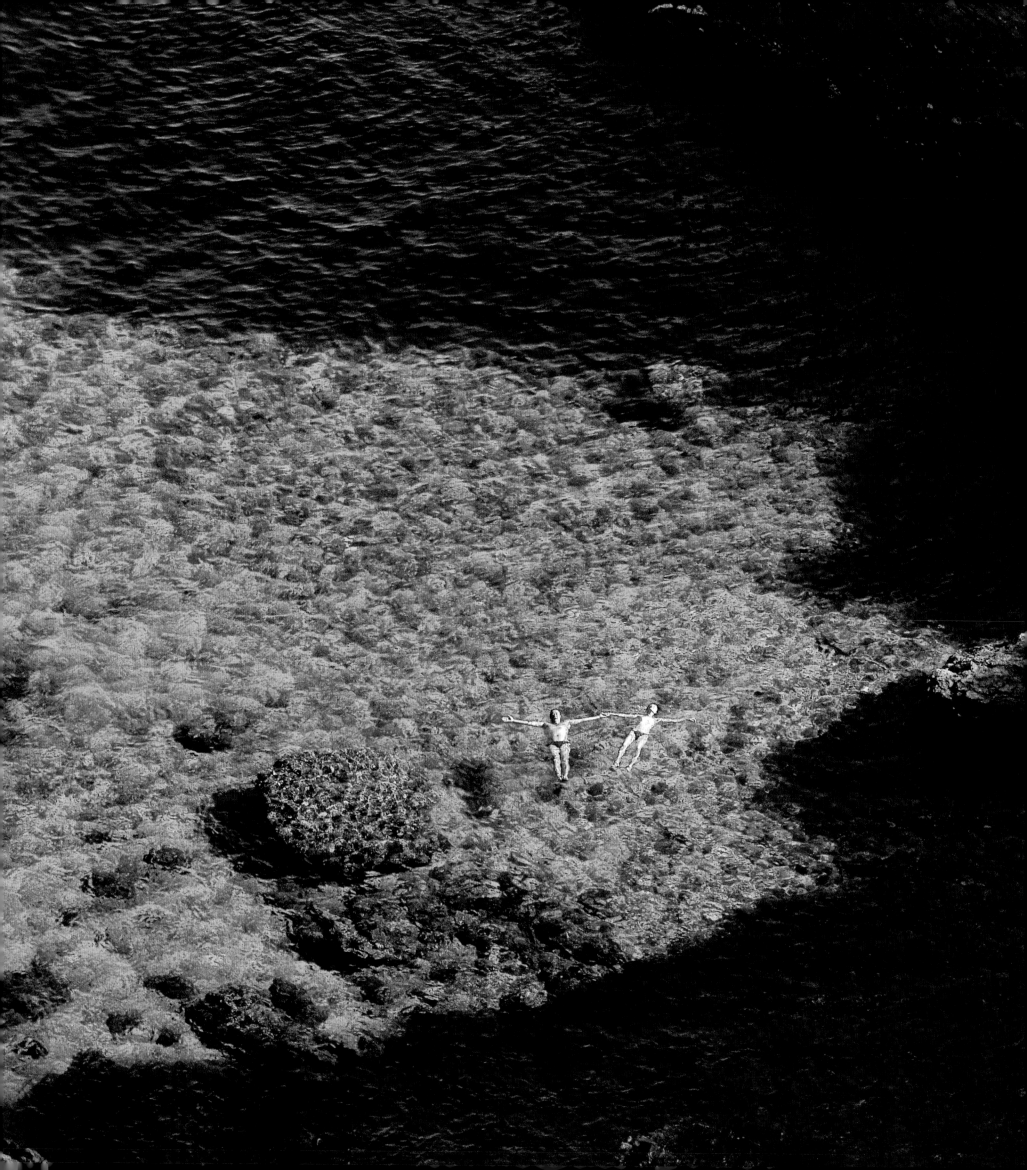

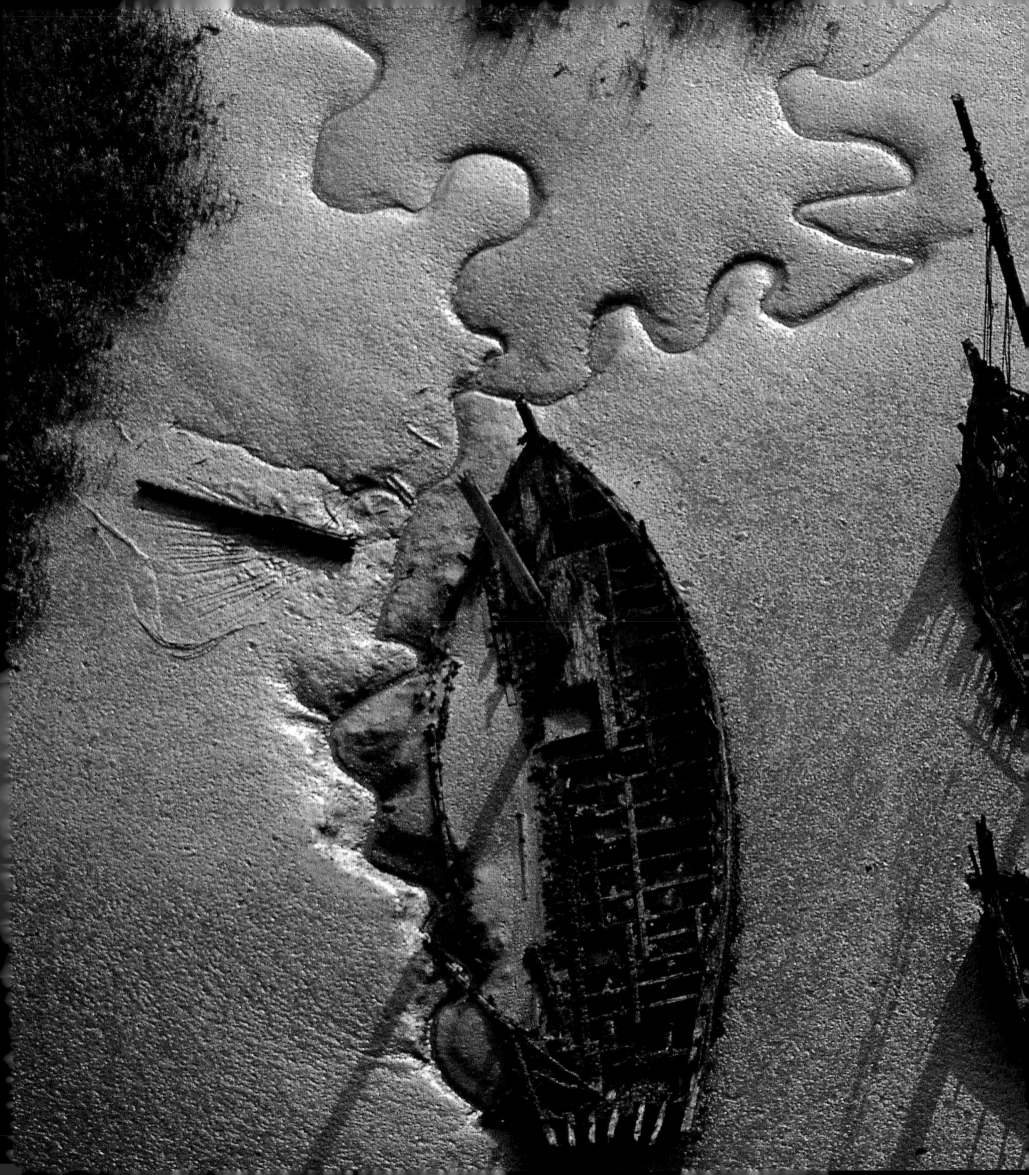

Pages 20–21

● **Between the sky and the sea, the clear blue waters of Cap Bénat.**
The transparent waters of the Mediterranean and the nearly deserted creeks of Cap Bénat can be reached by foot along the old customs paths lining the peninsula. Created under the First Empire to allow customs officers to keep an eye out for smugglers, these winding paths through the seaside pines have been progressively rehabilitated since the 1970s. They lead both to family beaches and nudist beaches, and, thanks to the sea's transparency, are excellent vantage points to appreciate the sea bottom. Dolphins can sometimes be spotted taking advantage of the clear waters of the Mediterranean coast.

Previous spread

● **The Kerhervy ships graveyard.**
Boats too old to be sailed disappear into the silt of the Kerhervy ships graveyard, in a loop of the Blavet River near Lanester (Morbihan). The first boats to wash up here in the 1920s were tuna boats from Groix Island. They were followed by dozens of decapitated dundees. Unlike ships with metal hulls, these rotting wooden ships will eventually meld into the landscape. But for every disarmed boat laid to rest after years on the water, how many potential wrecks still set out to sea?

This is literally the point where Man's work returns to the earth. Putrefaction begins. Building timber becomes part of nature again. This change of state is underlined by what looks like a lovely piece of a little puzzle in the upper part of the picture.—*PPDA*

Opposite

● **The Vosges Forest after the storm of the century tore through it.**
Thousands of conifers lying on the ground . . . The Vosges Forest (shown here in Dabo, in the Moselle region) was hit hard by the hurricanes that crossed France on the nights of December 26 and 27, 1999, with winds traveling at over 75 miles per hour. In Alsace and Lorraine, the volume of trees felled was estimated at over one billion cubic feet. Throughout France's 37 million acres of forest, these unusual storms, which seem to be symptomatic of climate change, caused over a million acres of windfall (trees knocked over by the wind). In conjunction with the effects of the drought of 2003, this disaster led to a 7 percent decrease in revenues for forest communities, or a loss of 100 million euros over five years.

When I saw this part of the forest devastated by the wind, I was simply overcome by the ravages the storm had left in its wake. My assistant, Françoise, is standing in the foreground, giving us a sense of the scale of the devastation.—*YAB*

This photo reveals man's extreme humbleness in the face of nature. Coming as they did on the eve of the year 2000, these storms seemed to be symbolic, like some kind of incantatory warning. Nature was reclaiming its rights by marking the land with long ugly scars.—*PPDA*

Opposite

● **Buren's columns at the Palais-Royal will soon be restored.**
Protest against these contemporary sculptures in the Cour d'Honneur of the Palais-Royal in Paris has now died out. They did initially arouse serious controversy when their creator, French artist and Venice Biennale Golden Lion winner Daniel Buren, installed them in 1986, to the point that construction was temporarily halted. With time, the columns, characterized by their pattern of black and white vertical bands, have become integrated into the gardens of this classically designed palace built in 1635. Today, they attract strollers and street artists. After years of wear and tear, tarnishing, and abuse by skateboarders, the columns are in serious need of restoration. They will soon be removed for cleaning, then returned to their original location, as part of the restoration of the Cour d'Honneur of the Palais-Royal. The cost of this project, which also includes the construction of two underground rehearsal rooms for the Comédie Française, is estimated at 2.6 million euros.

Though they've often been criticized, Buren's columns have become a lively, fun place for people to get together and children to play. And contrary to Les Halles, nothing was razed to build the columns.—*YAB*

When you look down on these columns from above, the impression you get is both enjoyably trivial and quite playful. They look like some kind of cross between sushi and dominos.—*PPDA*

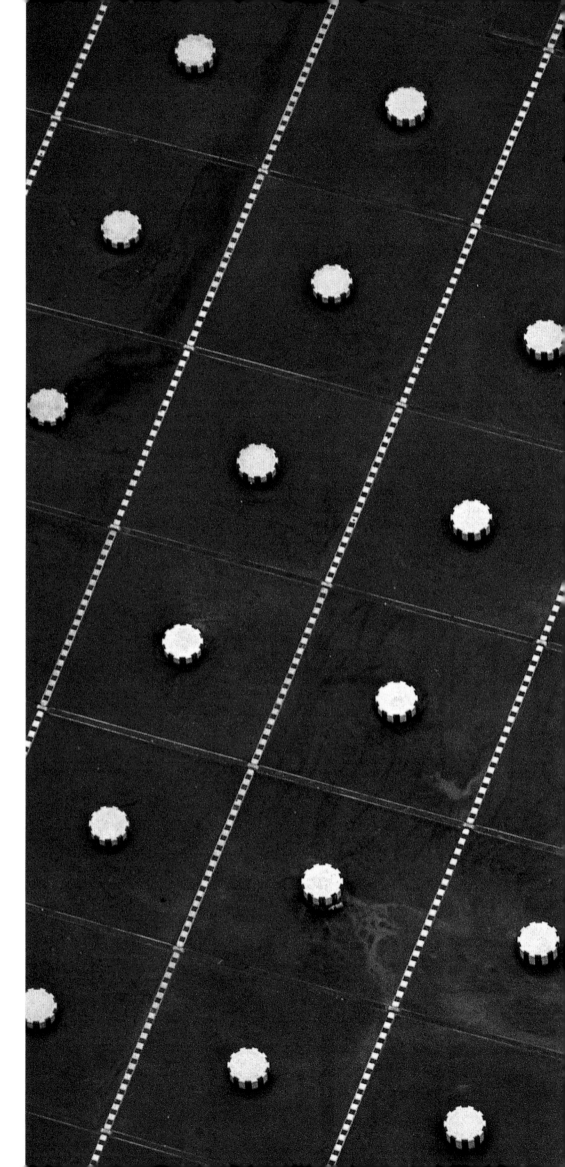

● **The bubble-palace in Théoule-sur-Mer.**
This astonishing moonlike spherical residence in Théoule-sur-Mer (Alpes-Maritimes) was conceived by Czech architect Antti Lovag in 1976. The property has since been expanded to occupy five acres of land and include a dozen suites, three large living rooms, two pools, an amphitheater, and a palm grove, alongside the main 21,500-square-foot building. The bubble-palace is a private residence that occasionally hosts special events, particularly during the Cannes Film Festival.

● **The Village des Sables on the beach at Torreilles.**
Round as wheels of Camembert, these concrete houses with individual gardens are part of a large development of 640 villas occupying 84 acres on the gigantic beach at Torreilles (Pyrénées-Orientales). Built in the late 1970s by the developer Merlin, these houses were once the subjects of considerable debate. Indeed, the construction of these yearly or seasonal rentals upset a rare, untamed natural site. But the vegetation has since grown in and the Village des Sables (Village of the Sands) has become integrated into the landscape, while the rest of the coastline is now protected by coastal preservation regulations.

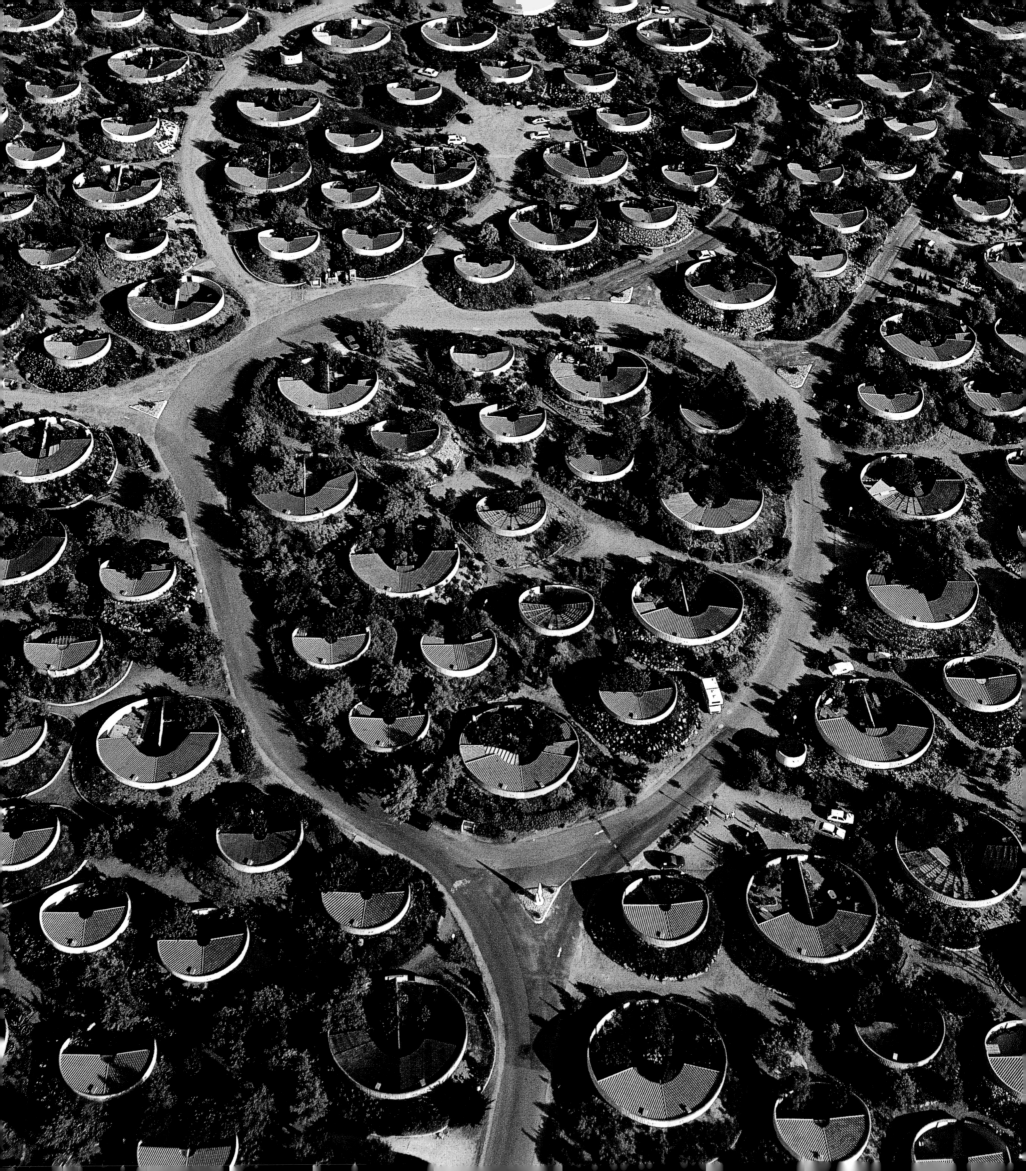

Left

● **The earth at rest in the area of Lyons.** This harvested corn field in the Lyonnais (Rhône) lies under winter's first snow. We have the relatively small size of fields in the Rhône to thank for these wonderfully curved furrows. In order to stay within the limited bounds of their own fields, farmers cannot use farming equipment in straight lines, but rather in the curving motions evidenced at left. In this area, cereals such as corn, wheat, and barley are grown as fodder for consumption by local cattle, particularly cows, which are numerous. There are 8,300 farms in the Rhône region, of an average size of 44 acres, as compared to the national average of 103 acres.

Right

● **Working the sea on the island of Oléron.** Oléron, in Charente-Maritime, is the largest French island on the Atlantic (67 square miles). The island's life is set to the rhythms of the tides that provide plankton for its oyster beds. Following the decline of its salterns at the end of the nineteenth century, Oléron converted to oyster farming. Producing oysters is a long haul, requiring more than three years to pass from the initial collecting of the spats to their maturing into fattened oysters, in specialized fattening ponds known as *claires*. Oyster farmers take advantage of low tide to sail through the oyster farms in flat-bottomed boats known as *lasses* and gather the precious shellfish.

When I take aerial photos, I am constantly looking for graphic patterns and geometric lines. I sometimes get the feeling that farmers use their tractors the way a painter uses his brush.—*YAB*

I also see it as a painting . . . And with this photo of Oléron, we're not so far from Monet and Sisley.—*PPDA*

Opposite

● **The art of the garden at the château of Versailles.**
The château of Versailles and its gardens (Yvelines) have been under extensive restoration for several years now. Begun in 1990 under Pierre-André Lablaude, chief architect for historic monuments, the project to replant the park (1,482 acres) was significantly hastened by the storm of December 1999, which felled some 1,500 trees at the château. The French gardens, initially conceived by André Le Nôtre, gardener to the Sun King, in the seventeenth century, have finally been restored to their original state. This garden restoration program has an annual budget of about 3,850,000 euros, which is regularly supplemented by fundraising drives.

Strangely enough, French gardens are made to be seen from the air. Though they're absolutely magnificent, I'm the only one to see them this way, and to rediscover the touch of the landscape gardener. When I'm in a helicopter, I often feel as though I'm wandering over a map.—*YAB*

French gardens, certainly, but also Arab calligraphy, with that ocher sand as a background! From the air you discover symbols you would never have been able to see from the ground.—*PPDA*

Page 34

● **The Notre-Dame-de-Lorette Cemetery.**
The Notre-Dame-de-Lorette Cemetery, in Ablain-Saint-Nazaire, in the Pas-de-Calais, is the final resting place of 40,000 bodies. At 67 acres, it is the largest cemetery in France. For the most part, those buried here are casualties of World War I. The cemetery was originally laid out along the frontline trenches that witnessed the deaths of nearly 100,000 men, and was classified as a "military burial ground" in 1920. Louis Cordonnier, the architect of the Basilica of Lisieux, is responsible for the ossuary and chapel in memory of the war dead. In total, France has 815 acres of "national necropolises." 730,000 soldiers have been laid to rest in these 265 military cemeteries.

I consider this picture to be a symbol. The military cemeteries in the north of France are impressive. So many people died here, millions of people. Once upon a time, people would fight to protect their countries, their borders, and their land. Luckily, today Europe is a country without borders, which prefigures what globalization should actually be.—*YAB*

I can't help but think of my paternal grandfather, who was eighteen when war broke out in 1914. He spent four years of his life, what should have been the most beautiful years of his life, in the trenches, to seize a thousand feet of land—a thousand feet that were probably lost within a month. . . . The so-called Great War claimed seventeen million lives in Europe. Yet today public opinion polls tell us the French's favorite people are the Germans. Did we really need to go through such horrors to achieve this?—*PPDA*

Right

● **Memento of the Sun King in Lyons.**
Set between the Rhône and the Saône, Place Bellecour is the thriving heart of Lyons (Rhône). It is accessible by subway, lined with boutiques, and constantly alive with open-air spectacles and the occasional political demonstration. What was once a swampy meadow was only acquired by the city in 1708, with the help of Louis XIV. Architect Robert de Cotte then designed the Place Royale to be dominated by a bronze statue of the Sun King. This effigy of the king was destroyed during the Revolution and replaced, in 1826, by Lyons artist François Lemot's rendition of the king on horseback, dressed as a Roman emperor.

We no longer immortalize our political figures by erecting statues of them in the town square. What is the contemporary symbol of power?—*YAB*

Like all the other rulers who had statues erected of themselves on horseback, Louis XIV was a conqueror king. All that conquering came at the cost of a lot of death and a lot of suffering. And yet this is how France was built. Before Louis XIV's reign, the size and influence of France were nowhere near as significant as they were by the end of his nearly three-quarters of a century on the throne.—*PPDA*

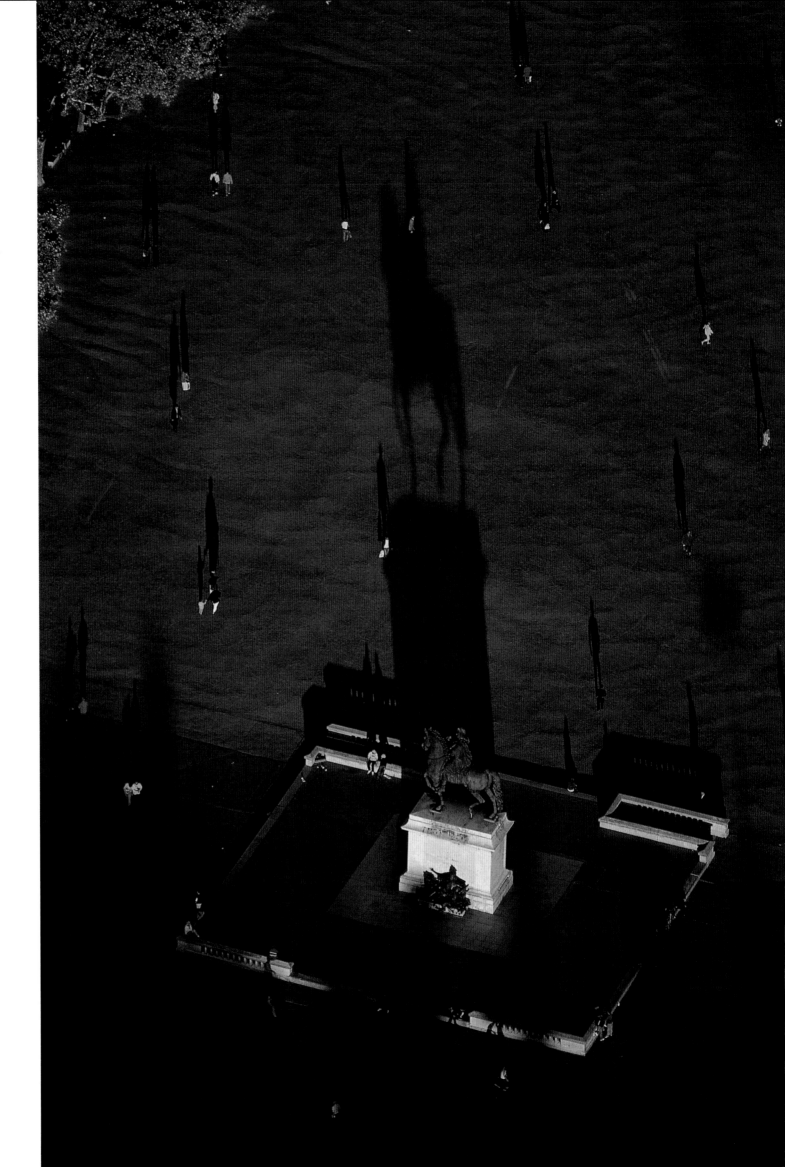

*Opposite and
following spread*

- **In Guérande, the salt marshes
  have come back to life.**
  This clay checkerboard is known
  as the "white heath" of the
  Guérande salt marshes, in the
  Loire-Atlantic. Twenty years ago
  the salt marshes were on the
  verge of becoming an industrial
  wasteland when some audacious
  salt makers took action and
  saved them. Now, following
  techniques inherited from the
  Middle Ages, locals use the sun
  to evaporate the brackish water
  and isolate sea salt. Salt harvesting takes place from June to
  September, the period during
  which the famed "salt flower"
  is gathered from the surface
  with a long rake known as a
  lousse. The area was classified
  as a national sanctuary in 1996.

Page 40

- **The embroidery of Vaux-le-
  Vicomte.**
  The château of Vaux-le-Vicomte
  is famous for the yew hedges
  traced out in front of it like
  embroidery. But who was
  responsible for that celebrated
  landscaping? The hedges were
  originally designed by André Le
  Nôtre, who was later to create
  the gardens of Versailles. Yet by
  1920, when a landscape gardener called Achille Duchêne
  "revisited" them, the hedges
  were completely neglected,
  and overgrown with weeds.
  Duchêne's restoration led to a
  controversy over the "copy-
  right" to the flowerbeds, which,
  by 2000, found his heirs facing
  off against the current propri-
  etor of the château and primary
  defender of Le Nôtre, Patrice de
  Vogüé. The case was resolved in
  2004, when the courts recognized Achille Duchêne's "personal touch."

Page 41

- **The Breton bocage and its
  crisscross of hedges and
  embankments.**
  As is typical of most imperme-
  able granite soil tilled since the
  Middle Ages, the Breton bocage
  (shown here in the Côtes-
  d'Armor) plays an essential
  ecological role, notably by regulating runoff water. Oak, beech,
  and chestnut hedges delineate
  properties and fields dedicated
  to cattle breeding and farming.
  They also harbor a diverse
  range of animals, including
  birds, insects, and small mammals. Often perched on the top
  of an embankment, these
  hedges follow the relief line,
  thereby helping to control
  flooding. Hedges limit soil
  erosion, help to drain the
  land, and slow the spread of
  pesticides and fertilizers used
  by the food-processing industry.
  The hedges of the Breton bocage
  were leveled in the 1960s and
  1970s to ease the passage of
  farming vehicles, but they
  have now been partially
  replanted. This replanting
  policy has been implemented
  as part of an effort at sustainable development.

The bocage forms a succession of little fields all over Brittany. As in the rest of
France, where a farm closes every twenty minutes, the Breton bocage is threatened by land consolidation.—*YAB*

These two photos express the contrast between arrogance and humility. At Vaux-
le-Vicomte, Superintendent Fouquet displayed his arrogance by trying to stun
Louis XIV with a château worthy of royal magnificence, but only succeeded in
bringing about his downfall. In the bocage, however, man modestly adapts to
nature.—*PPDA*

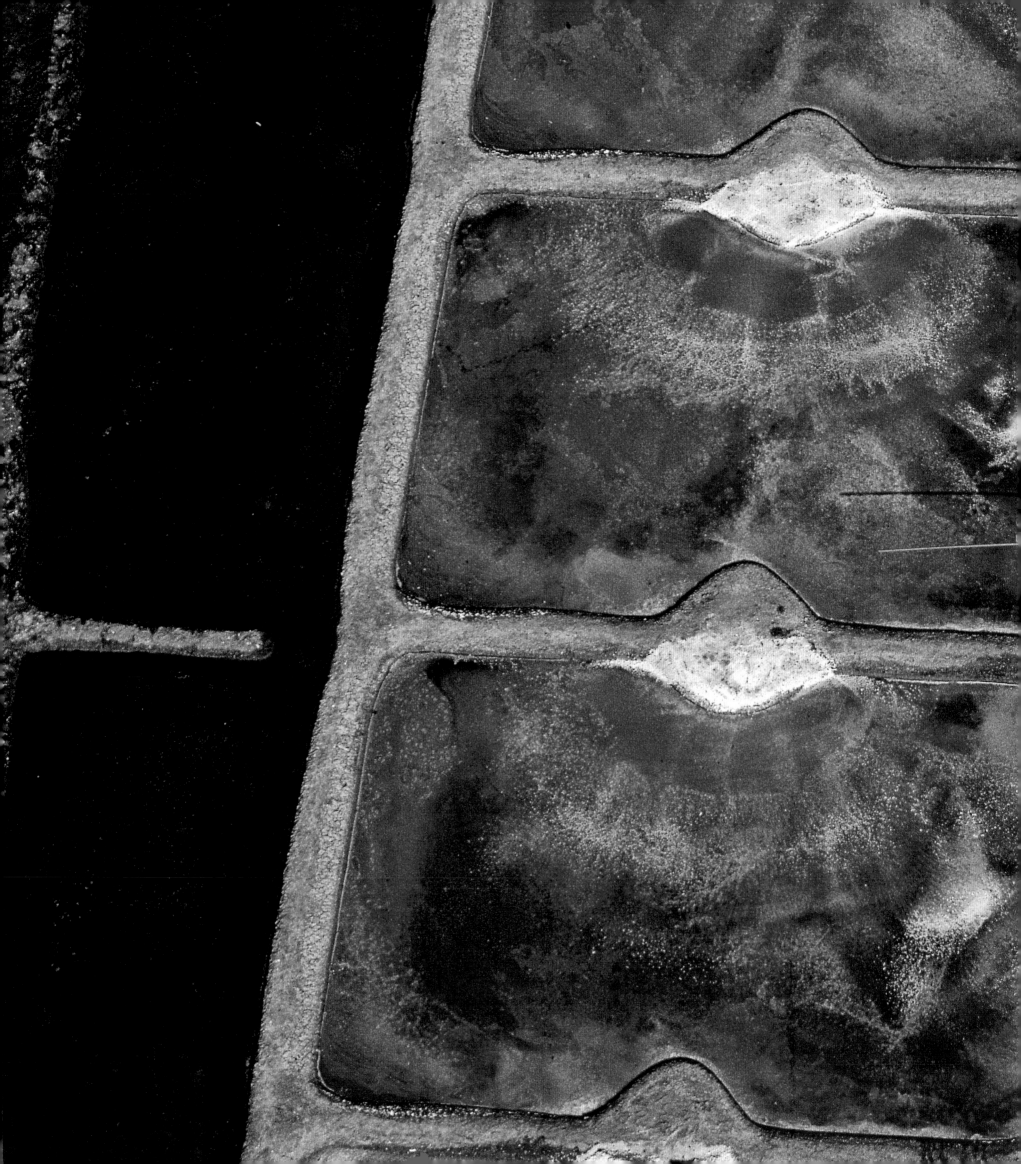

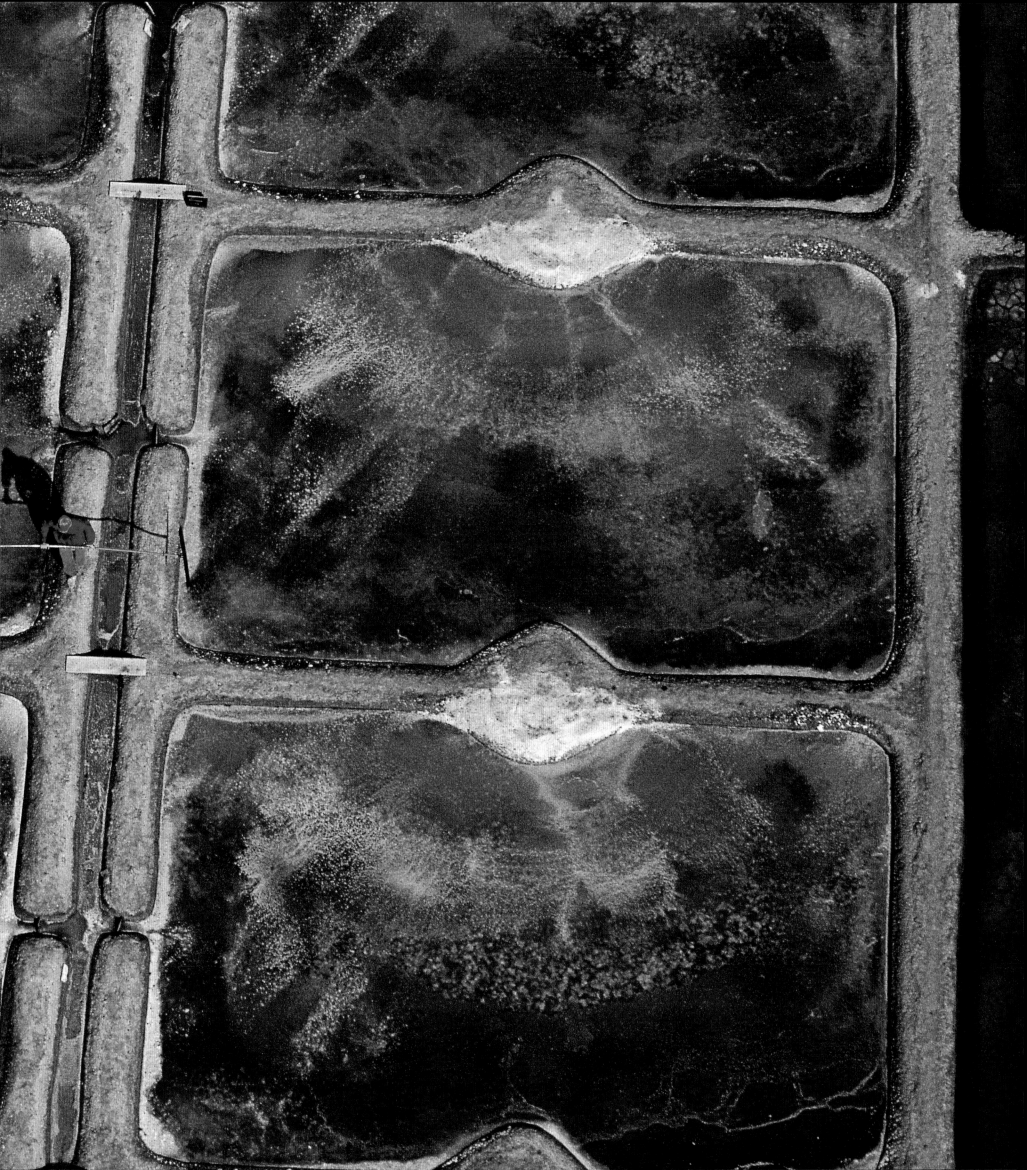

Opposite

● The Noé development is set to be demolished.
The construction of the Noé development in Chanteloup-les-Vignes (Yvelines) was entrusted to architect Émile Aillaud in the 1970s. His mission was to accommodate a working-class population, largely made up of immigrants, many of whom were employed in the Peugeot factory in Poissy, in this devel-opment of four thousand homes. Thirty years later, this artificial neighborhood has become a *zone urbaine sensible* (sensitive urban zone), and is set to be demolished according to the directives of the "Large City Projects." A new urban development, with parklands and individual houses, should replace it.

Following spread

● Sheep in the salt marshes of the Mont-Saint-Michel.
Mont-Saint-Michel Bay (Manche) occupies an approximately 200-square-mile depression regularly covered over when the spring unleashes the most powerful tides in the world. Yet its natural silting-up, at a rate of nearly 53 million cubic feet of sediment per year, has opened some ten thousand acres of grassland and salt marshes along the littoral, pro-viding about thirteen thousand sheep with land to graze on. The extension of the salt marshes has become worrisome, particularly since it is now threatening the Mont-Saint-Michel's identity as an island. A major project has recently been launched to ensure that this celebrated isle, crowned with a Gothic marvel that draws throngs of tourists and pilgrims, does indeed remain insular.

Seen from the air, Mont-Saint-Michel Bay looks like a shattered windshield, broken by a stone.—*PPDA*

Pages 46 and 47

● The rise of local produce.
The orchards of the Lyonnais Mountains (Rhône) are planted with a thousand acres of cherry trees around Bessenay, the cherry capital west of Lyons. The cherry business is expand-ing rapidly. Half the trees are less than a decade old, and the May to July harvest reaps up to eight thousand tons of cherries per year, placing the Rhône area third among French depart-ments growing cherries. The department also grows pears, apricots, and peaches, all of which are sold at the local markets, and benefit from consumers' attraction to "local produce" that defies the taste standardization practiced by the food-processing industry. This interest in local produce also carries over to breeding, which is another significant activity in the region. Ninety percent of milk production is delivered to dairy cooperatives specialized in making yogurt, fresh cream, and cottage cheese, all of which are highly appreci-ated on the local market. Overall, France produced 23 billion liters of milk in 2003.

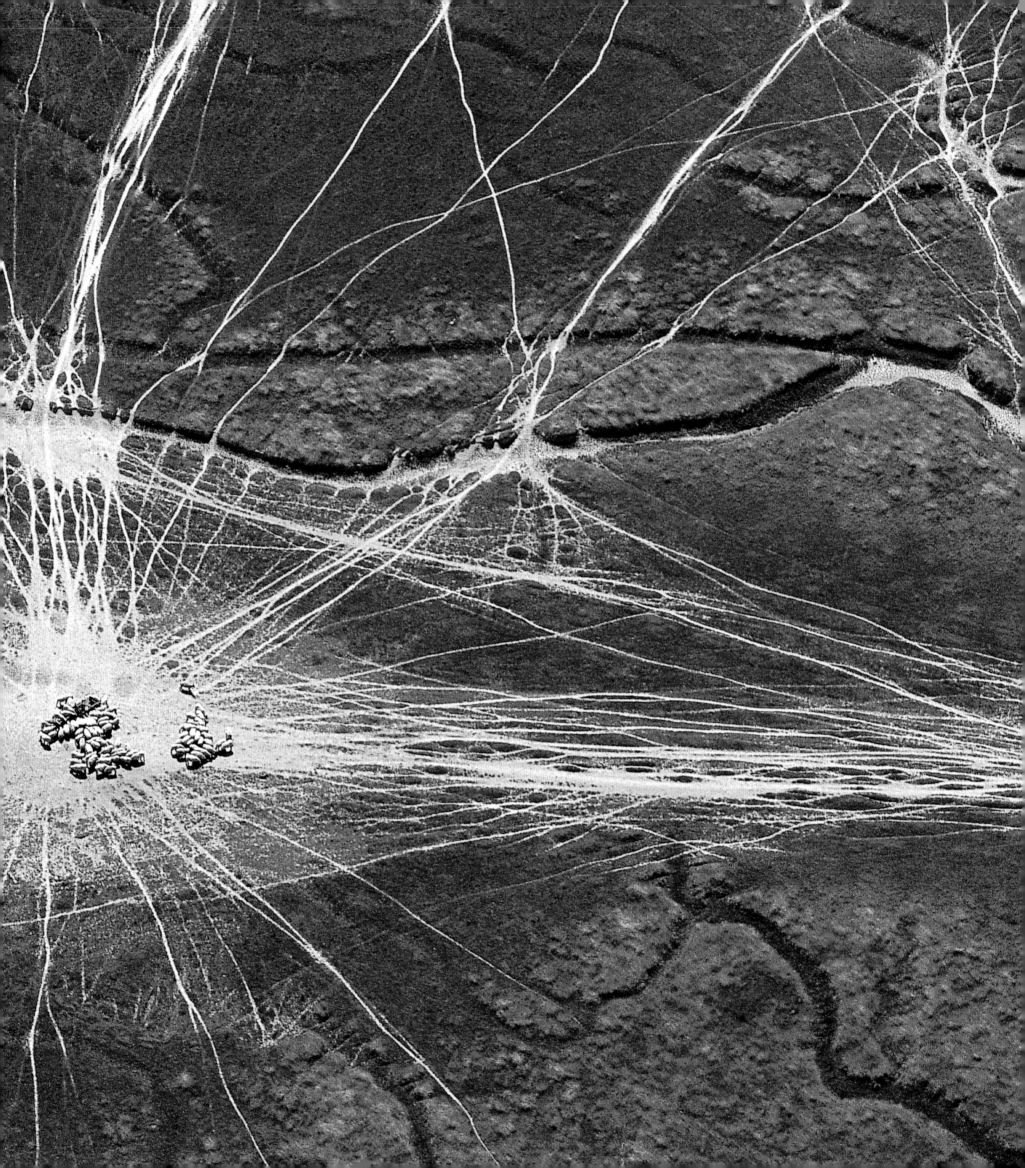

Left

- **The unshakable Eiffel Tower in Paris.**

It was only supposed to last as long as the 1889 World's Fair, yet it's still here. Named after its creator, Gustave Eiffel, the Eiffel Tower represents the triumph of nineteenth-century metallic architecture. Its construction on the Champ-de-Mars, in the 7th arrondissement, required some eighteen thousand different parts, assembled with 2.5 million rivets. The "iron lady" weighs almost ten thousand tons. It was originally 985 feet tall, but since 1929 it has gradually grown by about 65 feet due to the installation of a weather station and a network of television transmitters on its top level. About fifteen thousand visitors a day climb the Eiffel Tower.

Right and page 50

- **The Spirit of Liberty in Paris.**

The construction of the column of the Bastille, in the 12th arrondissement in Paris, was commissioned by Louis-Philippe in honor of the revolutionaries of the Trois Glorieuses (three glorious days) of July 1830. Inaugurated ten years later, the seventy-five-foot bronze column bore the names of the 615 people who died during those three days of revolt. Standing atop the column, the Spirit of Liberty takes flight toward the skies of Paris, brandishing the broken chains of despotism in his left hand and the torch of Civilization in its right. The statue was recovered with gold leaf by the Huber workshop of Paris on the occasion of the bicentennial of the Revolution of 1789.

I often use a zoom lens. It allows me to frame in such a way that I can isolate details in the landscape. This was the case with this picture, though I've also photographed the Spirit from a telescopic crane 260 feet above the ground.—*YAB*

Page 51

- **Low tide on the beaches of Vendée.**

With a total of 2,200 hours of sunshine per year and 155 miles of Atlantic coastline, Vendée wisely makes the most of its coastal assets. Fourteen seaside resorts, including Les Sables-d'Olonne and Saint-Jean-de-Monts, known as "the biggest sandbox in the West," reap the benefits of some 140 beaches of fine sand, the minimal incline of which allows the tide to sweep out a long way without endangering children at play. The tourist industry in this department of the Loire region employs eight thousand people in the off season and twenty-five thousand people in the high season.

I can still see myself in Brittany, with my parents, picking up seashells. There were six of us kids. I can still remember all of us running, waving our nets around, crying, "I got one! I got one!"—*YAB*

I have the same kind of memories, along with a recollection of nocturnal excursions to go sand-eel fishing. We would set out with our head lanterns and our rakes in search of the sand eels hiding in the gravel.—*PPDA*

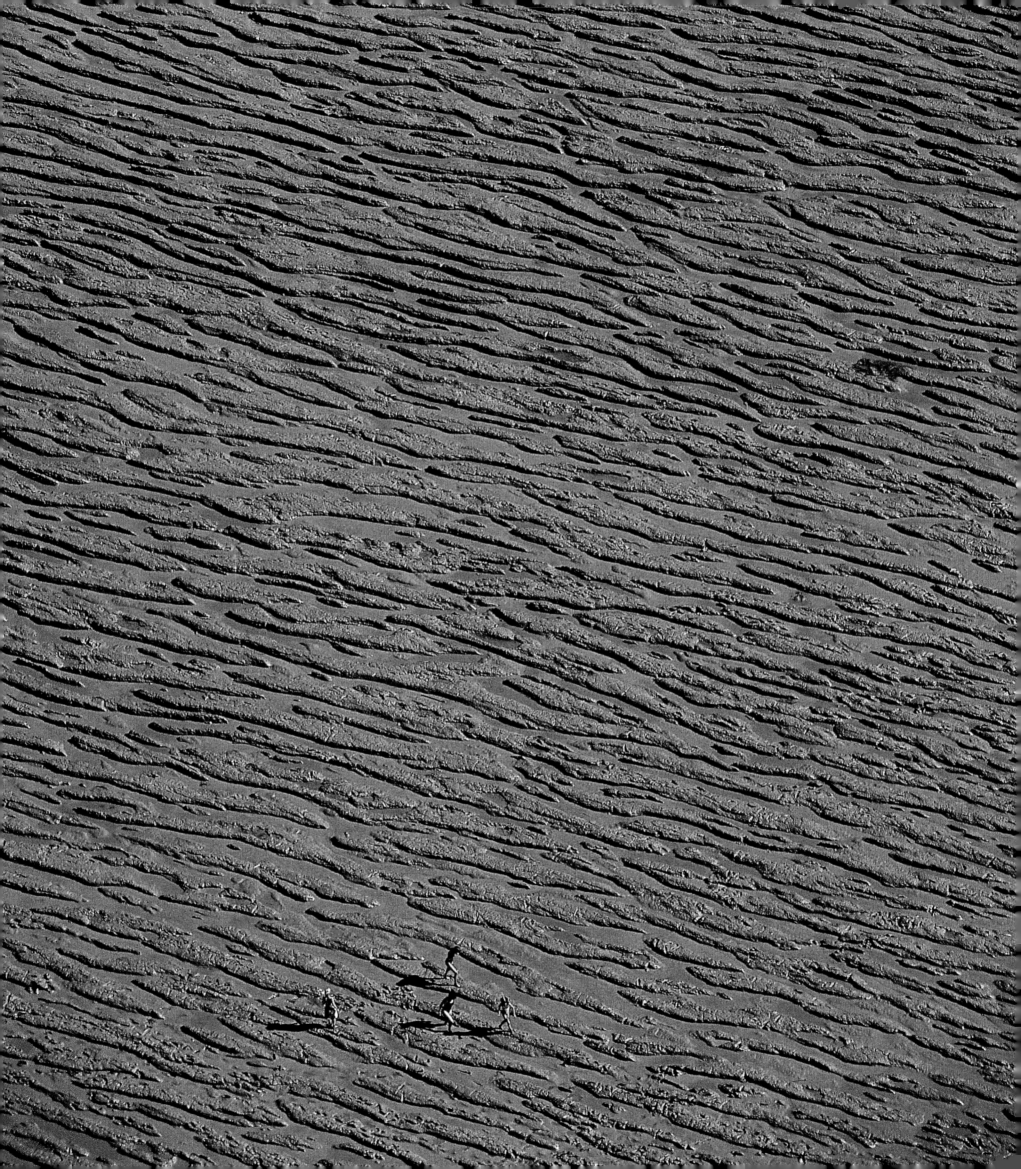

Opposite

● **Vestiges of the Atlantic Wall in Royan.**

The town of Royan, in Charente-Maritime, is situated on the estuary of the Gironde. In 1941, Royan was one of many towns along the French coastline to be fortified with casemates by the Nazis. The construction of the Atlantic Wall lasted two years, employed 250,000 men and required nearly 530 million cubic feet of concrete. After the Allied landings in Normandy, the Germans retreated here and held out in the "Royan pocket." The longest siege in the history of the Liberation ended on the night of January 4, 1945, when the British dropped 1,700 tons of bombs on the martyred town. The once unassailable blockhouses have since taken on lively colors.

A blockhouse is a vestige of war. Yet I find this blue casemate, surrounded by children playing on the beach, reassuring.—*YAB*

Unfortunately, a blockhouse is indestructible. In short, when it comes to war, to bloodshed and death, man is far better at constructing durable, solid objects than when it comes to survival, or just plain living.—*PPDA*

Following spread

● **The Beauduc lighthouse in the Camargue.**

Despite the significant risk of shipwrecks on the sandy shores of the Camargue (Bouches-du-Rhône), the Beauduc lighthouse on the dunes of the Pointe du Sablon wasn't built until 1902. Its construction was spurred by the sinking of a steamer from Marseilles, the *Pergame,* on January 1, 1898. The lighthouse's conical white freestone turret is 82 feet high. Though its light signals have been automatic since 2001, a watchman continues to keep an eye on the coast.

This photo doubly touches me, not only because I love the Camargue, but also because the lighthouse keepers are friends of mine. The sea is quite cloudy, because the Rhône carries a lot of alluvial deposits, but the beach is totally wild. People come here to recoup for a few days, far from the rest of the world.—*YAB*

The other surprising thing is that just a few decades ago this lighthouse was right by the water, and that the sands have since advanced, just like at Aigues-Mortes. So it isn't always the sea that wins!—*PPDA*

Previous spread

- **Mont Blanc, a top tourist attraction.**
The Mont Blanc massif in Haute-Savoie, in the French Alps, is 15,771 feet tall, and is the third most visited natural site in the world. This legendary peak remained untamed until the late eighteenth century, but is now ascended by countless climbers. In fact, climbers now have a choice of various routes to reach the summit, beginning with the so-called normal trail from Chamonix. During the June to September holiday season, up to two hundred and fifty people a day climb the Mont Blanc. The evolution of climbing-gear technology and performance have allowed for this democratization, which sadly constitutes an ecological threat to this extreme yet fragile environment.

When I am flying over the mountains, I am very sensitive to people climbing. I don't want to disturb them, because I know that up here silence is part of the experience.—YAB

It's true that it would be nice to be alone on France's tallest peak, which I was lucky enough to scale not too long ago. When you're all the way up there, you feel like the king of the world, because you can look over three countries. And because you suffered to get there.—PPDA

Opposite

- **The Mer de Glace (Sea of Ice) is threatened by global warming.**
The celebrated Sea of Ice, which opens onto the valley of Chamonix (Haute-Savoie), has been affected, like the rest of the Alps, by global warming attributed to the emission of greenhouse-effect gases. In the last ten years, this spur of ice, composed of three enormous séracs, has lost nearly ten feet in thickness at its highest elevation, and nearly thirty feet downhill, near the village of Des Mottets. Like the Sea of Ice, the great Alpine glaciers have seen a third of their mass melt away over the last century. This phenomenon could continue to accelerate, thereby threatening the future of low-altitude ski resorts.

This glacier is already worn out. You get the feeling it's been stitched up a thousand times, like a down-and-out boxer. It'll wind up pleading for mercy, before the last ring of the gong.—PPDA

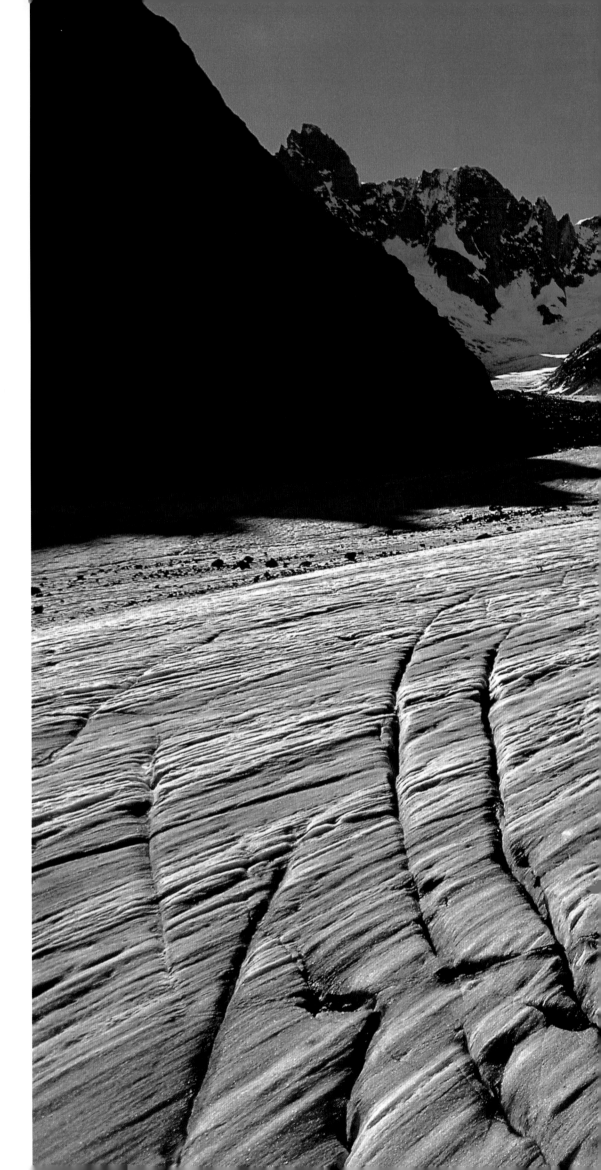

Left

- **The Saint-Exupéry TGV station near Lyons.**
Inaugurated in 1994, the Saint-Exupéry high-speed train station near Lyons (Rhône) manages to pay tribute to modern rail transportation with its futuristic metallic structures while providing a rail connection from the regional capital to Satolas Airport. Spanish architect and engineer Santiago Calatrava designed the train station to look like a giant bird on the verge of taking flight. The main hall's wings, which are supported by a white concrete structure, are spread to the sky, giving the building its dynamic. Trains that do not make a stop at the station speed through at 185 miles per hour.

Right

- **The Millau viaduct.**
Inaugurated in December 2004, the Millau highway viaduct in the Aveyron crosses over the Tarn valley at a height of 885 feet. It is the highest suspension bridge in the world. The heights of its seven pillars range from 250 feet to 1,125 feet. French architect Michel Virlogeux and British architect Norman Foster conceived this 8,000-foot-long work of art. Its three-year construction required 206,000 tons of concrete and 36,000 tons of steel. Thanks to the dilation flexibility of its joints, the roadway can withstand extreme temperatures ranging from -31° Fahrenheit in winter to 113° Fahrenheit in summer. Sensors and special panels attached to the bridge serve to evaluate and reduce wind strength. The viaduct, which is intended to last one hundred and twenty years, will have to be repainted in thirty.

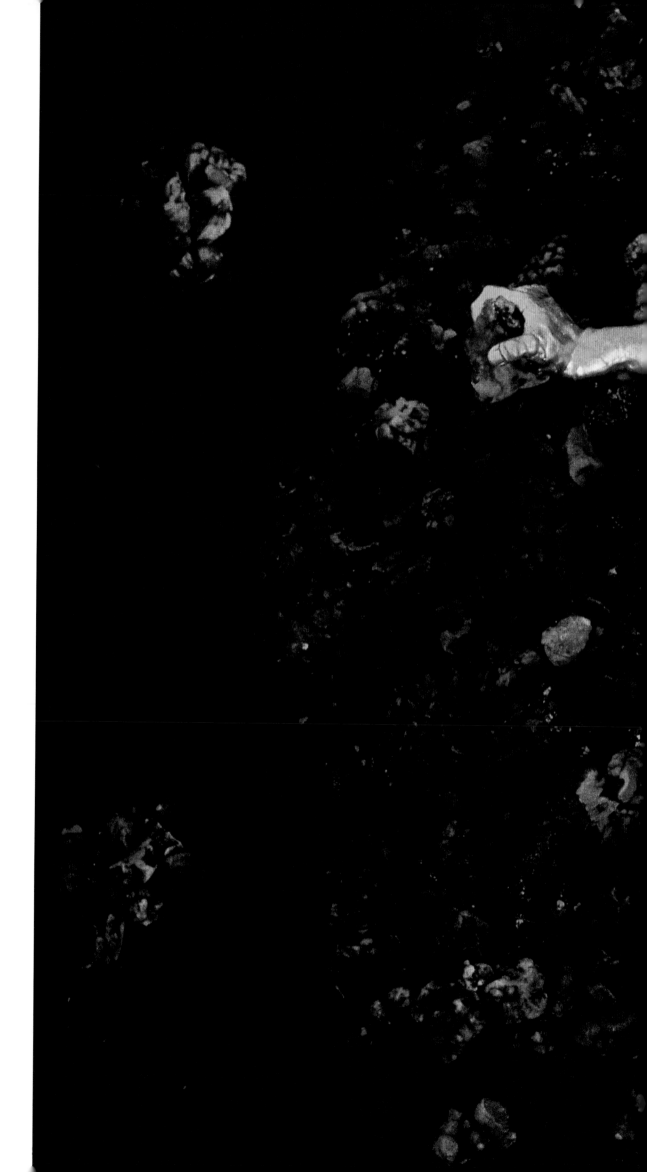

Previous spread

- **The abbey church of Sainte-Foy in Conques.**
The abbey of Sainte-Foy was founded in the ninth century in Conques, in the Aveyron, to house the relics of a young woman from Agen who was martyred and subsequently canonized. In the Middle Ages, this masterpiece of Romanesque art became an important center for pilgrimages. Largely destroyed during the Revolution, the church was saved in 1837 by the writer and historic monuments inspector Prosper Mérimée, who was stunned to find "such riches in this desert!" Born in Rodez, painter Pierre Soulages worked on restoring the abbey-church's stained-glass windows from 1987 to 1994. Limiting himself to black in order to, in his words, "reflect the light thereby 'transmuted,'" the artist ordered special glass from Saint-Gobain to recreate the 104 windows and achieve his vision.

Conques is an astonishing village for the way it hangs off the side of a hill, far removed from the rest of the world. When you're in a helicopter, you don't even see it coming. It only reveals itself at the last minute, peeking out of the depths of the forest when you're a mere three hundred feet from your objective.—*YAB*

One of the stops on the road to Compostela . . . If you follow the road on foot, you discover an exceptional aspect of France. When you reach Conques after having walked fifteen miles from the previous stopover, you are rewarded with the joy and relief of entering one of the most beautiful churches in the world.—*PPDA*

Opposite

- **The giant Encelade in the gardens of Versailles.**
In Greek mythology, the giant Encelade wanted to attack the residence of the gods. Enraged Athena made Encelade pay for his audacity by burying him in the lava from erupting Etna. As an absolute ruler, Louis XIV found the lesson edifying enough to have the Encelade fountain erected in the groves of Versailles (Yvelines) as a warning to overly ambitious courtiers. This lead statue of Athena striking down the giant was designed by Gaspard Marsy in 1676. It was restored and regilded at the end of 1997.

Opposite

● **The Val-de-Grâce in Paris.**
Anne of Austria, wife of
Louis XIII, founded the Val-de-
Grâce abbey in 1621 to thank
the heavens for granting her a
son after twenty-two years of
sterility. In 1645 she asked classical architect François Mansart
to add a church and a palace to
the abbey. Construction on this
second project was finished in
1647 under Jacques Lemercier.

Along with its cloister and
its gardens, the convent is a
model of seventeenth-century
religious architecture. It was
abandoned during the Revolution, then converted into a
military hospital in 1796.
Situated in the 5th arrondissement in Paris, the Val-de-Grâce
now contains one of the best
military instructional hospitals
in France.

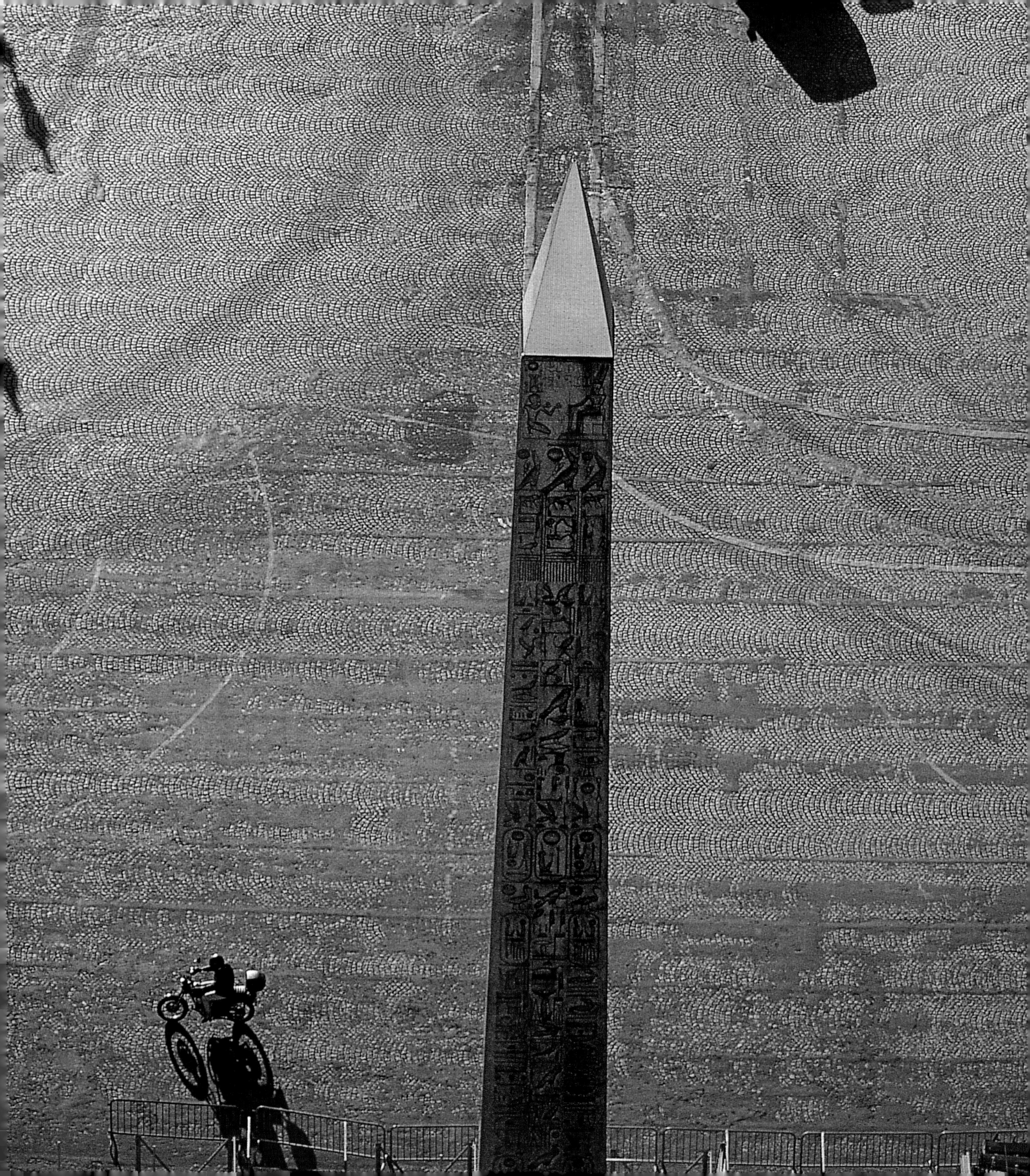

Left

● **The obelisk of the Concorde
in Paris.**
The Place de la Concorde, which
occupies more than 900,000
square feet in the 8th arrondissement, was laid out by
architect Jacques-Ange Gabriel
between 1755 and 1775. During
the Terror, in 1793, more than a
thousand people, including
Louis XVI and his wife, Marie-
Antoinette, were guillotined
here. The 227-ton, 75-foot-tall
obelisk was a present taken
from the 3,300-year-old Temple
of Luxor by Egyptian Pasha
Muhammad Ali and given to
King Louis-Philippe. Its erection
on Place de la Concorde on
October 25, 1836, drew over
200,000 spectators. Because
they were convinced the
obelisk's pinnacle had been
stolen, the authorities had its
top gilded. In 2000, urban
climber Alain Robert used his
bare feet and hands to climb the
obelisk without a harness.

Right

● **The fortified church
of Hunawihr.**
The square tower and pointed
roof of the fortified church of
Hunawihr (Upper Rhine) have
dominated the Alsatian vineyards of Colmar since the sixteenth century. Added to the
Historic Register in 1972, it is
home to a series of murals
devoted to the life of Saint
Nicolas, a very popular saint
in the region.

Below

● **The National Police changes its look.**

Last modified by designer Pierre Balmain in 1985, the uniform worn by National Police officers such as those seen here standing at attention during a Bastille Day parade in Paris, remained unaltered for twenty years. Patrolmen and officers finally inaugurated a new uniform during the Bastille Day 2005 parade on the Champs-Élysées. Designed by Balenciaga, this new uniform includes a soft cap, an ice-blue shirt, fatigue pants, and commando-style ankle boots. This 533-euro outfit, available in summer and winter styles, is intended to provide the 145,000 civil servants, captains, lieutenants, patrolmen, or security agents who will wear it with a more youthful image.

Opposite

● **The Fort of Brégançon, residence of the Republic.**

Standing on a 115-foot rocky peak in the commune of Bormes-les-Mimosas (Var), the Fort of Brégançon has left its military heritage in the past. Built in the eleventh century and reconverted several times, this fortress long served to protect the harbors of Hyères and Toulon. In 1919 the army decided to abandon it. In 1968, following General De Gaulle's overnight stay during his visit to celebrate the twentieth anniversary of the Allies' landing in Provence, the fort was named an official residence of the presidents of France. Soon modernized by French architect and Grand Prix de Rome winner Pierre-Jean Guth, Bregançon has been a vacation home for French presidents ever since.

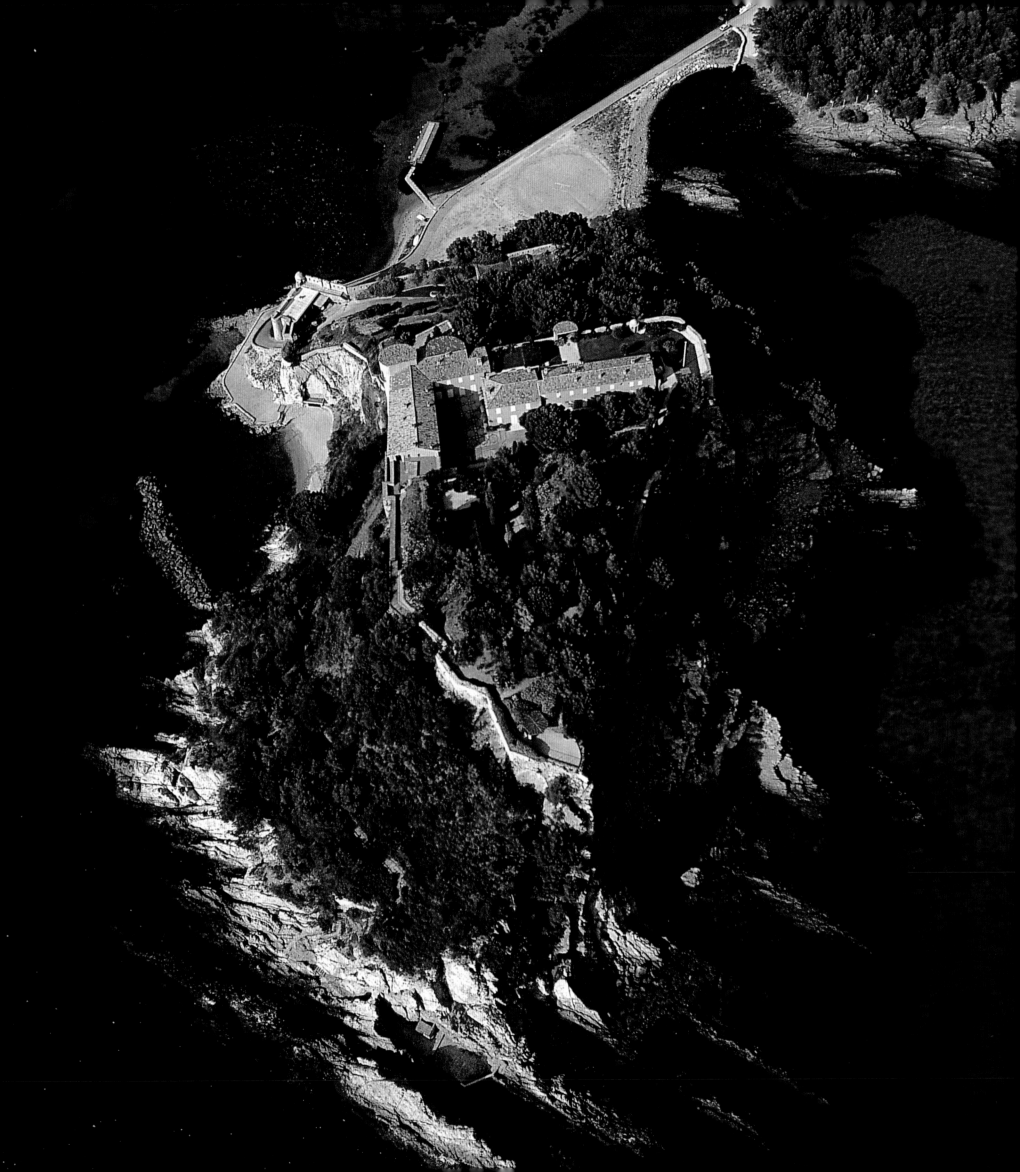

Opposite

- **The Notre-Dame-du-Haut chapel in Ronchamp.** The reconstruction of the chapel of Ronchamp (Haute-Saône) following its destruction under Allied bombs in 1944 was entrusted to Charles-Édouard Jeanneret, better known as Le Corbusier. His new concrete edifice was inaugurated in 1955. Along with the Notre-Dame-de-la-Tourette convent, it is the only religious monument constructed by the utopian architect also responsible for the Cité radieuse (Radiant City) in Marseilles, and considered one of the masters of modern architecture.

I consider Ronchamp to be one of Le Corbusier's most moving structures. It is said the design of this chapel was inspired by the Algerian mosque of Al Ateuf. It is magnificent in the evening light.—YAB

Below

● **Cycling is a priority in Greater Lyons.**
The installation of a bicycle path along the banks of the Rhône, in the Parc du Confluent (also known as the Parc de Gerland) in Lyons (Rhône), has contributed to the growth of cycling as a non-polluting mode of transportation in France's second-largest metropolitan area. The city plans to extend its 185-mile network of bicycle paths to 310 miles by 2010. In the spring of 2005, the city also launched "Service Vélo'v" (Bike Service)—a service that allows Lyons residents to rent one of two thousand city-owned bikes in exchange for a modest fee.

Opposite

● **The Tour de France on the Mont Ventoux.**
Since it was created in 1903, the Tour de France bicycle race has become an athletic event-cum-national holiday, and remains firmly entrenched as France's favorite summer cliffhanger. Every year, the twenty stages of the 2,170-mile Grande Boucle (Big Loop) provide competitors with numerous challenges, such as the ascension of the 6,263-foot Mont Ventoux, in the department of Vaucluse. The Tour draws a total of twelve million roadside spectators a year.

The Tour is part and parcel of France's identity. Summer without the Tour de France is simply unimaginable. Some twelve million people line the roads to see the competitors with their own eyes. As for those who watch on television, many are drawn by the opportunity to see the same kind of aerial landscapes this volume aims to provide. In 1967 British cyclist Tom Simpson dropped dead when he reached the summit of Mont Ventoux. Since then, cyclists have always stopped at the top to honor him with a moment of silence.—*YAB*

I once followed the Tour de France on a motorcycle. I was struck by this genuinely popular spectacle's passionate yet convivial atmosphere. As the most popular sport in France, bicycling is constantly expanding, despite the fact that our cities are ill-adapted to the daily practice of bike riding.—*PPDA*

Opposite

● **The towers of the Sainte-Croix Cathedral in Orléans.**
Battered by the Wars of Religion and ravaged by Protestants in 1568, Sainte-Croix Cathedral in Orléans (Loiret) was rebuilt by the kings of France over a period of several centuries. Henri IV, a converted Protestant, broke ground on the new structure in 1601. Architect Jean-François Trouard designed the 265-foot towers in a Gothic "fantasy" style in the eighteenth century. The central spire rises 374 feet. Devoted to the Cult of Reason during the Revolution, the cathedral had its towers "decapitated" by Allied bombings in 1944. It has since been perfectly restored.

Page 78

● **The strange patterns of the streets of Paris.**
Beginning with Baron Haussmann's major remodeling of the layout of the capital under the Second Empire, it appears to have become standard practice to carve new streets into the urban fabric. A good example of this approach is rue Marcadet, in the 18th arrondissement, whose name was reportedly drawn from an area once known as the Mercade, or Mercadé. The 1.25 mile-long rue Marcadet has erased all traces of the byways that preceded it on the path to Montmartre.

Page 79

● **The Great Pyramid of the Louvre in Paris.**
The Pyramid of the Louvre, in Paris's 1st arrondissement, was part of President François Mitterand's Great Works construction project. It was erected in the courtyard of the old palace of the kings of France, and was inaugurated in 1988. The pyramid is an astonishing technological feat on the part of its Chinese-American architect I. M. Pei. Indeed, the 71-foot-high structure is composed of 673 glass lozenges and triangles assembled on a 95-ton metallic armature. The translucent structure serves as an entrance to the Louvre Museum, which contains thirty-five thousand art objects and is visited by more than six million people a year. Since June 2005, these priceless collections have also been able to be viewed on the museum's new Web site.

Pages 80–81

● **Sowing season in the fertile Beaujolais.**
The north of the Rhône department is largely composed of prairies that run into the hills of the Beaujolais (shown here near Cublize). In this area, goats and cows produce milk used in local cheeses such as the cenvard or the cabrion. Farmers also devote 12 percent of available farmland to growing cereals such as wheat and corn, which are then stockpiled to feed cattle during the winter. On average, cultivated plots here are about two hundred and fifty acres in size. The area sustains about 640 working farms.

Pages 82–83

● **Training at the Maisons-Laffitte hippodrome.**
Occupying 227 acres along the Seine, the Maisons-Laffitte equestrian training center (Yvelines) is one of the oldest such establishments in France. It was founded in the eighteenth century on the grounds of a residence belonging to the Comte d'Artois, one of Louis XVI's brothers, and a lover of thoroughbreds. Currently managed by the France Galop Association (France Gallop Association), the center permanently trains some eight hundred horses, such as those seen here on the Adam round. The hippodrome has the longest gallop track in Europe (6,560 feet), and hosts some thirty equestrian meets a year.

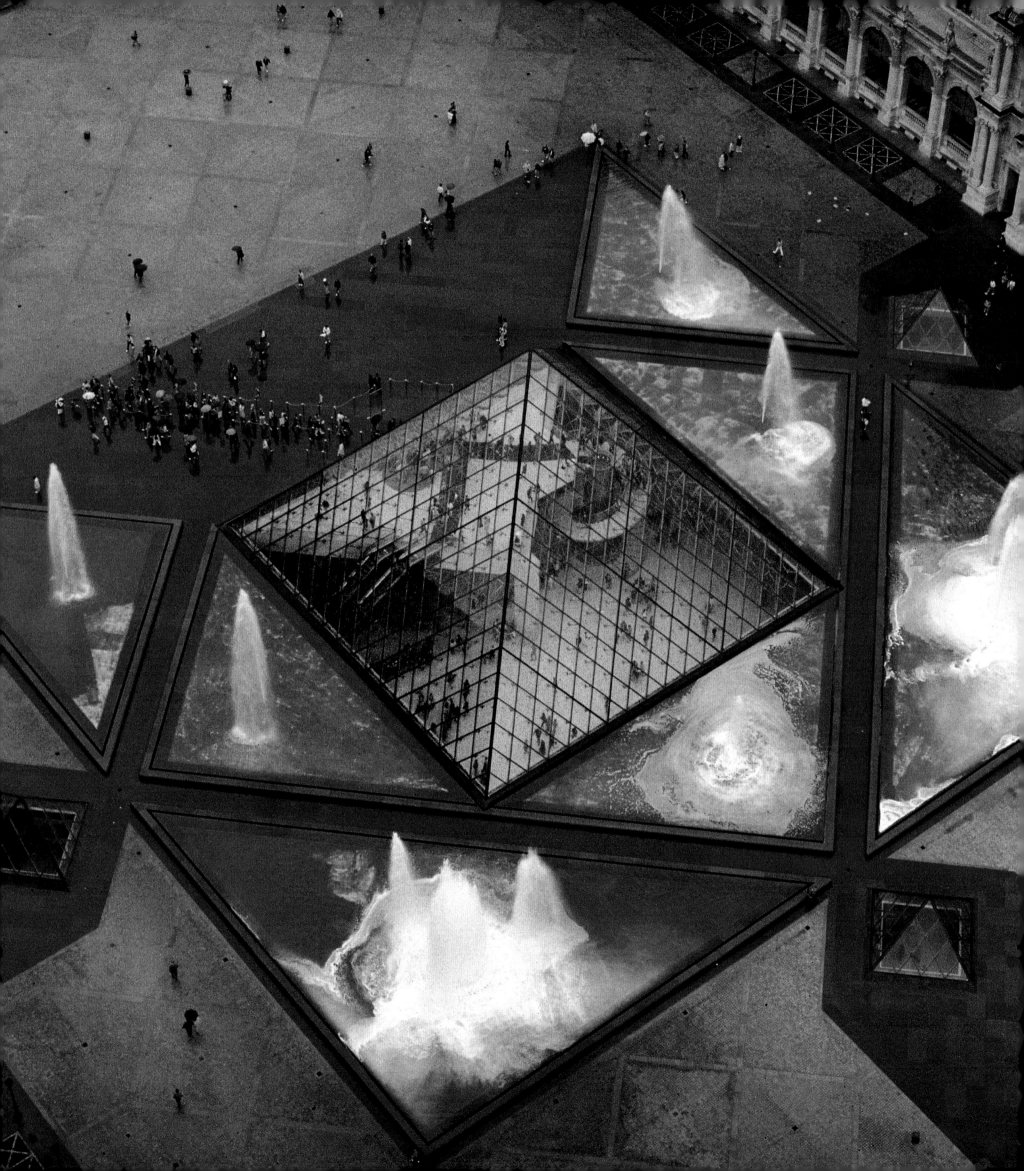

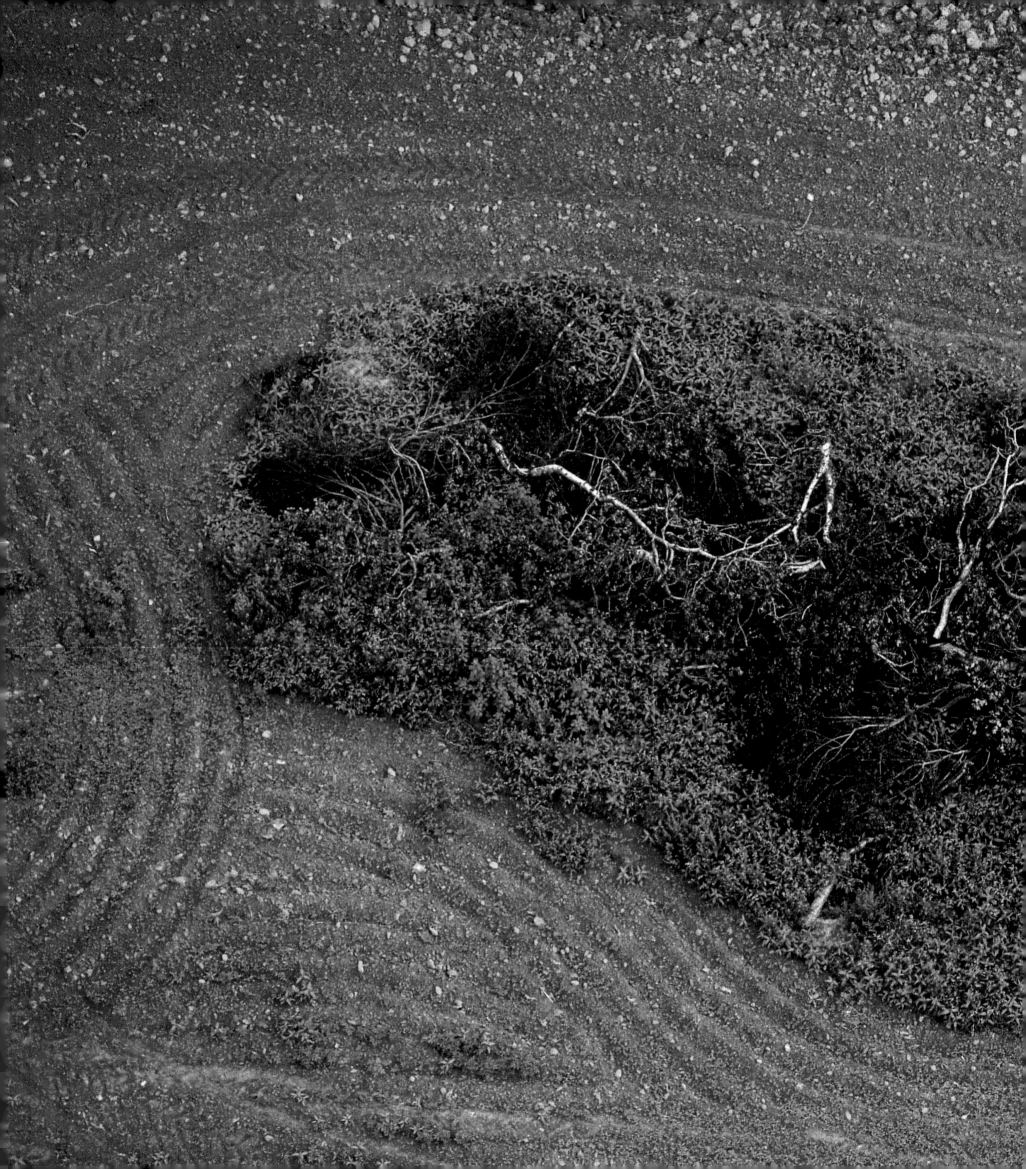

Previous spread

- **Overproduction of cider apples in Brittany.**
Along with Normandy, Brittany is one of France's major producers of cider apples. A powerhouse in the early twentieth century (with nearly 14 million hectoliters produced in 1900), the cider industry has steadily declined to the point that annual consumption of cider is now estimated at one million hectoliters, or less than two liters per inhabitant per year. Despite the rejuvenation of the orchards (1.5 million trees in Brittany) through the planting of low-stemmed trees since the 1980s, overproduction remains a constant problem in areas such as this one, near Plougrescant, in the Côtes-d'Armor. Though the cider, apple juice, and pommeau industry (pommeau is a local drink of Calvados and cider) only makes use of about 203,000 tons of apples per year, production is estimated at 500,000 to 600,000 tons, a significant amount of which is wasted.

Opposite

- **Lavender spreads color through Haute-Provence.**
By 1992 lavender production had reached a low point of 25 tons a year. Today, cultivation of this wild flower frequently found on arid land is booming again, as can be seen here near Sarraud, on the plateaus of the Vaucluse. Lavender (11,366 acres) and its hybrid, *lavandin* (40,771 acres), sustain 2,400 farmers in Haute-Provence. In 2004, after distillation, these plants provided 71 tons of fine lavender essential oils and 1,250 tons of *lavandin* oils for perfume and aromatherapy. This revival directly contributes to local economic development, as well as providing a tourist attraction.

Pages 88–89

- **Bivouac on top of Mont Blanc.**
Since it was first ascended by Jacques Balmat and Michel Paccard on August 8, 1786, the legendary Mont Blanc has been drawn out of its splendid isolation. Climbers no longer hesitate to bivouac on its flanks, while the Company of Chamonix Guides (Haute-Savoie), founded in 1821, organizes annual summer trekking expeditions on the glorious peak. Good weather is essential for these excursions to be a success. According to a local saying, "If the Mont Blanc puts on a cap (of clouds), he promises a storm," and "if he smokes his pipe (by stirring up snow flurries), he predicts a great wind."

Pages 90–91

- **Reforestation in the Ariège Pyrenees.**
After World War II, the section of the Pyrenees in Ariège was used to rapidly grow the conifers needed for reconstruction. The conifers were planted in strips beneath the original beeches, which favored their rapid development by providing them with shade and moisture. "Exotic" species imported from North America, such as Douglas or Vancouver pines, were also introduced to the area. Today, the ecological balance is off-kilter. Beeches are coming back in strength, spreading their boughs over the conifers and suffocating them. These problems are managed locally by the National Forest Office in Foix, which tries to ensure the well-being of reforested massifs such as this one near Seix.

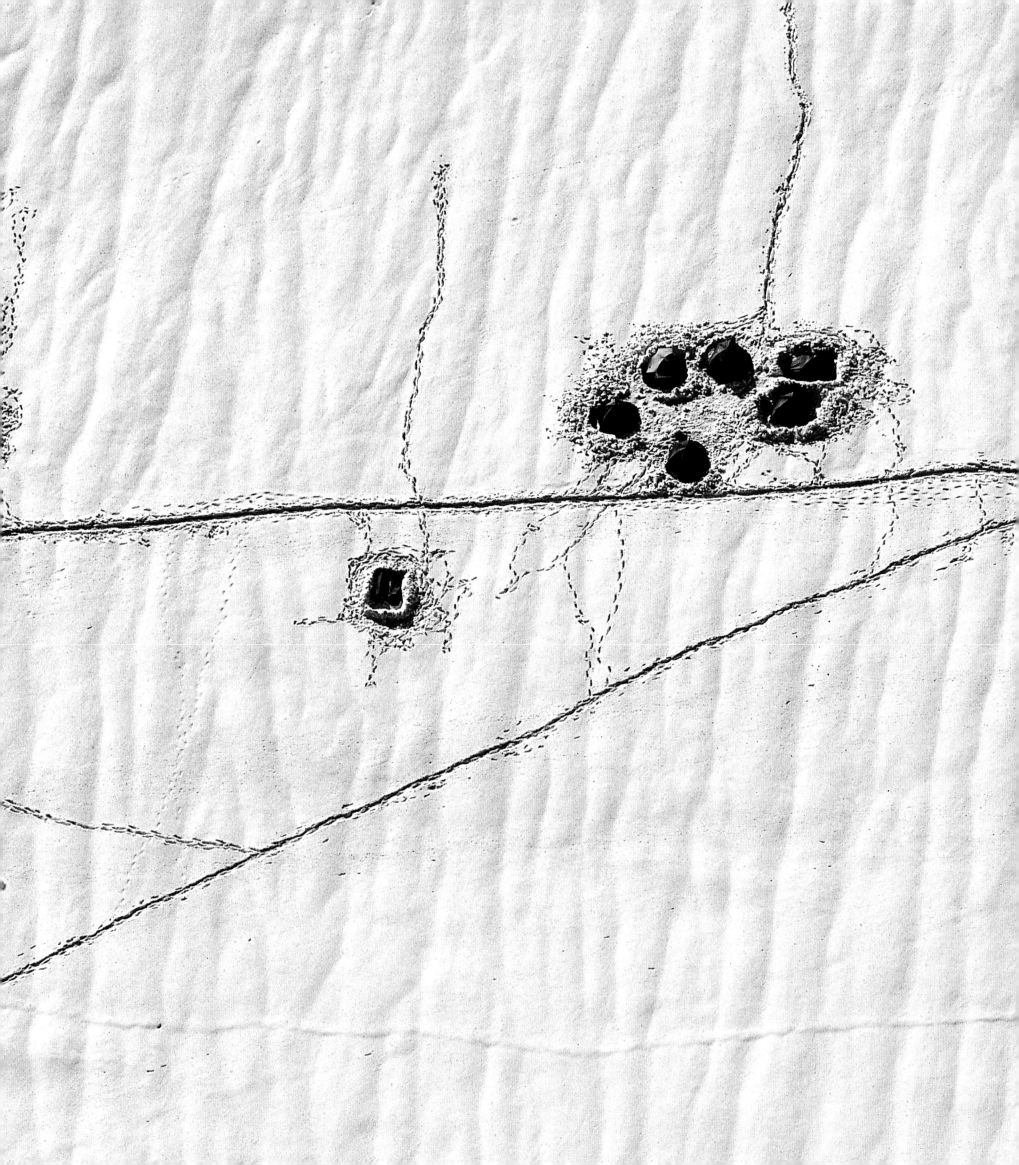

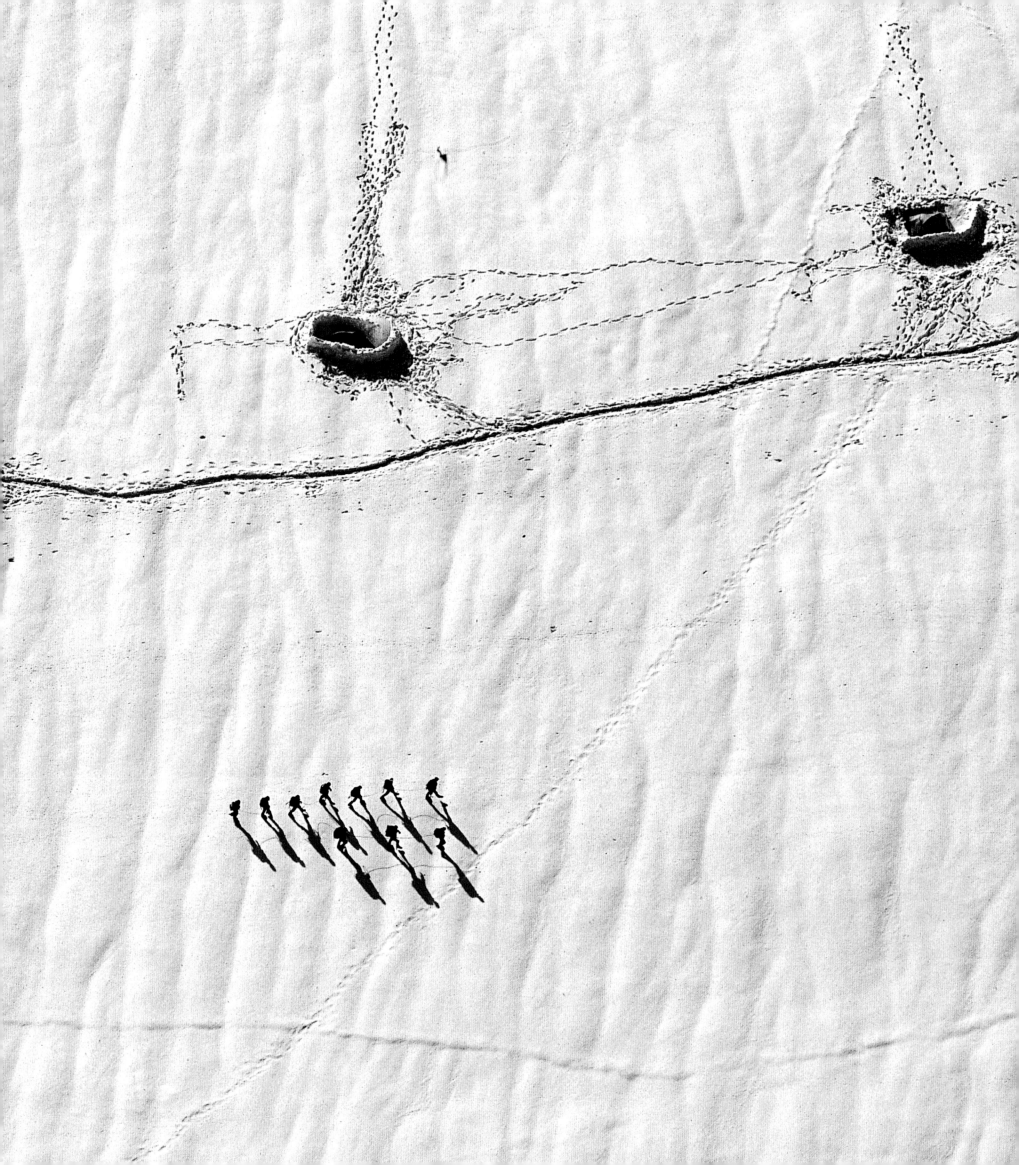

Previous spread

● **Reims, the coronation cathedral.**
Though most of the construction of the Gothic cathedral of Notre-Dame-de-Reims (Marne) was finished in 1275, the seven spires initially planned for by the builders were never added to the edifice. The cathedral's current towers were erected in the fourteenth and fifteenth centuries. Twenty-five French kings have been crowned here, from Louis VIII, in the primitive cathedral of 1223, to Charles X, in 1825. The sole exception to this long lineage was Henri IV, who was crowned in Chartres in 1594. For many centuries, the monarchy considered this unction the sign of the divine right to rule. The cathedral was bombed during World War I, but it has since been restored and named a UNESCO World Heritage Site.

I thought I would take a classic shot of the cathedral's facade, but I was drawn to the light on the chevet, which gives a totally different take on the building.—*YAB*

I was born at the foot of this cathedral. Half a century later, I'm finally flying above it!—*PPDA*

Above and opposite

● **The Royal Saltworks of Arc-et-Senans.**
The Saltworks of Arc-et-Senans (Doubs) is a unique relic of French industrial architecture during the Enlightenment. It was built by Claude-Nicolas Ledoux in a neoclassical, or Palladian, style, from 1774 to 1779. Franche-Comté salt was extracted here by evaporating saltwater in wood ovens. Workshops and housing for the workers were arranged in semi-circles around the director's residence. The Saltworks was closed in 1895, but was eventually bought back by the local council and restored. It is a UNESCO World Heritage Site.

With its perfectly symmetrical patterns, the Saltworks of Arc-et-Senans really seems to have been made to be seen from the air.—*YAB*

Opposite

● **Place Stanislas in Nancy.**
Place Stanislas is the heart of
the city of Nancy (Meurthe-et-
Moselle). It was laid out in 1752
by the ex-king of Poland,
Stanislas Leszczynski, an
enlightened ruler who had
become duke of Lorraine following his daughter Marie's marriage to Louis XV. In fact,
everything about this square,
from the classical pavilions
designed by architect Emmanuel
Héré to the gates of the palace
by Jean Lamour, were intended
to dazzle the French ruler.
Today, the palace is Nancy's city
hall, but a statue of Louis XV
continues to look over the
square. This World Heritage Site
is one of the most beautiful
groupings of eighteenth-century
French architecture around.

Below

● **The Volcanoes of Auvergne Regional Nature Park.**
Founded in 1977, the Volcanoes of Auvergne Regional Nature Park extends almost one million acres over the departments of Puy-de-Dôme and Cantal. The château of Montlosier sits at the heart of the park. It was built at the beginning of the nineteenth century in Aydat (Puy-de-Dôme), and currently houses a center for information about the region, specifically its geology (including scale models of volcanoes) and its fauna and flora. The château is open year-round and is also used as a lodge. Unfortunately, the "Vulcania" European Center for Volcanism, which was opened in 2002 near Clermont-Ferrand on the initiative of Valéry Giscard d'Estaing, the ex-president of the regional council, has disappointed expectations. It received 628,000 visitors in its first year, but by 2004, annual visitors were down to 420,000, and the center was operating at a 2-million-euro deficit.

Opposite

● **The Puys volcanic chain in Auvergne.**
Dominated by the 4,806-foot peak of the Puy de Dôme, the Puys chain includes about a hundred volcanoes in a 31-mile area west of Clermont-Ferrand (Puy-de-Dôme). The first eruptions here took place some seventy thousand years ago. Some of the Strombolian-type volcanoes' craters have become lakes. Other Pelean volcanoes have been known to belch out fiery clouds in their day. These Massif Central landscapes in the Volcanoes of Auvergne Regional Nature Park are unmatched in the rest of France.

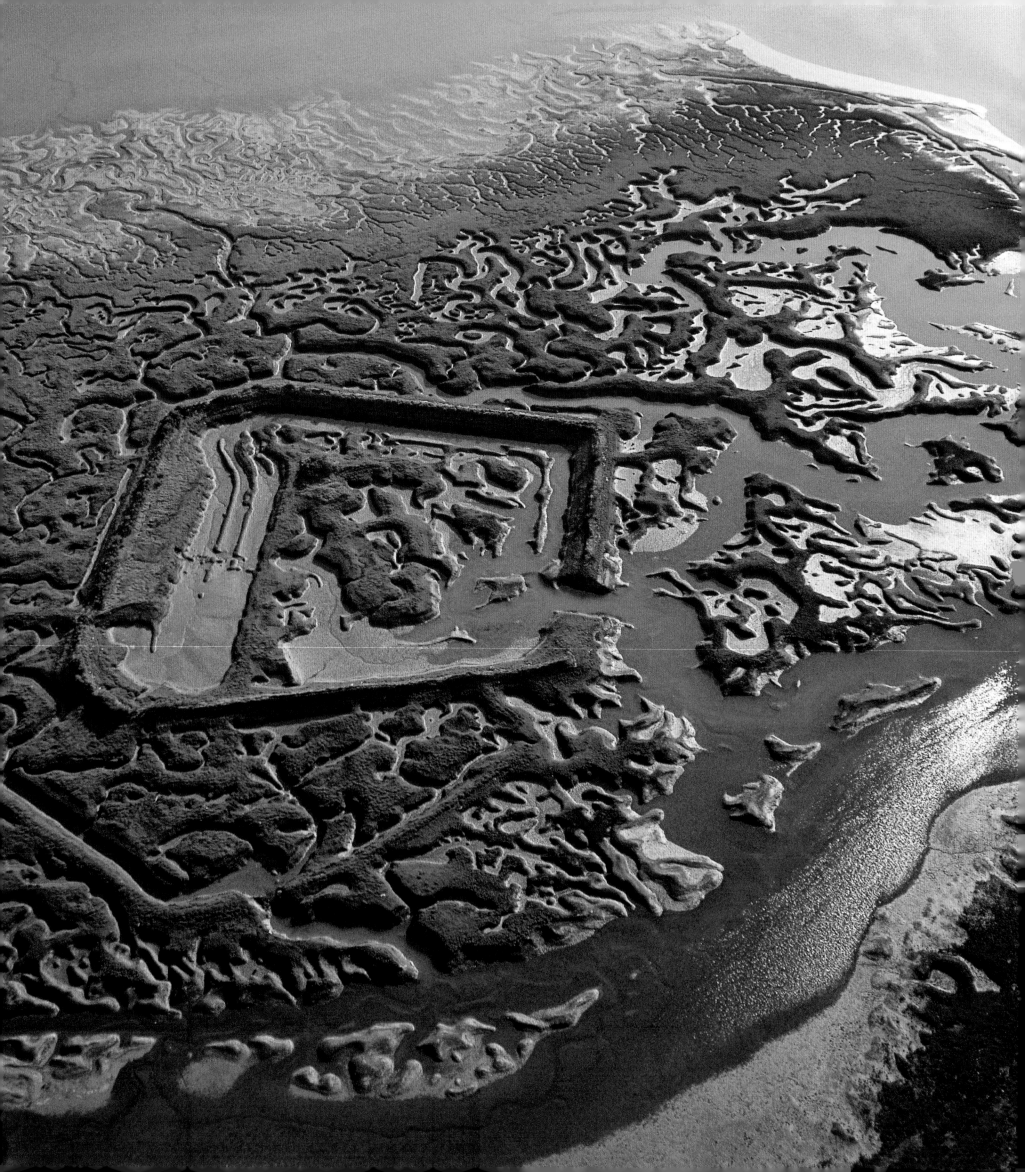

Left

Saint-Suliac, an old Viking encampment.
The Breton village of Saint-Suliac (Ille-et-Vilaine) is considered one of the most beautiful in France. It preserves traces of its foundation by Vikings over a thousand years ago. The ruins of an old fortified encampment set up in the estuary of the Rance by these ferocious longship-borne invaders who came from distant Scandinavia in the eleventh century have remained trapped in the mud. Today, the ruins are difficult to access even at low tide.

Right

A labyrinth of corn.
Initially devised in 1995, the concept of the "Labyrinthus," a huge treasure hunt through a maze of specially sculpted corn stalks, has been tremendously successful. The Labyrinthus at the foot of the medieval town of Cordes-sur-Ciel (Tarn) has now been replaced by a downtown "Garden of Paradise," devoted to medieval floral art, but Labyrinthus parks have continued to spring their verdant traps in several regions, including Alsace and the Midi-Pyrénées. The only inconvenience to this leisure activity is that its reliance on corn drains large amounts of water.

Following spread

Fog over the Loire valley.
Morning fogs produced by ambient humidity due to overnight temperature drops are frequent in the Loire valley. Here they are shown cloaking the countryside between Nantes and Ancenis (Loire-Atlantic), conferring a romantic feel to the royal river as it flows to its estuary.

I don't mind if some of my pictures, such as this shot of a steeple poking out of the fog, are reminiscent of postcards. After all, a postcard can be a picture you feel like sending to those that you love.—YAB

Fog is like cotton. It envelops things, dulls sound, and makes everything cleaner. To me, this picture is representative of Julien Gracq's Loire.—PPDA

Opposite

● **Fixey, the oldest Romanesque church on the Dijon coast.**
The Romanesque church of Fixey, in a hamlet near Fixin (Côte-d'Or) is registered as a historic monument. Initially built in A.D. 902, then altered in the eleventh and twelfth centuries, this small chapel dedicated to Saint Antoine was once a dependence of the Abbey of Saint-Bénigne in Dijon. Its glazed-tile steeple is typical of Burgundian architectural traditions, and its geometric motifs are reminiscent of the colored roofs of the famous Beaune Hospices. Set in the heart of a region celebrated since the Middle Ages for its wines, the church overlooks the Fixin vineyards. These vines growing on rocky limestone soil have produced *appellations d'origine contrôlée* wines, since 1936. An *appellation d'origine contrôlée* is a registered designation of origin that guarantees a product's provenance.

Above

● **The marché d'Aligre, one of the oldest markets in Paris.**
Since the market stalls of Les Halles moved to the suburbs, in the early 1970s, the marché d'Aligre, in the 12th arrondissement, has taken over as the "belly of Paris." Created in 1779 and rebuilt in 1843 to cater to the cabinetmakers of the Faubourg Saint-Antoine, the market continues to serve this now-trendy neighborhood near the Bastille. Open every morning except Monday, the marché d'Aligre's colorful stalls offer food products from the entire world. A flea market on its edges now draws antiques shoppers on the prowl for a bargain.

Today the heart and soul of Paris only survives in small neighborhoods, which always develop around a market. But finding such an inviting area and isolating it from the rest of the city, from cars and all the rest, is a rare feat in a metropolis of two million inhabitants, in a megalopolis of twelve million.—*PPDA*

Following spread

● **The gardens of Villandry put nature on display.**
The gardens of the Renaissance château of Villandry (Indre-et-Loire) were returned to their original splendor following the château's restoration by Doctor Joachim Carvallo at the beginning of the twentieth century. Anticipating city dwellers' enthusiasm for outdoor activity, the aesthete Carvallo domesticated nature to put it on display and recreate historic gardens in the spirit of their respective eras: He planted medicinal herbs for the garden of the Middle Ages, laid out Italian-style gardens for the Renaissance, and classical-style gardens, complete with a play of water, for the era of Louis XV. As for the vegetable garden, its caretakers alternate cabbage, beets, carrots, and pumpkins from one season to the next, and maintain a triennial rotation so as to avoid deteriorating the soil.

Opposite

• **The new suburbs of Marne-la-Vallée.**
The opening of the Disneyland amusement park in the Brie plains in Marne-la-Vallée (Seine-et-Marne) has led to a rapid build-up of the surrounding area. Indeed, Disneyland Europe has generated some forty-three thousand jobs in the region, whether by direct employment or its economic impact, thereby significantly modifying the appearance of what was once a rural area and is now an urban agglomeration of new cities and suburban housing zones.

Page 110

• **A welcome rainfall in the Cher.**
Rain sustains crops during a drought near Bourges, in the Cher. Global warming has made lack of water a serious concern for farmers. Over the last thirty years, the surface area devoted to irrigated farmland has sharply increased in France, from 1.9 million acres in 1970 to 6.5 million in 2000. Yet at 35,144 cubic feet per inhabitant, France's annual water consumption is slightly below the European average of 43,055 cubic feet per inhabitant.

Page 111

• **Harvest season in the Lot.**
Generally speaking, grape seeds mature one hundred days after the grapes reach full bloom. The harvest date therefore has a crucial impact on the quality of the wine a vineyard's grapes will produce. Depending on the types of vine and of soil, the harvest season generally takes place between August and October. Here in the Lot, grapes used for Cahors wine are harvested manually, a method that requires expensive labor, and that is currently tending to be replaced by the mechanized grape harvesting techniques introduced in France in the 1960s.

Page 112

Junkyard in Saint-Brieuc.
How many wrecked, rusted, and unusable vehicles does this junkyard, some nine miles from Saint-Brieuc (Côtes-d'Armor), have piled up? Each year, eight to nine million cars throughout Europe, including two million in France, are scrapped, causing insurmountable pollution problems. A European directive requiring 80 percent of these wrecks to be recycled by 2006 has recently been passed, causing a boom in the scrap market. Metals are bought for 50 to 150 euros per ton, and well-preserved mechanical components are brought into the salvage circuit.

Page 113

Anchorage near the Glénan islands.
This sailboat near the Glénan islands (Finistère) is just one of the many sailboats regularly sailing off the coasts of Brittany. Once an elite activity, sailing experienced a major boom in the 1990s. Today there are about four million amateur sailors in France, with approximately seven hundred thousand boats registered for leisure activities. Concurrently, France has imposed itself as a force to be reckoned with in boat construction, largely due to the Bénéteau factories in Vendée, which are the global leaders on the recreational sailing market. Ports have grown with sailing's increased popularity: there are 165,000 berths available, as well as open anchorages along the coast. The other side of the coin is that 80 percent of sea rescue operations are aimed at getting amateur sailors out of trouble.

Opposite

The high mountain pastures at the foot of the Aiguilles de Varan.
The Aiguilles de Varan, in Haute-Savoie, form an imposing wall of minerals in the Alpine landscape. The 8,648-foot Aiguille Rouge (Red Peak) and the 8,346-foot Aiguille Grise (Gray Peak) are both formed of crystalline rock. At the foot of these peaks, grassy mountain pastures extend into vast prairies on which herds of dairy cows graze during the summer transhumance.

Left

● **A doe roams free in the Chevreuse valley.** Founded in 1985, the Haute-Vallée de Chevreuse Regional Nature Park (Yvelines) constitutes an authentic ecological corridor in the Paris area. Forests such as the forêt de Rambouillet occupy about 40 percent of its 59,304 protected acres. Does, stags, and boars find abundant supplies of food here, including in areas within striking distance of urban zones, such as this colza field near Cernay-la-Ville. The regional park, which has a stag as its emblem, organizes fall outings to listen to these large mammals belling during the mating season.

These gigantic colza fields near Cernay-la-Ville shelter hundreds of stags and does. When I fly above them in a helicopter, the animals are startled, and I get to see them spring out among the flowers. It's a spectacular sight.—*YAB*

Seen from the air, colza and sunflowers seem to infuse nature with extraordinary warmth. It's the color of summer, a color that fills us with hope and patience.—*PPDA*

Right

● **The rooster, a typically French symbol.** This rooster on the steeple of the basilica of Notre-Dame-de-la-Délivrance in Quintin (Côtes-d'Armor) could single-handedly symbolize the French spirit. Yet the origins of this jingoistic emblem are uncertain. Apparently, the Romans already associated it with our ancestors, using the same Latin word, *gallus,* to refer to the fowl and the Gauls. In any case, by the sixteenth century, François I had adopted the white rooster as his emblem, and Louis XIV later used it to decorate the Gallery of Mirrors at Versailles. The rooster survived the revolutions and reappeared in World War I propaganda, standing on his spurs in defiance of the Germanic eagle. It made a triumphant return during the Liberation and, at General De Gaulle's request, appeared on the first new stamps printed in 1944.

The zoom lens has changed aerial photography, and our perception of the sky. You can now capture astonishing images in the sky, such as this rooster standing apart from the rooftops.—*YAB*

What a beautiful symbol the rooster is! It has the arrogant, sometimes insufferable bearing of the French, and that extreme vanity when it's surrounded by its hens. But it also knows how to be brave, including in extreme conditions. It really does reflect the French character.—*PPDA*

Opposite

• **The ocher quarries of the Vaucluse.**

Ocher is a very sandy ore colored by an iron hydroxide known as goelithe, which is found in the Vaucluse, around Roussillon, Apt, and Gargas. The rich color spectrum of ocher, which extends from brown to bright red and from yellow to dark orange, has led people to use it as a pigment since antiquity. Its industrial extraction was developed in the nineteenth century. In 1929, at the industry's peak, forty thousand tons of ocher were extracted for use in dyeing manufactured products such as rubber boots, linoleum, cigarette filters, etc. Today the Gargas quarries are the only ones still in use, but interest in ocher has been on the rise. For instance, using ocher to paint the walls of a home has become an attractive proposition because it follows environmental norms. The Conservatory of Ocher and Applied Pigments in the old Mathieu factory in the Roussillon receives thirty thousand visitors a year, as well as offering introductory courses.

I waited for the end of the day, when there was nearly no one around, to photograph this fracture of red land lined with a little greenery. The two hikers reveal how impressive the scale of the site is.—*YAB*

The only other place I've found this kind of red was in the heart of the Tenere desert.—*PPDA*

● The Notre-Dame-de-Fourvière basilica in Lyons.

Opposite

The Notre-Dame-de-Fourvière basilica in Lyons (Rhône) is home to the Black Virgin that has allegedly saved the city on several occasions over the centuries, protecting it from the plague in 1643, from cholera in 1832, and from the Prussian invasion in 1870. This last miracle convinced archbishop Ginoulhiac to honor the statue by building it a shelter worthy of its power. The neo-Byzantine basilica was designed by Lyons architect Pierre-Marie Bossan (1814–1888). It remains a highly popular tourist destination, and also includes a museum. In the spring of 2005 the museum exhibited the clothing of the late Pope John Paul II: about sixty garments, most of which were designed by Italian designer Stefano Zanella, who was responsible for a radical new direction in liturgical fashion.

I took this picture on September 11th, 2001. It was beautiful out. We had just learned about the terrorist attacks in New York, but we didn't yet realize their extent. We had turned the radio off to work in peace. Suddenly, we saw a police helicopter coming toward us, signaling for us to land immediately. For two hours, everybody had been wondering what our helicopter was doing flying over the city when everyone was traumatized by the sight of those airborne attacks.—*YAB*

This golden light fits Lyons perfectly. It's quite a discrete city. The way it rises and falls between the Rhône and the Saône has a certain gentleness to it.—*PPDA*

● The Great Arch of La Défense.

Following spread

The Great Arch of La Défense in Puteaux (Hauts-de-Seine) was designed by Danish architect Otto von Spreckelsen. It was inaugurated on July 14, 1989, in honor of the bicentennial of the Revolution. This gigantic cube spans 360 feet from front to back, and has thirty-seven floors and a roof terrace, all accessed by elevator. Its 300,000 tons rest on four huge girders and twelve bearing surfaces. Thanks to its large esplanade and its skyscrapers housing the headquarters of several large corporations, La Défense is the biggest business hub in Europe.

I consider the arch to be a total success.—*YAB*

Frankly, it's the only success in all of La Défense. The rest is very chaotic. Since the famous La Défense development plan, buildings have been thrown up here and there without any rhyme or reason. The arch is not well served by its immediate environment.—*PPDA*

The problem with La Défense isn't so much the architecture as the urban planning. You have to circle around on foot for hours before you have any sense of where you are.—*YAB*

Left

● **The ephemeral art of the garden in Chaumont-sur-Loire.** The park at the château of Chaumont-sur-Loire (Loir-et-Cher) has hosted the International Gardens Festival since 1992. The seven acres of gardens were redesigned by Belgian landscape gardener Jacques Wirtz, who conceived thirty interconnected plots representing the stylized leaves of a Virginia tulip tree. Every summer, French and foreign artists exhibit ephemeral blossoms on a set theme: "Memory" in 2005, "Playing in the Garden" in 2006.

Right

● **A cold spell hits the fruit trees of Lorraine.** Lorraine has a Continental climate, with harsh winters that leave the fruit trees covered in frost, as can be seen in this photo of trees on the banks of the Seille river (Meurthe-et-Moselle). With about 300,000 cherry-plum trees planted on those slopes that receive direct sunlight, the region is responsible for 70 percent of global cherry-plum production. The cherry plum is a fleshy fruit harvested at the end of summer. Each tree produces about 175 pounds of cherry plums.

Page 126

● **The port of Nantes-Saint-Nazaire.** The autonomous port of Nantes-Saint-Nazaire (Loire-Atlantic), the fourth largest international port in France, stretches over the estuary of the Loire, some 30 miles from the ocean. It processes more than 32 million tons of merchandise per year, of which 77 percent consists of hydrocarbons. The oil terminal established in Donges is equipped to receive 150,000-ton ships. The refinery, whose flare towers peek out of the fog in this picture, covers about 740 acres and processes more than 8 million tons of crude oil per year. Overall, the port of Nantes-Saint-Nazaire employs 5,000 people, and generates another 25,000 jobs in the region.

Page 127

● **The Tévennec lighthouse in the Raz de Sein.**
Sailing between the Pointe du Raz and the Isle of Sein (Finistère) has always been dangerous, to the point that shipwrecks were once a common occurrence here. In 1869, it was decided to build the Tévennec lighthouse on the islet of the same name in order to allow sailors a fighting chance among the currents and the reefs. After six years of labor, the lighthouse was first illuminated on March 15, 1875. Yet "dark tales" began to circulate about it. Breton writer Anatole Le Braz established its legend as a "cursed place" by recounting that lighthouse keepers had died on the job and returned to haunt the islet. Initially fueled by gas, then by propane, the Tévennec lighthouse, which is no longer inhabited, has been powered by solar panels since 1994.

This little lighthouse near Ouessant was caught in the eye of the storm. I had to wait for the wind to die down to take this photo, but the water was still foaming.—*YAB*

A lighthouse always reassures a sailor in a storm. Of course, you don't want to get too close; that would be a bad sign. All in all, though, I think the lighthouse will always be the most spiritual human construction.—*PPDA*

Previous spread

● **Saint-Laurent-des-Eaux, one of the first French nuclear-power plants.**
Saint-Laurent-des-Eaux (Loir-et-Cher) was the second French nuclear-power plant after the plant in Chinon (1963). It has been generating power from the banks of the Loire since 1969. Two of its reactors were permanently shut down in 1992; two reactors opened in 1981 are still operating. Saint-Laurent-des-Eaux belongs to EDF (Électricité de France), and employs about 700 people. With twenty-five nuclear power stations spread throughout the country since the oil crisis of 1973, and fifty-eight active reactors generating a total of 63,200 megawatts of power, France generates 78 percent of its electricity through nuclear power (in other words, an approximately 50 percent rate of independent power).

Opposite

● **The Trimouns talcum quarry.**
The talcum deposit in Trimouns (Ariège) formed about three hundred million years ago. Talcum consists of a magnesium silicate found in crystalline shale soil. Though prehistoric humans already used talcum for their rock paintings, its industrial usage did not begin until the nineteenth century. About eight tons of earth and rubble must be removed to extract one ton of talcum, which must then be ground to a powder in flour mills. Today the open-air quarries in Luzenac have about three hundred full-time employees and one hundred seasonal laborers. This talcum deposit is considered the largest in the world.

Previous spread

● **The Punta di Rondinara in Corsica.** The Punta di Rondinara between Porto-Vecchio and Bonifacio, in southern Corsica, is slowly eroding and creating beaches of fine sand. It offers a stunning example of the astonishing relief of the Isle of Beauty, an incomparable mix of peaceful gulfs facing out on the open sea and arid, abrupt mountains dominating the water. Inaccessible and highly coveted, Corsica (3,351 square miles) was considered an island citadel for many centuries. It continues to proclaim its uniqueness.

It's no coincidence that Corsica is called the Isle of Beauty. Corsica and the Polynesian islands are the most beautiful islands I have seen. Corsica gave birth to Napoleon, who would become a great French war leader. As a warrior, he had a dark side, but he was also an absolute genius. The Corsican people have a deeply committed desire to preserve their roots and their coast. They have been tremendously successful in doing so.—*PPDA*

Left

● **Bairols, a village perched in the mountains of Haute-Provence.** The Roman-tiled houses of the picturesque village of Bairols (Alpes-Maritimes) huddle atop a rocky peak rising 2,723 feet above the Tinée valley. For many years, life here was difficult, punctuated by summer heat and winter chills, to the point that the village was nearly abandoned. Yet today, Bairols's medieval alleyways, covered passages, and old facades have been renovated, and the village, which is surrounded by a 3,459-acre nature preserve, now boasts 114 inhabitants and a renewed lease on life.

Right

● **The walled town of Talmont-sur-Gironde.** The citadel of Talmont-sur-Gironde in Charente-Maritime is sheltered by its thick ramparts. It was founded in 1284 by King Edward I of England, who was also ruling over Aquitaine and the banks of the Gironde. The fortified town's narrow hollyhock-lined streets and low white houses with pastel shutters sit on a peninsula towering over the estuary. The Romanesque church of Sainte-Radegonde stands on a sheer cliff overlooking the water, which continues to draw fishing enthusiasts to the area for plaice fishing.

Opposite

● **Flooding in Taponas in the department of the Rhône.** Built near the Saône at an elevation of 575 feet, Taponas (population 572, Rhône) is particularly proud of its islands and its *lônes,* branches of the river filled up by alluvial deposits. Here, alder and dogwood send their roots deep into the water and take on the appearance of thriving mangroves. One can also spot yellow water lilies and numerous heron colonies. Yet from March 20 to 23, 2001, catastrophic flooding disrupted this paradisiacal atmosphere. Taponas is only one of some 310 communities whose 556,000 inhabitants live under the constant threat of sudden floods.

Even a flood can lead to a visually satisfying image. I tried to abstract the disaster and focus on the graphic pattern made by these trees.—*YAB*

You get the feeling it isn't the first time around for these trees! This area must flood one or two times a year . . . Once in a while, the Saône needs to stretch out. The trees don't seem to mind.—*PPDA*

Opposite

● **Agriculture at the gates of the city.**

The future of agriculture in the urban periphery (such as in this area in the Yvelines) presents problems. In the Yvelines, for instance, farming cereal and tree cultivation occupy more than 43 percent of the surface area, despite the fact that the department's limited number of farms (1,270 in 2000) employ less than 0.5 percent of the population. On the other hand, the city tends to impinge on farmland, placing electricity pylons in garden allotments, turning fields into unofficial trash dumps, or disgracing tractors for blocking the road. In an attempt to harmonize these varying points of view, the upcoming "law on the modernization of agriculture" will encourage crop rotation and the diversification of landscapes, and will favor food-processing industries associated with new crops such as green peas and colza.

The garden allotment is a typically French institution. The concept was introduced at the end of the nineteenth century, then experienced a real boom after World War II. Working the land in this way frees the mind. It would be great if every French citizen could have his or her own parcel of land.—*YAB*

I find them beautiful because they convey a particular image of happiness. Having your own parcel of land is so important! On the other hand, these pylons are hideous. They disfigure the French landscape, while in England and Sweden all the electricity cables are underground. These massive Erector Sets don't even have the excuse of a graceful appearance.—*PPDA*

Following spread

● **The martyred village of Oradour-sur-Glane.**

Life came to a stop here on June 10, 1944. Four days after the Allied landing in Normandy, the Waffen SS of the Reich division stationed in the Haute-Vienne was issued an order to "clean out the sector." They surrounded the village of Oradour-sur-Glane. The men of Oradour were killed on the spot, while women and children were gathered up and massacred in the church. The village was then pillaged and burned. 642 bodies were recovered from the ruins, but only one in ten was identifiable. Today, two thousand people populate the rebuilt Oradour-sur-Glane, and the martyred village has been made into a Memorial Center. It receives 300,000 visitors a year.

I was very moved when I photographed Oradour-sur-Glane. This martyred village is a symbol of absolute horror. The photo barely conveys the extent of the horror.—*YAB*

I visited Oradour with my eldest son. When you reach this ghost village, silence comes over you. You just don't have a right to speak any longer. You look, then you close your eyes; you realize there were lives here, life, plain and simple.... Then came treachery, evil, and pain.—*PPDA*

The Gallo-Roman city of Diodurum near Jouars-Pontchartrain.
The actual extent of the Gallo-Roman city of Diodurum, near Jouars-Pontchartrain in the Yvelines, wasn't scientifically established until aerial photographs taken in 1976 led to four years of salvage excavations carried out from 1994 to 1998. These excavations allowed experts to study the ruins before the site disappeared under the embankments of the N2 highway. The ruins of a Cistercian farm, the ferme d'Ithe, built over the site in the eleventh century, are currently being considered as the foundation for a scientific and historical study center. The collection of ancient objects found at Diodurum could eventually be gathered here, thereby ensuring the posterity of this ancient "City of the Gods."

The ruins of the city of Diodurum were discovered near Jouars-Pontchartrain. Extending over several acres, Diodurum was one of the biggest Gallo-Roman cities built around Paris. Since archaeologists could not dig up the whole area, they only searched the location of the new road.—*YAB*

This picture eloquently depicts both the geological and the historical strata of France, a country built on numerous civilizations, including, of course, the Roman.—*PPDA*

Opposite

An installation by the sculptor Arman.
Erected in 1982 in Jouy-en-Josas (Yvelines), in the gardens of the Fondation Cartier (now located on Boulevard Raspail, in Paris), this sculpture by Armand Fernandez, better known as Arman, is titled *Long-Term Parking.* Long term is an apt description: the sculpture is practically unmovable. It consists of a pile of sixty cars held in place by concrete. *Long-Term Parking* was intended to follow the dictates of new realism, an aesthetic movement founded in 1960, with the aim of "poetically recycling urban, industrial, and advertising reality." Born in 1928 in Nice, and later naturalized American, Arman was one of the main forces behind new realism, along with artists such as César and Niki de Saint-Phalle.

This is a sculpture by Arman, whose main subject matter is accumulation. The sculpture interests me as a photographer, because I'm always drawn to any kind of pile-up: tires, wrecks, barrels.—*YAB*

Page 144

The French dream of owning a home.
The development of residential suburbs such as this lot in the Yvelines was a result of the French desire for home owning spurred by the economic boom of the Trente Glorieuses. The "peri-urbanization" phenomenon, which saw long rows of frequently identical houses being built, began around Paris in the 1970s, then spread through the provinces. Today, cities are tending to expand into the countryside, eating into rural zones to form a second peripheral belt in which bungalows, prefab houses, and restored farms rub elbows. This "rurbanization" is leaving the French landscape in tatters.

According to opinion polls, the average French citizen's greatest dream is to own a house.—*YAB*

To live in your own place, with your family . . . It's an image of happiness aspired to by an entire population.—*PPDA*

Page 145

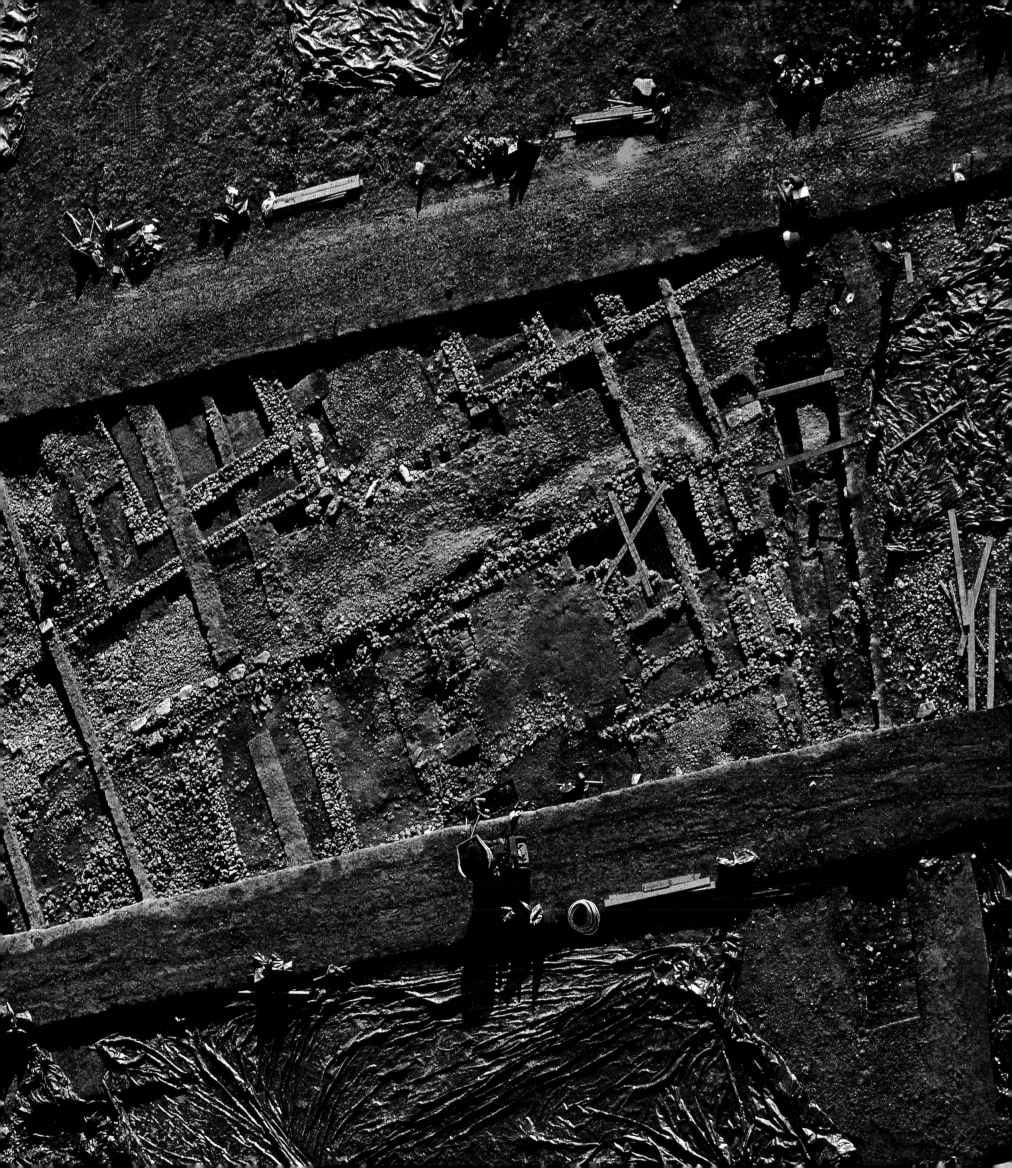

Left

● **The medieval construction site of Guédelon.**
Embarked upon in 1998, this unusual construction project in Treigny, in the Yonne, is devoted to building a fortified castle using the materials and methods of the twelfth century. The construction, which was initiated by its current overseer Michel Guyot, a devotee of historical buildings, should take about twenty years to complete. Artisans with specializations in carpentry, quarrying, stone carving, masonry, and lime burning are rediscovering lost techniques as they set about erecting defensive curtains and dungeons. The site is intended for historical and scientific research as well as for pedagogical projects. It was visited by two hundred and twenty thousand people in 2004, of which eighty thousand were children.

Right

● **Disneyland Resort Paris in Marne-la-Vallée.**
Since its opening in 1992, this amusement park in Marne-la-Vallée (Seine-et-Marne) has imposed itself as the most popular tourist destination in Europe, with more than twelve million visitors a year. The park sits on 323,000 square feet in the vicinity of Paris, and can be reached by car or by train, thanks, in part, to the construction of a special high-speed-train station in 1994. Euro Disney's combination of spectacular attractions with hotels, a golf course, some sixty restaurants, and as many stores has generated forty-three thousand jobs in the region. About twelve thousand people are employed in the Euro Disney Park itself.

I really enjoy the parallel between this artificial château built in a few months and a real castle being built using the materials and methods of the Middle Ages over a period of about twenty years. Once the castle is finished, the plan is to build a Cistercian abbey, following the same approach.—*YAB*

● **Hog farm in Haute-Normandie.**

This sow is probably one of the last to be raised in the open air in Brionne, in the Eure. This department in Haute-Normandie, though specialized in agriculture, only has about a dozen extensive hog farms left. This kind of farm allows the animals (about thirty per acre) plenty of room to frolic and ensures that their nutrition is strictly controlled, enabling the production of high-quality meat identified by a red label. Yet today many hogs are raised "soil-free," on duckboards in enclosed buildings, at a significantly reduced cost.

I am deeply opposed to industrial livestock raising, which restricts animals' movements and requires sows to be immobilized with straps so they don't crush their piglets. Life must be respected in all its forms.—*YAB*

Another reason to oppose these intensive hog farms is that they cause liquid manure runoff, which produces nitrates. The spread of nitrates in water, and, particularly, seawater, results in green algae, which disfigures our coastlines.—*PPDA*

● **Vacationing near Saint-Raphaël.**

The beaches of the Mediterranean coast, seen here near Saint-Raphaël (Var), always attract the summer crowds. Yet mass tourism, which was characteristic of the last few decades, seems to be slowing down. Today, the French are breaking up their holidays and diversifying them. Only 43 percent of the French now spend their summer vacation at the beach, versus 46 percent ten years ago. While the countryside remains a popular weekend destination, for longer vacations, trips abroad are now tending to replace idle days on sunny beaches.

I just got back from a trip to Algeria. Over there, people don't like the sun. They all have beach umbrellas. Here in France, sunbathing culture is dominant, and the beach remains a crucial place.—*YAB*

This extreme concentration of people seems strange when you think of all the hundreds of deserted coastal areas in France. Maybe it's a surviving strand of the herd instinct.—*PPDA*

Below

● **The private beaches of Saint-Tropez.**
Deckchairs and beach umbrellas come at a premium in Saint-Tropez (Var), where several private beaches with restaurants, cold drinks, and towel rentals attract a privileged clientele. However, the shore, or the part of the coastline between the sea and the highest point reached by water at high tide, is part of the coastal public domain and remains, in principle, open to all.

Opposite

● **The redevelopment of the mining country.**
In 1945, 1.4 million tons of coal were extracted in Hénin-Beaumont (Pas-de-Calais). By 1973, the last mine was closed, and the mining town had to turn its attention to redevelopment. Taking advantage of their town's geographic position eighteen miles from Lille and close to several European capitals, Hénin-Beaumont's twenty-seven thousand inhabitants are now banking on the service industry. A 500-acre area containing five economic development zones has been created to lure new companies to the town, and local mining cottages have been entirely renovated. The improvement of this part of the area's architectural heritage has come to represent urban renewal.

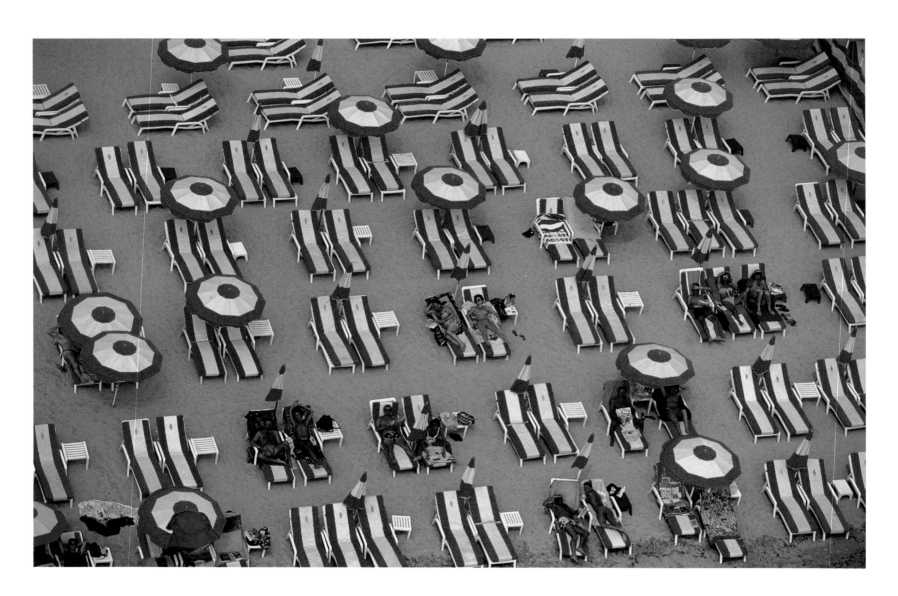

Following spread

● **The Entressen dump, Marseilles' garbage can.**
The Entressen dump in the plain of Crau, forty-three miles from Marseilles (Bouches-du-Rhône), is one of the largest open-air dumps in France. The detritus piling up here for nearly a century now covers about two hundred acres, and builds up at a rate of six hundred thousand tons per year. Whenever the wind blows, sheep in nearby pastures find themselves grazing among plastic bags carried by the mistral. Following an official warning from the European Commission, the urban community of Marseilles committed to closing the Entressen dump by the end of 2006. It will be replaced by an incinerator located in Fos-sur-Mer.

This is the biggest garbage dump in Europe. The day I went there, the wire fencing had been torn and the wind had spread thousands of plastic bags over the Camargue. Every year, the French throw away three million plastic bags. Every day, this dump receives fourteen hundred tons of garbage.—*YAB*

Entressen symbolizes megaconsumerism, but also everything that wasn't properly planned for: How is it possible that the second-largest city in France didn't consider other waste disposal methods earlier? Nowadays, we have become aware of the pollution caused by plastic bags, and many supermarkets have stopped using them.—*PPDA*

Below

● **Black tide off the Basque country.**

On November 19, 2002, the oil tanker *Le Prestige* ran aground off the coastline of Spanish Galicia, severely polluting the Atlantic coastline all the way up to France by unleashing its cargo of 77,000 tons of fuel on the Gulf of Gascogne. The fisher-men of Saint-Jean-de-Luz (Pyrénées-Atlantiques) were poorly equipped to combat this black tide. They are shown here gathering balls of hydrocarbon with their landing nets. A year after the shipwreck, traces of oil still speckled the beaches. The cost of this catastrophe was esti-mated at over one billion euros.

These fishermen are picking up fuel from the wreck of the *Prestige* with landing nets! Despite the fact that the oil industry is the biggest industry in the world! I find it pathetic, and absurd.—*YAB*

Like all nature lovers, I am furious with those who entrusted the transportation of oil, a noble material, to unscrupulous charterers. What a ter-rible price to pay for a little bit of profit.—*PPDA*

Opposite

● **Wastewater purification in the Marne.**

The purification of wastewater, as seen here near Châlons-en-Champagne (Marne), remains problematic in France, where collection of wastewater is still insufficient: only 35 percent of domestic water is decontami-nated. In 2004, the European Court of Justice condemned this French tardiness, due to a lack of technical facilities. A Euro-pean Union directive requires that by the end of 2005 all French communes be equipped to reprocess all wastewater collected.

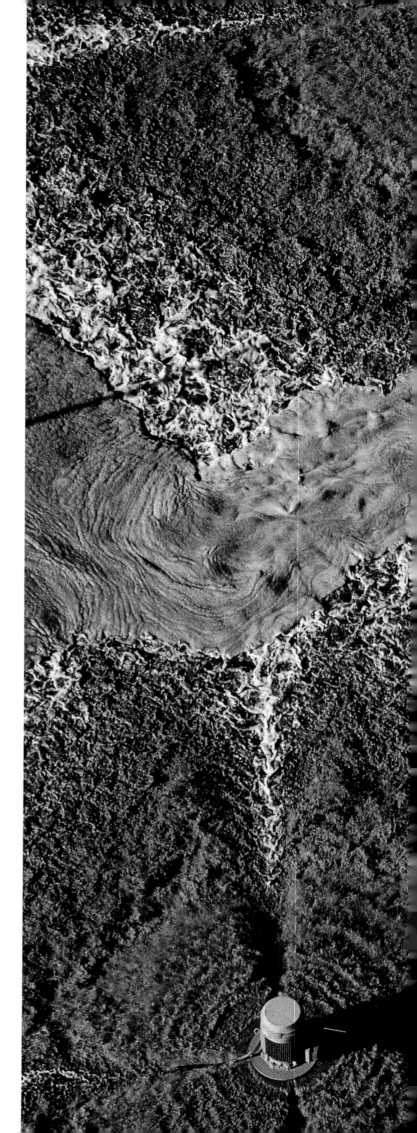

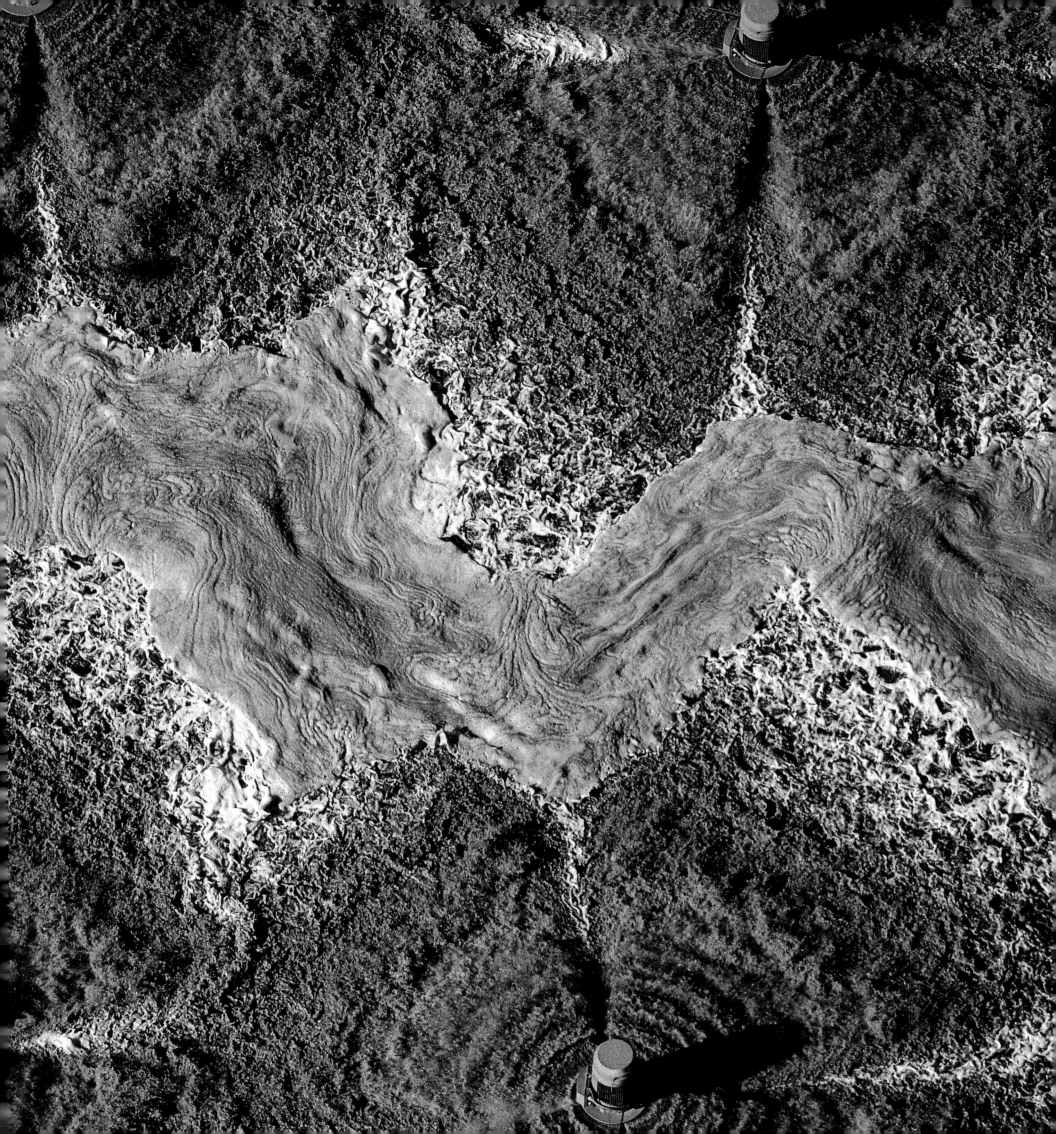

Left

● **"Challenger," the headquarters of the Bouygues corporation in Guyancourt.** Officially named "Challenger" but nicknamed "the Versailles of the modern era," this futuristic property in Guyancourt (Yvelines) is the headquarters of the Bouygues corporation, an international construction, telecommunications, and media company. Designed by American architect Kevin Roche, "Challenger" was built on a seventy-four-acre lot in 1985. The buildings are covered in a synthetic membrane that reflects sunlight to the ground and repels dust. The gardens are the work of British landscape artist Sir Shepeard. The water basins lining the central path serve as reservoirs for watering the plants or in case of fire. Bouygues employs 113,300 people in eighty countries.

The Bouygues château is a little over the top, but, all in all, I'm quite fond of it. I'm glad there are people who make their wildest dreams reality.—*YAB*

François Bouygues had wagered that one of the biggest conglomerates in the world could have its headquarters in the heart of the country. The Bouygues employees who work here seem happy to be surrounded by greenery. It's certainly better than being crammed into an office block.—*PPDA*

Right

● **The gleaming dome of the Invalides in Paris.** The Hôtel des Invalides, in the 7th arrondissement in Paris, is the largest architectural structure in Paris. It was founded in 1670 by Louis XIV to "host and house all officers and soldiers, whether maimed or old," of his armies, which amounted to some four thousand men. Today the old military residence serves as the Museum of the Armies. The royal church of Saint-Louis-des-Invalides was built by Jules Hardouin-Mansart and crowned with its famous dome in 1690. In 1989, on the occasion of the bicentennial of the French Revolution, the dome was regilded for the fifth time in its history: the gilding required 550,000 gold leaves, or more than 22 pounds of precious metal.

As soon as I began photographing Paris from the air, I was drawn to certain places that I have since tirelessly returned to. This is certainly the case with the dome of the Invalides, which shines like a gold coin in the heart of the city.—*YAB*

All those coats of fine gold seem to act like a magnet for the dome's beauty. And somewhere beneath it all, one might just run into Napoleon's ghost.—*PPDA*

Opposite

● **The agricultural plains of the Beauce.**
The Beauce plains nature area covers 2,895 square miles over five departments (Loiret, Essonne, Yvelines, Eure-et-Loir, Loir-et-Cher). Long considered France's granary, the Beauce is now diversifying its crops. Though it continues to produce soft wheat for flour and hard wheat for pasta, the Beauce is gradually giving up on corn, which drains too much water, and sunflowers, which are ill adapted to the local climate. However, it is growing increasing amounts of vegetables: green beans, peas, and spinach for the food-processing industry (canned and frozen foods) and even so-called *beauceronne* potatoes used for McCain French fries. In this region, one in ten members of the working population works the land.

I remember carrying bales of hay with pitchforks at my grandfather's place. The bales were heavy, but we could still carry them. Today everything is mechanized, and when I fly over the countryside, I don't see a soul. There are only one million farmers left in France, a little under 4 percent of the working population.—*YAB*

Like many people I know, I helped gather hay when I was little. I was fascinated by the way the reaper moved, and by the swing of the pitchfork as it raised the cut wheat to the sky.—*PPDA*

Opposite

- **Art in the heart of nature.**
American sculptor Richard
Serra is one of the most audacious artists of the twentieth
century. Born in San Francisco
in 1939, Serra developed into a
leading minimalist artist. His
background in minimalism led
him to give up on the traditional usage of the pedestal in
order to directly engage his
works with their natural surroundings. Serra also uses
unusual materials such as rubber or melted lead. This gigantic
metal sculpture installed in the
gardens of a private residence
in the Yvelines is intended to
create a specific dialogue with
its environment.

Page 164

- **The Sautour park in
Les Mureaux.**
The town of Les Mureaux was
once surrounded by vineyards,
but over the years its location
in the Yvelines at the crossroads
of the Vexin and Normandy has
subjected it to rapid change. In
1843, Les Mureaux was industrialized by the construction of
the Paris-Rouen railroad. Then,
beginning in 1950, it became the
bedroom community for
employees of the Renault
factories in Flins. Despite its
large housing developments,
which have now been reno-
vated, the 79,072-acre town has
devoted half of its surface area
to parkland. The Sautour park,
which includes an artificial hill
and a lake, is open to walkers
and cyclists on a year-round,
permanent basis.

Right

● **Pilat, the highest dune in Europe.**
The Pilat sand dune at the mouth of the Bay of Arcachon (Gironde) consists of 2 billion cubic feet of sand standing 345 feet tall. At 8,858 feet long and 1,640 feet wide, the dune is the largest sand formation in Europe. It continues to grow thanks to sand from the neighboring Arguin sandbank being carried to it by winds, tides, and strong currents. Yet with over a million visitors per year, the dune is becoming a victim of its fame. It was finally named a Significant National Site, in order to preserve its rare characteristics and its environment. In 1994, a site rehabilitation operation was carried out here.

Following spread

● **The Élysée Palace in Paris.**
In the eighteenth century, the Élysée Palace was one of the first private mansions to be erected in the fields of the Faubourg Saint-Honoré, which was then at the gates of Paris. Architect Armand-Claude Mollet and his successor Alexandre Hardouin built the Hôtel d'Évreux between a courtyard and a garden. In keeping with the fashion of the time, they followed a classical style, though they did allow themselves a great deal of ornamental flourish. Renamed and registered as a "National Treasure" at the beginning of the nineteenth century, the Élysée has served as the presidential residence since 1873. Over the years, the palace has been endlessly modified according to the tastes, whims, and needs of its residents, beginning, shortly after 1873, with the installation of a telephone line.

On a personal, sentimental level, I'm quite fond of this perspective. It's hard to imagine that this is the absolute heart of power in France, with its two little ventricles on the side. All the power is concentrated in tiny little offices. Even important advisors are housed in garrets, to the point that when elections roll around every five years everyone fights tooth and nail to gain a few feet! The apartment known as the "duty room" is on the corner facing the place Beauvau and the Ministry of the Interior. Quite a symbol! Every night, a different advisor sits up here, in order to wake the president, if need be, or to take an important decision.—*PPDA*

Below

● **At the edge of the water in an old sand quarry.**
This little cabin floats in an obsolete industrial zone, a 2.5-acre body of water abandoned after the closing of the Groupe des sablières modernes (GSM—Modern Sand Quarries Group). The GSM mined aggregates here in Carrières-sous-Poissy, in the Yvelines. A private association took advantage of the fact that the land couldn't be built on, because it was located in a flood zone, to obtain permits to install thirty chalets for fishing and weekend getaways. The inclusion of similar structures into the development of the nearby banks of the Seine is currently under consideration.

Opposite

● **The Dents de scie, a housing development for workers in Trappes.**
The Dents de scie (Sawtooth) housing development, built in 1931 in Trappes (Yvelines), was saved from demolition by its inclusion on the Additional Register of National Monuments. In 1992 architect Antoine Grumbach rehabilitated these moderate-rent houses once reserved for railroad employees working at the town's important marshaling yard. He retained their initial simplicity, along with their terraced roofs and small gardens, but made them far more functional. Some tenants have lived here since this living, evolving part of the national heritage was first opened.

Opposite

● **The last *burons* in the
pastures of the Aubrac.**
The basalt mounds of the
Aubrac, in Aveyron, provide
abundant pastures at elevations
of 3,600 to 4,600 feet. In the
eighteenth century, the *cantalès,* herdsmen who watched
over large herds of black-eyed
cows, built *burons* throughout
this area. *Burons* were stone
cabins made of irregularly
shaped slabs of stone. They
served the *cantalès* as shelters
during the transhumance (from
May 15 to October 13) and as
cheese dairies. In 1883, it was
reported there were three hundred *burons* on the *causse,* the
limestone plateau in south-cen-
tral France. At the beginning of
the twentieth century, twelve
thousand seasonal workers were
using the *burons* to make seven
hundred tons of tomme de
Laguiole cheese a year. By the
1950s, only fifty-five *burons*
were still in use, of which only
two remain today.

I've hiked in this area, leaving Aumont-Aubrac in the direction of Conques.
I was with a friend who was a local, but had never walked on the road to
Compostela. He couldn't get over it: it was as though he were discovering another
country. —*PPDA*

In summer, only cows venture to graze on these windswept, treeless plateaus.
This *buron* is a reminder that cheeses were once produced here. —*YAB*

Opposite

- **Vacationing in Vendée.**
Due to its temperate coastal climate and its relaxed lifestyle, Vendée is the third-most-popular tourist destination in France, after the Var and the Hérault. The department currently welcomes about five million visitors a year, of whom roughly 15 percent are foreigners. These visitors account for thirty-six million overnight stays booked in hotels and rural cottages, but also, on campgrounds. This family-oriented, highly popular form of open-air accommodations has been evolving of late: camping grounds are being better integrated into their environments, and are beginning to offer "modern conveniences."

Below

- **A herd of sheep in the Somme Bay.**
The gigantic Somme Bay (17,300 acres encompassing the estuaries of the Somme and the Maye) bristles with peculiar vegetation. Halophyte plants that sustain themselves in seawater grow between the sand and the marshes, forming a salt marsh regularly submerged by the spring tides. Here a herd of 3,500 sheep roams free as it grazes on the salt marsh during the transhumance. The number of animals allowed on the salt marsh is strictly controlled to limit pollution. Sheep that spend one hundred to three hundred days on the salt marsh are given a red label to certify the high quality of their meat.

Following spread

- **The wind-power plant in Avignonet-Lauragais.**
The wind-power plant in Avignonet-Lauragais (Haute-Garonne) was put in service in November 2002 as part of the Éole (Aeolian) Program. Placed in a double line on the crest of a hill north of the town, in the part of an agricultural area known as "Brésil," each of these ten 165-foot-diameter windmills uses the prevailing winds to produce 800 kilowatts of electricity. Wind power is clean power, meaning it does not produce waste. Fourteen regions in France now have wind-power plants. With a total of 390 wind-generated megawatts in 2004, France is ranked sixteenth among countries that use wind power, far behind Germany (16,628 MW), Spain (8,623 MW), and the United States (6,725 MW).

Wind-power plants may be charming to look at, but they are, above all, essential components of the effort to produce new, nonpolluting power sources. The number of wind-power plants in France hardly lives up to the possibilities offered by its coastlines and topography. With these geographic assets, France could be the global number two in wind-power production, but it is far behind its European neighbors.—*YAB*

I prefer it when wind-power plants are in the sea. They look like modern-day lighthouses, and are better integrated into the landscape.—*PPDA*

Left

- **The Southern charm of Pélissanne.**
Curled up along the banks of the Touloubre River, Pélissanne (Bouches-du-Rhône) is best discovered on foot. Thanks to its opulent economic past as a crossroads of the Aix and Salon regions and a stop on the road to the Alpilles, Pélissanne has retained some splendid seventeenth-century facades. The shade of the town's plane trees and the coolness of its public fountains contribute to its Southern charm.

The diversity of roofs in France is fascinating. When you're flying, roofs serve as landmarks to help you determine which region you're in: slates north of the Loire and tiles in the South.—*YAB*

Right

- **The countryside in Paris.**
Once a rural area, the east of the capital was industrialized and developed throughout the nineteenth century, leading to the construction of individual workers' houses, particularly in what are now the 19th and 20th arrondissements. Now that they've been renovated, these houses provide an oasis of calm in the heart of the city, particularly when they are outfitted with a small garden. It is estimated that about ten thousand of these Parisian houses have been preserved. Frequently used as artists' studios, they have also become highly desirable homes.

Following spread

- **Paris flows with the Seine.**
Nestled between two branches of the Seine, the Ile de la Cité bears witness to Paris's origins as Lutetia, the Gallic capital of the Parisii conquered by the Romans in 52 B.C. The Frankish kings established their residence in Paris beginning with the reign of Clovis in the sixth century. The construction of the first palace of the Louvre, a royal residence on the right bank, was begun by Philippe Auguste, the Capetian king whose reign (1180–1223) reinforced monarchic power. The Louvre continued to be constantly modified, enlarged, and embellished until the advent of the Second Empire. In 1793, it was converted into a museum, and in 1988, I. M. Pei's Great Pyramid was inaugurated in its courtyard.

Paris is the sum total of all the civilizations that have lived in the area and all the centuries the city has lived through. It all starts with the Ile de la Cité, behind the Ile Saint-Louis. Everything is harmonious, possibly due to the loops in the Seine. And then there's the Louvre, the old royal residence that was turned into a museum.—*PPDA*

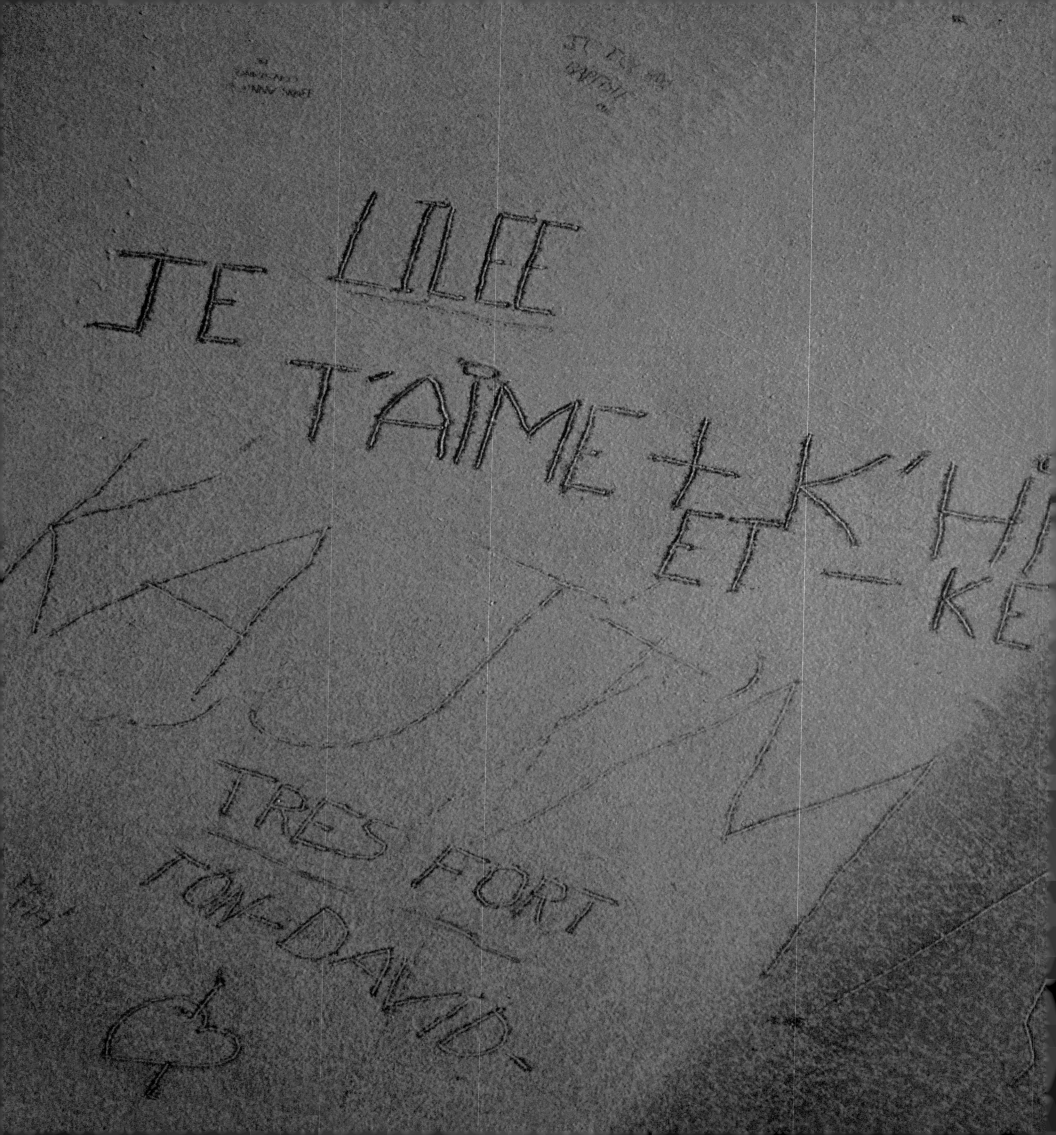

Opposite

● **Text message lingo conquers the beaches.**
Traced in ten-foot letters in the sand of this beach near the Mont-Saint-Michel (Manche), this romantic message has adopted the new spelling

developed for text messaging. This symbol of contemporary trends will soon be washed away by the rising tide.

You can't really tell, but the letters are about ten feet tall! It's written in the language of today, text message language. I also like the idea that the tide will soon sweep over the letters, just like in the Yves Montand song, "Les Feuilles mortes"(Dead Leaves).—*PPDA*

Above

● **A "heartthrob" house in Fréhel-Sables-d'Or-les-Pins.**
This unique house with an inclined roof in the shape of a playing card heart was conceived in Fréhel-Sables-d'Or-les-Pins in 1974 as a residence for its architect, Martine Abraham. It is made of wood-covered reinforced concrete, with a curved

balcony on the second floor. Large plate-glass windows offer 360-degree views of the surroundings, including a breathtaking view of the sea. Thanks to its centimeter-thick windows, the house is a passive solar dwelling, and was a forerunner of the current enthusiasm for environmentally sound habitats.

Left

● **Brittany, an agricultural region.**
In order to raise itself to the top tier of French agricultural regions, Brittany has worked since the 1960s at developing an intensive agriculture. Ten percent of Brittany's working population is now employed in agriculture. Aside from raising cattle, growing vegetables is the area's leading economic activity, notably along the northern shoreline, around Saint-Pol-de-Léon (Finistère) and Paimpol (Côtes-d'Armor), where these farmers are planting cauliflower, one of the region's leading products. Numerous other fruits and vegetables, including potatoes, cranberry beans, tomatoes, and, especially, the celebrated Breton artichokes (accounting for 75 percent of French artichoke production), make up the local produce. These water-intensive cultivations concentrate 26 percent of irrigated land in Brittany.

Right

● **Mussel beds in Saint-Brieuc Bay.**
Part of the three hundred square miles of Saint-Brieuc Bay (Côtes-d'Armor) is planted with posts, known as *bouchots,* or mussel beds. Clusters of mussels are attached to the posts for fifteen to twenty-four months, during which they feed on plankton brought to them by the tides. Saint-Brieuc Bay, one of the seven mussel-producing bodies of water in North Brittany, produces six to seven thousand tons of mussels per year, second only to the ten thousand tons collected in the Mont-Saint-Michel area. Shellfish farming, which includes the farming of oysters and mussels, is a fragile marine activity. It is dependent on the quality of coastal waters, but also on water temperature. The heat wave in the summer of 2003 therefore led to the development of toxic microalgae.

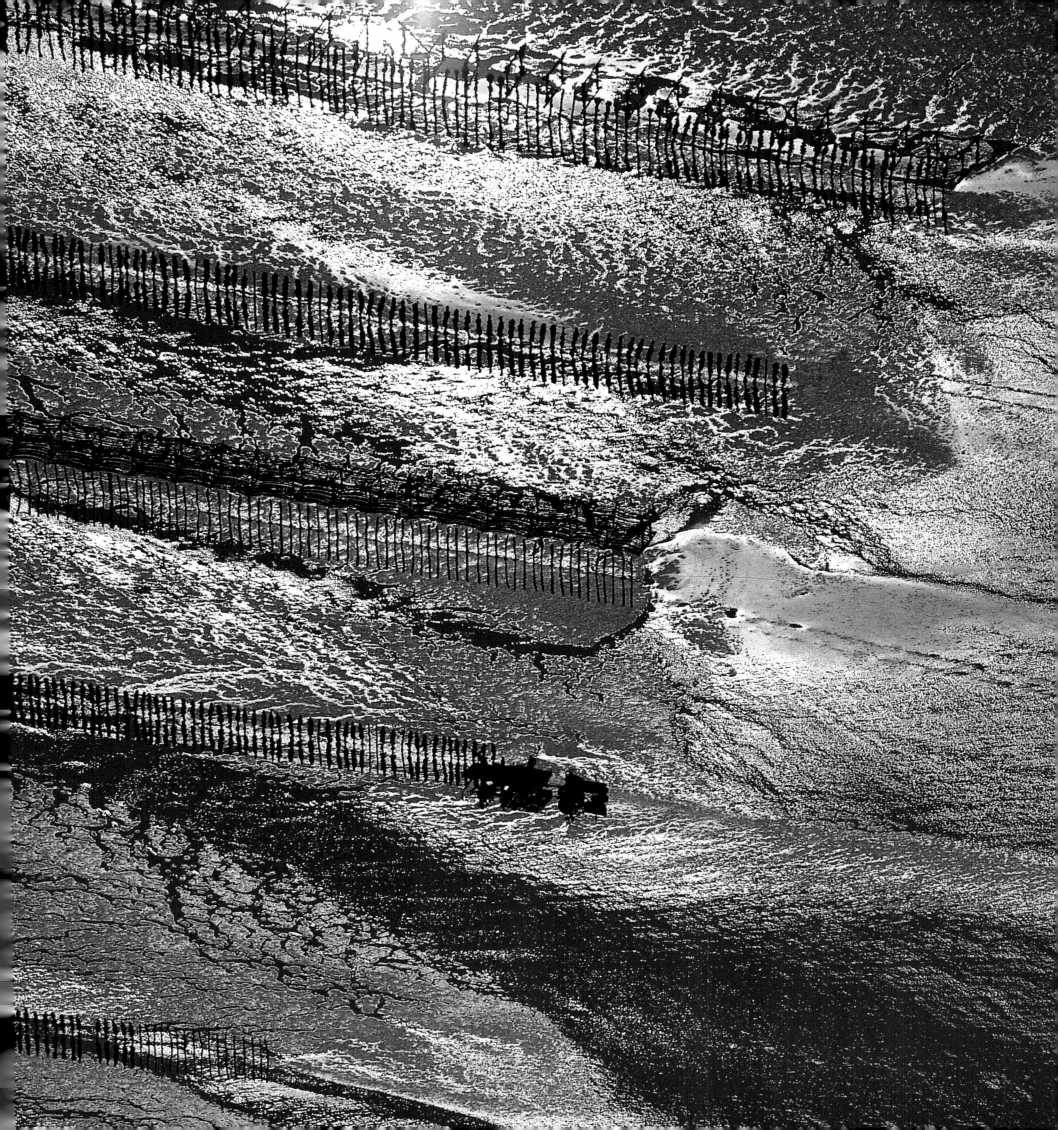

Left

● **Old tide mills.**
For many centuries, Brittany
was home to about a hundred
working tide mills such as these
in the Côtes-d'Armor. The mills
were set up on protected bodies
of water, such as estuaries near
the sea. Water would accumu-
late with the incoming tide,
then set the wheels of the mill-
stone in motion as it washed
away with the ebb tide. Millers
would work night and day to
the rhythm of the tides. The
grain to be milled would be
delivered on little sailboats,
which would then return to
land with the bags of flour.
Some of the mills remained in
use until the 1960s. Today they
are most frequently used as
vacation homes.

Right

● **The *calanques* in Cassis.**
The *calanques* in Cassis, near
Marseilles (Bouches-du-Rhône),
are formed of ancient river valleys that were flooded by the
sea. Limestone from these rocky
inlets was long used for construction, particularly in the
nineteenth century, when
calanque limestone was used
to build the port of Alexandria,
in Egypt, and the base of the
Statue of Liberty, in New York.
Today, the *calanques* have
been returned to nature and
planted with Aleppo pines.
Their hundred miles of marked
footpaths attract one million
visitors a year.

Pages 186–87

● **Ramatuelle.**
Built on the side of a hill, the village of Ramatuelle (Var) sits safely enclosed in its ramparts. With its steep alleys and pink tile roofs, Ramatuelle is easily one of the most picturesque sites on the Saint-Tropez peninsula. Actor Gérard Philipe owned a family home here called La Rouillère, a *mas* surrounded by seventy-one acres of vineyards and parasol pines. The star of *Le Cid* and *Till l'Espiègle* died in Paris, at the age of thirty-six, and was buried in Ramatuelle on November 28, 1959. His grave has since become a pilgrimage site.

For me, Ramatuelle is, first and foremost, Gérard Philipe. I've often gone to see his grave. The village has remained very authentic, in an area that is less and less so, where silicone and Botox are becoming the rule.—*PPDA*

Page 188

● **Limoux, home of the** *blanquette.*
Fifteen miles from Carcassonne in the Aude, the narrow streets of the town of Limoux annually host one of the oldest carnivals in France, a tradition that reportedly goes back to the sixteenth century. Pierrots and masked *godils* keep the festivities rolling while the *blanquette,* a locally produced sparkling wine, flows freely.

Page 189

● **The château Saint-Léger in Saint-Germain-en-Laye.**
The château Saint-Léger was built in a park in Saint-Germain-en-Laye (Yvelines) at the end of the nineteenth century. For several decades it served as the headquarters of the Institut de recherche de la sidérurgie (IRSID—Institute of Steel Metallurgy Research) installed here in 1946. When work was done to modernize the structure in the eighties, architect Dominique Perrault added a sprawling conference room (three hundred seats), built entirely beneath the building. Hence the impression that the manor is surrounded by a moat full of water, which is actually just glass panels reflecting the sunlight! When IRSID was moved to Lorraine, the property was bought by Ford France to be used as its corporate headquarters.

Opposite

● **The "Loire Grandeur Nature" Plan.**
The Loire is now free of the pollution that was threatening it at the beginning of the 1990s. Abandoned by boat transportation at the end of the nineteenth century and damaged by the extraction of aggregates throughout the twentieth century, Europe's last wild river found its poorly maintained waters being clogged by vegetation, and suffocated by algae (as shown here near Digoin, in Saône-et-Loire). The implementation of the decennial "Loire Grandeur Nature" (Full-size Loire) Plan by the Ministry of the Environment in 1994 reversed this negative trend by developing and maintaining the riverbed and the river's dead branches. Thanks to this economic and environmental development program with an annual budget of 2 billion francs (totaling 330 million euros over the ten-year period), salmon has found its way back to the spawning beds.

What a beautiful tableau. It's reminiscent of Monet's *Water Lilies.*—*PPDA*

I am never tired of photographing nature. The more I fly, the more I'm aware of its beauty.—*YAB*

Following spread

● **The seals of the Somme Bay.**
Two of the twenty types of seals known to man can be found in Somme Bay. This 17,300-acre indent on the coast of Picardy is home to a few gray seals and to about one hundred common seals that make up the largest common seal colony in France. Fully adapted to life in estuaries, common seals spread out at high tide to catch six to nine pounds of fish per day, then regroup on the sand banks at low tide. The suckling of young seals born in June and July exclusively takes place on the sand. Long hunted for its fur, to the point that by the 1980s it was threatened with extinction, the common seal is now thriving. Seals do remain vulnerable to pollution, however, and observing them requires great discretion.

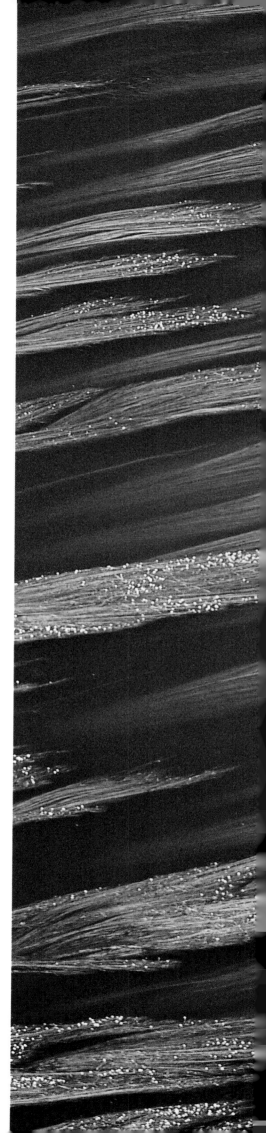

Pages 194–95

● **The house in the dunes was defeated by the sea.**
This solitary house in the place known as Ker Emma, in Plounévez-Lochrist (Finistère), no longer exists. It was defeated by the sea, carried away by dune erosion, and finally demolished in 2000. The house was initially a simple kelp-gatherer's hut, without running water or electricity. After World War II, a man who loved the area bought the cabin and named it after his wife: Ker Emma, or Emma's Place in Breton. Other properties in North Brittany are similarly threatened by the erosion of the dune ridge, which, in some areas, can recede some forty feet per year under the power of the tides.

The house has disappeared. The sand had receded to the edge of the house. By the time it was torn down, the water was lapping at its walls.—*YAB*

Once again, nature has the last word—it does not like to be challenged on its own turf.—*PPDA*

Previous spread

● **The island of Molène, a biosphere reserve.**
Anchored in the currents of the Iroise Sea, at the tip of the Finistère, the island of Molène (237 acres) and its archipelago were classified as "Biosphere Reserves" by UNESCO in 1988. The island's rocks are home to a colony of gray seals under the observation of the Océanopolis scientific institute in Brest. Up to 132 species of fish and crustaceans live in these waters. The lives of Molène's 264 inhabitants are set to the schedule of the *Penn ar Bed* shuttle boat. The *Penn ar Bed* makes the one-hour trip to and from the Continent several times a day.

Molène makes me happy. Perhaps because this island, the most westerly island in France along with Ouessant, has remained on the solar hour. The woman who owns Molène's only restaurant will invite you for lunch at 11 A.M.! And for before-dinner drinks at 5 P.M. Everything is two hours out of sync with the Continent!—*PPDA*

Opposite

● **The port of Saint-Tropez.**
First drawn out of obscurity in the 1950s, the port of Saint-Tropez (Var) has now become an international attraction. Its two docks cover 22.2 acres and can accommodate up to 800 ships, yachts, and large sailboats (up to 230 feet long for a 15-foot draft). The harbormaster's office proudly proclaims the port's status as an "authentic sea hotel," complete with innovative commodities such as internet access, grooms, and baggage checkrooms. Seven thousand ships of widely diverse provenance put in at Saint-Tropez over the course of a year, adding up to about twenty thousand individual overnight stays.

Saint-Tropez is also a beautiful, authentic village, the praises of which have been sung by our greatest writers. But the truth must be told: when summer comes, the port is human bombast at its worst, a veritable festival of vanity. What are those big ships doing facing the café terraces? Who's looking at whom? What's the sense of this game of false mirrors? Saint-Tropez was once a lovely little fishing village, with little sailboats and beautiful blue wherever you looked. One day, the *pointus*, the local fishing boats, should be able to take back their place and send the bigger ships out to open sea. But is that really what they're cut out for?—*PPDA*

Page 200

A national navy tugboat.
Built in 1992, the *Kéréon* (named after a lighthouse on the neighboring island of Ouessant) is one of the seven national navy tugboats operating out of Brest (Finistère). Eighty-two feet long and twenty-seven feet wide, with an eleven-foot draft, the *Kéréon* helps military vessels in Brest harbor to maneuver in and out of the port. It also occasionally heads out to open sea, as can be seen in this picture taken near the Isle of Sein. Two Abeilles, high-sea tugboats also stationed in Brest, attend to the safety of civil ships sailing on the particularly busy and dangerous Ouessant shipping lane. Despite these safety measures, the tip of the Finistère, which is notorious for its high winds and treacherous currents, can still see accidents such as the December 1999 wreck of the *Erika,* a tanker carrying thirty-seven thousand tons of fuel.

Page 201

The Briare Canal Bridge.
The Briare Canal Bridge in the Nièvre allows barges sailing the canals to cross over the occasionally turbulent waters of the Loire. Inaugurated in 1896, this 2,171-foot bridge was, at the time, the most ambitious metallic structure in France. The Eiffel Company, known for erecting the tower of the same name in Paris, built the bridge's bases. At the turn of the century, the canal bridge was crossed by approximately twenty-five ships per day, or ten thousand per year. Today freight transportation has been replaced by leisure sailing, much to the dismay of environmentalists who have calculated that every barge convoy could take seventy trucks off our roads.

I'm very fond of the contrast between the Loire, which can be truly wild, and the peaceful canal passing over it. A boat sailing on a bridge is always a surprising sight!—*YAB*

Every time I've sailed on a barge, I've had the impression I was moving at human speed. And bargemen are very endearing people.—*PPDA*

Opposite

The aftermath of fire in Provence.
Every year, dryness and the mistral conspire to spread devastating fires through the forests of the South of France, sometimes destroying homes and putting human lives in peril. In 2003, the year of the heat wave, it was particularly difficult. Some 152,077 acres of wood and scrub went up in flame in the Mediterranean South (seen here near Valensol, in the Alpes-de-Haute-Provence), with a third of the damage focused on the Var. According to statistics, 55 percent of fires are due to carelessness, 20 percent to malicious intent, 5 percent to lightning, 5 percent to garbage dumps, 6 percent to trains and electric lines, and 9 percent to miscellaneous causes. The best method of prevention remains the systematic cleaning out of undergrowth, once ensured by grazing cattle.

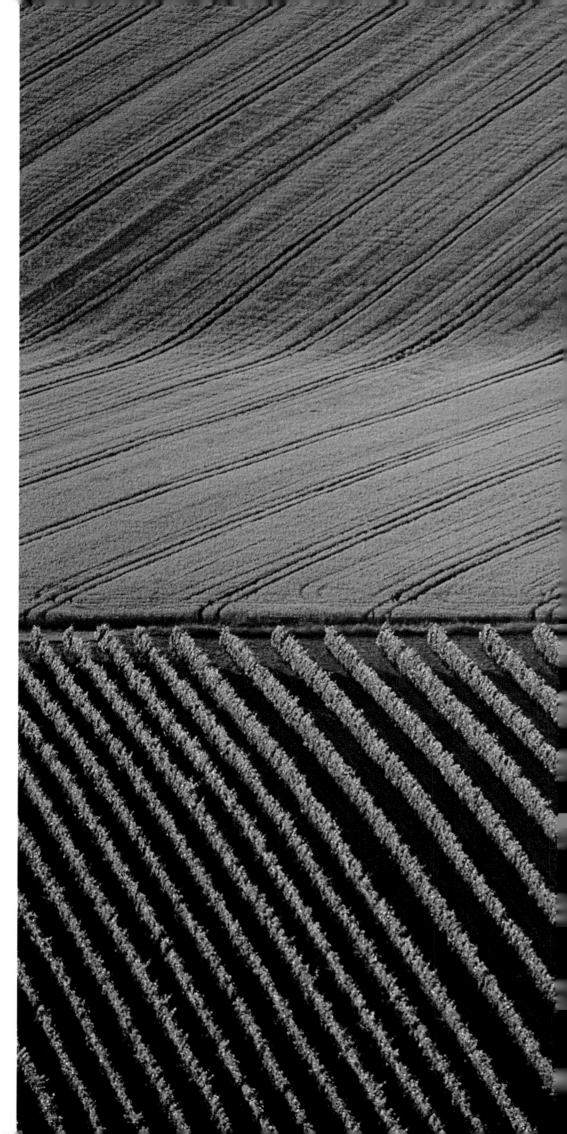

Opposite

● **The Cognac region.**
The area in Charente, where cognac is produced, was only delineated by official decree in 1909, but the vineyards have been in the region since the third century. The area is divided into six different vineyards, from the Grande Champagne to the Fins Bois, forming concentric circles around the town of Cognac (population 16,000). The vine is cultivated on plots of land varying in size from 32,100 acres to 2,700 acres. Eau-de-vie, which is obtained by distilling various white wines, is aged for at least thirty months in new oak vats. In 2004, exports of cognac, which is particularly appreciated in Japan, among other places, accounted for 16 percent of total exports of French wines and spirits.

● **In the old-fashioned way.** The invention of washing machines and dryers has not eradicated the practice of hanging up laundry to dry in the sun (seen here in Brittany). This method of drying, which is both economical and environmentally friendly, gives laundry an unbeatable sheen.

This kind of picture is a gift, a chance offering. —YAB

Laundry snapping in the wind like a childhood memory. —PPDA

Opposite

Below

● **The château of Jarnioux in the Rhône.**
Celebrated for its six glazed-tile towers, the château of Jarnioux (Rhône) has been spared by the many wars that have raged since its construction in the Renaissance style in the fifteenth century. Today, it is registered as a historical monument. Outfitted with a drawbridge, the château also has several interior courtyards, one of which forms a terrace over a hamlet built of attractive light-ocher limestone. This southern part of the Beaujolais wine region is sometimes nicknamed "the Beaujolais of golden stones" because every village in the area once had its own quarry.

Opposite

● **Grape harvest in the Beaujolais.**
The vineyards of the Beaujolais extend over 54,000 acres in the north of the Rhône department. The area's entire wine production is given an *appellation d'origine contrôlée* (registered designation of origin) that guarantees its exclusive origin. The region produces some famous wines, such as brouilly (73,000 hectoliters per year from 3,212 acres of vineyards), chiroubles (20,000 hectoliters from 914 acres), juliénas (34,000 hectoliters from 1,482 acres) and moulin-à-vent (3400 hectoliters from 1,606 acres). Every fall, about forty thousand people, an increasing number of whom are from Eastern Europe participate in the grape harvest (shown here near Corcelles-en-Beaujolais). The arrival of Beaujolais Nouveau on the third Thursday of November is celebrated around the world.

Following spread

● **Near Montmélian, the capital of Savoie wines.**
Contrary to popular perception, outside of its highly mountainous areas, Savoie enjoys a relatively temperate climate. The area gets about 1,600 hours of sunshine per year, which is ideal for growing wine grapes. The Allobroges, a Gallic people, were the first to develop vineyards in the area (seen here near Montmélian). They were also the first to use barrels to store wine, rather than the amphora used by the Romans. Savoie wines, which obtained an *appellation d'origine contrôlée* (registered designation of origin) in 1973, are rapidly expanding these days, to the point that fallow land is being replanted throughout the region. The local vineyards currently cover 3,212 acres and produce 130,000 hectoliters of wine per year, of which 80 percent are white wines such as crépy or roussette.

Opposite

● **The old village of Gruissan.**
Every summer this village,
wrapped in concentric circles
around the ruins of the
medieval château of Gruissan
and the Barberousse tower
erected in the twelfth century
to defend the port of Narbonne,
experiences an incredible
population explosion: the
population of 3,100 off-season
inhabitants expands to 60,000
summer revelers! Gruissan
(Aude) does enjoy an exceptional location, within easy
reach of the big beaches of
Languedoc-Roussillon.

Above

● **The traditional countryside.**
Raising cattle and working the
land were long the essential
resources of the rural world of
Alsace. Every farm such as this
one near Colmar had some
farmyard animals and a few
sheep. An ecomuseum encompassing seventy traditional
homes in Ungersheim, on the
Upper Rhine, has kept this
country lifestyle alive in the
face of extinction. Farmers here
follow the age-old local prac-
tices of harvesting hemp and
white cabbage, shearing sheep,
and drying tobacco.

● **The medieval city
of Martres-Tolosane.**
Seventeen hundred inhabitants
live on either side of the ring
of trees that has replaced the
ramparts of the medieval city
of Martres-Tolosane (Haute-
Garonne). Famous as of the
eighteenth century for its
earthenware factories, nine of
which are still active, the city
developed around its dungeon
and the church of Saint-Vidian.
Like many other towns in the

area, Martres-Tolosane attracts
many Britons interested in buying houses. The Haute-Garonne
reportedly has a population of
1,800 Brits, versus 2,400 in the
Dordogne and 700 in the Gers.
According to the National Institute of Statistics and Economic
Study, the number of Brits living in France since 1999 has
doubled. But the boom in real
estate prices has now incited
them to start looking farther
north, toward the Limousin.

Opposite

● **American-style villas
on the Côte d'Azur.**
These neo-Provençal villas with
direct access to gardens, parking
spaces, and pools were built in
the hills of Grimaud-Beauvallon
(Var) with an unbeatable view
of the Gulf of Saint-Tropez. For
several years now, real estate
developers have been turning

away from overpopulated, heavily built-up fishing villages and
taking hold of the last plots of
land available for construction
on the foothills of the Maures.
The residential developments
currently being constructed
are introducing a highly Ameri-
canized concept of urbanism to
the area.

The French market for pools is experiencing a real boom.—*YAB*

Pools have become an added requirement to the French dream of having a convivial home.—*PPDA*

Following spread

● **The château of Versailles,
a World Heritage Site.**
Registered by UNESCO as a
World Heritage Site, the
château of Versailles (Yvelines)
is an enduring testament to the
glory of Louis XIV. In 1661, the
Sun King decided to enlarge and
embellish a hunting lodge that
had belonged to his father,
Louis XIII. Work on the site
lasted until 1690, at a cost of
60 million livres. The palace
became a showcase for architects Louis Le Vau and Jules

Hardouin-Mansart and was imitated throughout Europe, from
Peterhof, Peter the Great's
Russian Versailles in Saint
Petersburg, to Sans Souci,
Frederic II of Prussia's château
in Potsdam. The gardens of
Versailles, which were designed
by André Le Nôtre, contain
nearly three hundred vases and
statues. These fragile artifacts
are subject to the wear and tear
of time, and can now be
"adopted" by patrons interested
in restoring them.

It isn't easy to obtain an authorization to fly over the château of Versailles. It's
also very difficult to photograph it in its entirety, even from the air. But I'm fascinated with the idea that in a mere thirty years a simple hunting lodge was
transformed into one of the most stunning châteaux in the world.—*YAB*

In any case, the photo is astonishing. It seems like the château is being reflected
in a pair of sunglasses.—*PPDA*

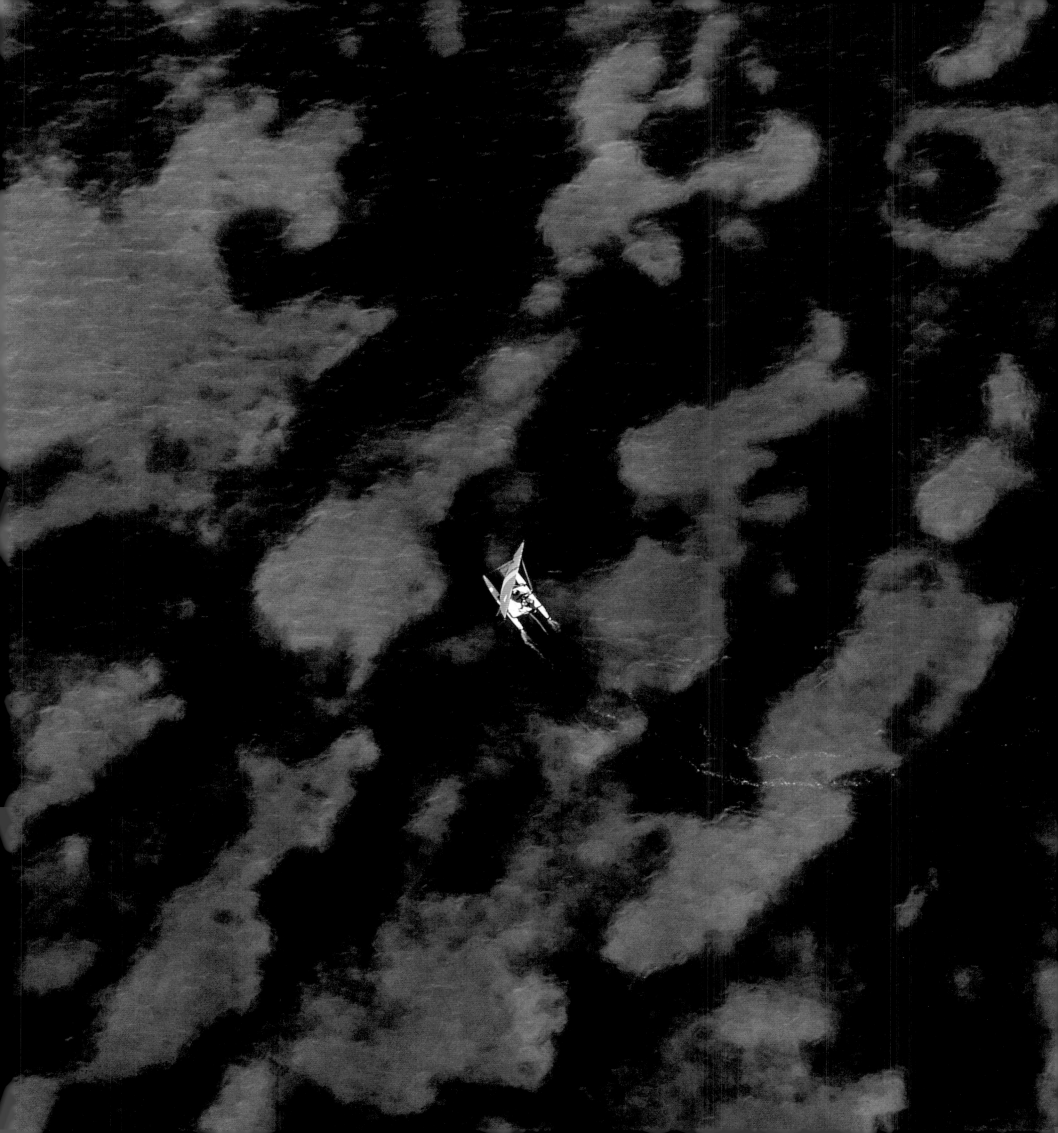

Page 218

The Old Harbor in Marseilles.
Marseilles (Bouches-du-Rhône), or rather the Phocaean city that preceded it, was first settled in the sixth century B.C., when sailors from Phocaea discovered its extraordinary 148-acre stretch of sheltered, smooth water. A first 130-foot-deep, 5-acre dock was dug here in the first century B.C. In the sixteenth century, the Old Harbor (better known as the Vieux-Port) was fortified by François I. Louis XIV had these defensive structures reinforced in order to keep watch over the harbor and to arm a powerful fleet of galleys. In the eighteenth century, the Old Harbor, which could be reached by Marseilles's most important street, the Canebière, was at the center of the local economy. Today, while the new docks on the outskirts of the city have made Marseilles into the second-largest port in France, the Old Harbor's pontoons continue to dock innumerable traditional boats known as *pointus*.

These *pointus* that you see in the South are as old as Marseilles's harbor. They are part of the family heritage and are passed from one generation to the next.—*YAB*

We're looking at the heart of a city that is very strongly attached to its singularity. Marseilles recently celebrated the two thousand six hundred years of its existence.—*PPDA*

Page 219

On the open sea near the Glénan islands.
The transparent waters of the Glénan archipelago (Finistère) attract many leisure sailors, but also the big catamarans that eagerly take on the world's oceans.

Opposite

Chenonceau, the jewel of the Val de Loire.
One of the most famous châteaux of the Val de Loire, the château of Chenonceau (Indre-et-Loire) attracts 750,000 visitors a year. This elegant and charming château is often referred to as the château *"des dames"* ("of the ladies") because it was built by Catherine Briçonnet, before Diane de Poitiers, mistress of King Henri II, moved in in 1547. Its construction on the foundations of an old fortified mill in the bed of the Cher River lasted from 1513 to 1521. Diane de Poitiers was also responsible for the bridge linking her château to the other bank of the river, a bridge on which Queen Catherine de' Medici would later have a 195-foot, two-tiered gallery erected. Today, the château's 172-acre park includes two 40,000-flower symmetric gardens dedicated to the women who inspired the site.

I try to avoid châteaux, because they're photographed so frequently. But this one is magnificent. During World War II, the demarcation line happened to be drawn through the hospital that had been set up in the château. Many French men and women took advantage of that hospital to enter the Free Zone.—*YAB*

Following spread

The Glénan archipelago off the coast of the Finistère.
In the words of seaman Olivier de Kersauson, the Glénan archipelago is "a cross between Brittany and the Pacific." Though it may feel more like the Pacific, it is found in the Atlantic, ten nautical miles from the coast of Concarneau (Finistère). The combination of a specific limestone deposit known as marl and the clearness of the sea floor gives the archipelago's water the colors of a tropical lagoon. Eight of its thirteen sandy, windswept islands are habitable, or inhabited in the summer, but only Saint-Nicolas, which has shuttle service to the Continent, is a vacation destination. As for the famous Glénans nautical center, it is always operating at full capacity. With four islands at its disposal, the leading sailing school in Europe initiates fourteen thousand students a year to the joys of sailing.

Previous spread

● **Flooding in Port-d'Ouroux-sur-Saône.** The Saône valley and its damp prairies have always been subject to floods. The dikes erected along the riverbanks in the 1850s are generally sufficient to protect the region's villages, yet in recent years the increased water levels reached by floods, have forced locals to organize themselves to be able to survive on their own for several days in the floodwater. During this flood, firemen used boats to make daily rounds delivering food and mail, as well as medicine.

Left

● **Haut-Kœnigsbourg, a neo-Gothic fortress.** Looming from a 2,483-foot rocky promontory, the château of Haut-Kœnigsbourg (Lower Rhine) has had a tumultuous history. The first Kœnigsbourg (royal château in German) was destroyed in 1462 and soon replaced by a fortress capable of withstanding technological advances in artillery. This version of the château burned down in 1633. In 1899, the Alsatian town of Sélestat gave the ruins of the château to Kaiser Wilhelm II on the occasion of one of his visits to the region, which had been under German rule since 1870. Scrupulously restored in the neo-Gothic style by architect Bodo Ebhardt, the renovated château became French by the Versailles Treaty signed at the end of World War I. The château is classified as a historic monument and has enjoyed the added draw of a medieval garden since 2001.

I think this is where the Jean Renoir film, *La Grande illusion*, with Jean Gabin, Erich von Stroheim, and Pierre Fresnay was shot.—*PPDA*

Right

● **Notre-Dame de Strasbourg.** Built between the eleventh and fifteenth centuries, the Gothic cathedral in Strasbourg (Lower Rhine) dominates the narrow streets of the old city. Thanks to its 465-foot spire completed in 1439, the cathedral was the tallest building in Europe until the nineteenth century, when it was outdone by modern spires such as the one in Rouen (485 feet) and the one in the German town of Ulm (528 feet). The sculptures were destroyed during the Revolution and later replaced by copies. Following the 1944 bombings at the end of World War II, the cathedral was extensively renovated. It has been registered as a World Heritage Site since 1988.

Notre-Dame de Strasbourg's stone was heavily damaged by pollution. Today diesel engines aren't allowed in its immediate area.—*YAB*

Part of this cathedral's charm is that it was never finished.—*PPDA*

● **The fortified town of Neuf-Brisach.**
Located two and a half miles from the Rhine, France's natural border with Germany, the town of Neuf-Brisach (population 2,100, in the Upper Rhine) has always played a defensive role in French history. Fortified by Vauban during the seventeenth century and considered the "most beautiful diamond of the French crown" by King Louis XIV, Neuf-Brisach was long the base of a military garrison. This old stronghold, which also serves as a port on the Rhine canal, now takes advantage of its surroundings to maintain a presence as one of Alsace's tourist draws.

● **Port-Camargue, an exceptional marina.**
In 1967 this site was nothing but sand dunes and swamp. Following an intensive mosquito clearing, it was transformed by architect Jean Balladur into one of the biggest marinas in Europe, with a total of 4,860 berths. The construction of the Port-Camargue marina (Gard) was finished in 1985. This maritime development in the commune of Grau-du-Roi is a year-round home to one thousand of the city's 6,500 inhabitants.

● **Gravelines, Vauban's citadel.**
An ex-herring fishing port between the banks of the Aa River and the Côte d'Opale, Gravelines (population 12,650) was first fortified in 1610. But this Flemish town made part of France by the 1659 Peace of the Pyrenees was further entrenched behind its brick defensive walls by Marquis Sébastien Vauban. In 1680, Louis XIV's head superintendent of fortifications had bastions and a deep moat built around the city. These ramparts allowed Gravelines to hold off German troops for a whole week in May 1940, thereby permitting 340,000 allied soldiers to evacuate Dunkirk and reach England.

232

Below

● **The roller coaster at the Astérix amusement park.**
Since its opening in Plailly (Oise) in 1989, the forty-nine-acre Astérix park has imposed itself as the second-most-popular French amusement park, with 1.8 million visitors during the seven months (April to October) it is open annually. While remaining faithful to the concept behind its success,

namely, "the most Gallic park of them all," it also regularly offers new attractions, such as this wood roller coaster known as "Zeus's Thunder." This 3,900-foot-long circuit is one of the highest in Europe, with hundred-foot drops negotiated at 50 miles per hour.

Opposite

● **The Arc de Triomphe in Paris.**
Commissioned by Napoleon in honor of his Grande Armée, the Arc de Triomphe in Paris's 8th arrondissement was finished in 1836 and inaugurated by King Louis-Philippe. In conceiving this 164-foot-tall, 147-foot-wide monument, architect Jean Chalgrin modeled his work on examples from antiquity. The

arch has four bas-reliefs, including the Marseillaise, sculptor François Rude's homage to the volunteers who enlisted to defend the endangered nation in 1792. Since 1920, the Arc de Triomphe has been the resting place of the Unknown Soldier, an anonymous victim of World War I. The torch of memory is lit here every day at 6:30 P.M.

Following spread

● **The Ratonneau Island lazaret off Marseilles.**
Ratonneau is one of the four islands composing the Frioul archipelago off Marseilles (Bouches-du-Rhône). The island long served as a quarantine center for ships coming from the Orient, many of which carried

diseases such as the plague. In 1820 a yellow-fever epidemic forced authorities to rethink the Ratonneau lazaret and, two years later, to build the Caroline hospital. The fortress-like establishment was conceived to meet the requirements of the era's hygienists: excellent ventila-

tion to avoid miasma, impassable walls, and interior regulations as strict as a prison's. In 1970 the city of Marseilles provided the island with a 700-berth marina, and the hospital became a curiosity.

Page 236

Page 237

The Mont-Saint-Michel.

The "marvel of the Occident" was built between the eighth and sixteenth centuries in the Mont-Saint-Michel Bay (Manche). It has recently been the object of a massive dredging campaign intended to return it to the sea. Indeed, salt marshes creeping up on the base of the Mont-Saint-Michel at a rate of seventy-four acres per year have deprived the rock of its insularity. The site is also a victim of its own success. The onslaught of nearly three million annual visitors has led Mont-Saint-Michel to be disfigured by thirty-nine acres of shoreline parking lots. Significant hydraulic work should modify the flow of the Couesnon River to produce a "flushing" effect that will drag alluvial deposits to the open sea with low tide.

The present sea wall will be replaced by a 1.75-mile linkspan allowing the waters to move freely. Access to Mont-Saint-Michel will be by shuttle, while a new parking area in the place known as La Caserne will provide parking for 4,150 vehicles. The total cost of this project is estimated at 220 million euros. Like other prestigious monuments, the Mont-Saint-Michel, which is a UNESCO World Heritage Site, is included as a scale model in the "France Miniature" amusement park opened in 1991 in Élancourt (Yvelines). France Miniature's models make some hundred and fifty attractions such as the château of Chambord, the Stade de France, and the Eiffel Tower available to visitors in a single swoop.

The old saying has it right: "The Couesnon in its folly placed the Mont in Normandy." The Couesnon is the little river that separates Normandy from Brittany. Until the fifteenth century, it flowed to the right of the Mont-Saint-Michel, which was therefore Breton. Today it's Norman. But forget about all those squabbles. The important thing is that Man was able to build such a magnificent, immutable thing on that little rock. And I'm not even talking about the spirituality, practically the holiness, that seems to emanate from the place. The monks didn't do all that work for their own edification, but for the world's. It's no coincidence that this is the most heavily visited French monument outside of Paris. It's the finest thing Man can achieve.—*YAB*

The Mont-Saint-Michel is being silted up, a victim of Man's contradictions, of Man's tendency to irrigate any old way, to tamper with age-old bocage, to pollute without even realizing it. Now we're searching for ways to make the sea return to where it belongs . . . by 2020, we hope.—*PPDA*

Opposite

Under the protection of the Archangel Michael.

Cleaned and restored, the Archangel of the Mont-Saint-Michel, the "Prince of the Celestial Millennia," continues to watch over the pilgrims who have been crossing the bay to visit the abbey since the Middle

Ages. Every year, forty thousand people put on shorts and take off their shoes to attempt this now-touristic feat under the leadership of an expert guide. Leaving from the Bec d'Andaine and crossing the sands of the bay at low tide takes two hours.

The Archangel was recently restored. He has now been returned to his perch, from which he watches over the Normans . . . and the Bretons! Gold and silver play off one another in a perfect combination of the work of Man and the work of Nature; the quintessence of what each does best.—*PPDA*

● **The Grande Borne, a bygone model of contemporary urbanism.**

Built from 1967 to 1971 on farmland belonging to the towns of Grigny and Viry-Châtillon (Essonne), the Grande Borne has seen better days. Its architect, Émile Aillaud, a disciple of Le Corbusier, had imagined an exemplary low-income housing development encompassing thousands of homes in its then-futuristic curves. But the Grande Borne was isolated by highway A6, and was short on all the essentials: schools, day-care centers, shops. In 2000 the development's deterioration led authorities to consider tearing it down in the context of the "Grand Projet de la Ville" (Large City Project).

Man wasn't made to live in these highly concentrated environments. After World War II, these developments were built in response to a general sense of panic. They were the fruit of a lack of reflection. People who should not have been drawn to them were drawn to the big cities. There was an overall failure on the part of urbanism and architects. Now, thirty years later, we're tearing places down! Of course, you can find happiness anywhere, but providing people with this kind of environment is not offering them the best conditions for positive development.—*PPDA*

● **The Ile aux Oiseaux (the Isle of Birds) in the Bay of Arcachon.**

The Ile aux Oiseaux, once known as Teste Island, sits at the heart of the Bay of Arcachon (Gironde). Its 741-acre high-tide surface area extends to three times that at low tide. This untamed island covered in heather and thistles long served as a pasture for cows and horses from local farms to take advantage of its reputedly tonic grasses. During the last century, fishermen built *tchan-quée* cabins (meaning "built on stilts" in Gascon) to protect themselves from the tides. The colonies of birds that gather on these cabins have wound up giving this easily accessible little paradise a new name.

Opposite

● **The sea gardens
at La Tremblade.**
The Marennes-Oléron oyster-
farming basin stretches across
the estuary of the Seudre, in
Charente-Maritime. Several
small ports, such as L'Éguille,
Étaules and, especially, La
Tremblade (shown here), at the
mouth of the river, are responsible for producing sixty thousand tons of oysters a year.
Access channels have been
placed throughout the mosaic of
fattening ponds that uniquely
characterizes local oyster farming. About twenty oyster busi-
nesses are represented in the
120 brightly painted oyster-
farming cabins on the port.

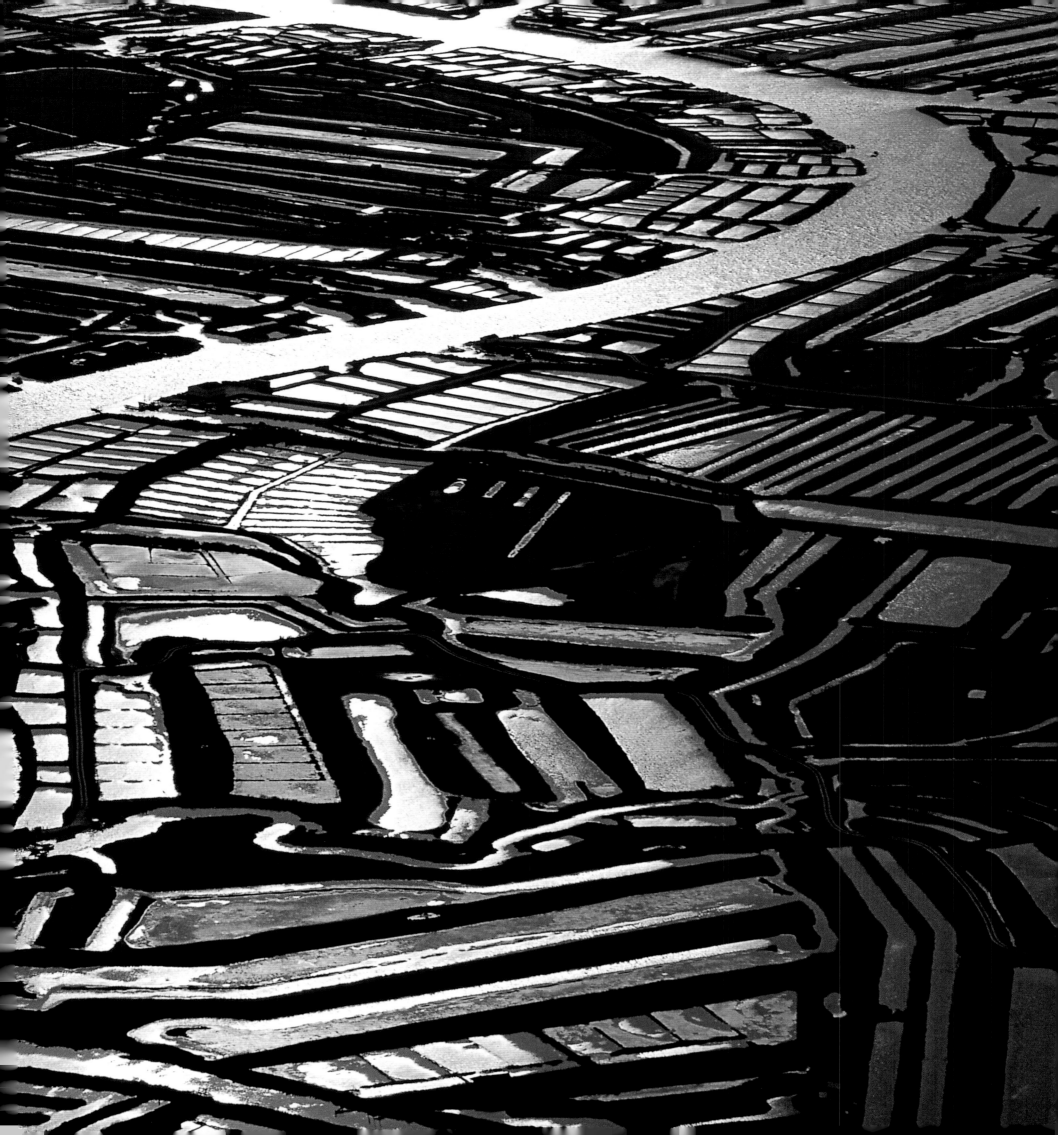

Opposite

● **Chambord, François I's hunting lodge.**

The architect responsible for Chambord (Loir-et-Cher) remains a mystery, though certain sketches of the château have been attributed to Leonardo da Vinci. Chambord was commissioned by François I. The process of building it was one of the lengthiest of the sixteenth century (1519–1547), and required the labor of 1,800 workers. The 511-foot-by-383-foot structure has 440 rooms, 365 windows, 365 chimneys, 13 staircases, and 800 capitals, pilasters, and pinnacles pointing at the sky in a profusion of stones and slates. Chambord towers over a 13,442-acre state park. The only royal residence to have been left in its original state, inside and out, Chambord has also been registered as a national hunting reserve since 1947. But since the election of President Jacques Chirac in 1995, hunting here has been strictly limited to what is required for environmental purposes, such as regulating the number of boars or foxes.

Page 246

● **The Renault-Flins parking lots.**

The construction of the Renault automobile factories in Flins, in the Yvelines, began in the 1950s, on a 553-acre plot of farmland, which led to the Flins site's "factories in the fields" nickname. Some 3.5 million cubic feet of soil had to be displaced to level the assembly-line platform. In 1999 Renault reached a partnership agreement with Japanese manufacturer Nissan. Today, 270 Twingos and 890 Clios come off the assembly line in Flins every day and are parked in these massive parking lots before being shipped out. The factory currently employs six thousand people.

Page 247

● **Bringing back forgotten fruits.**

For several years now, the Hautes-Alpes chamber of agriculture has been collaborating with the National Alpine Botanic Conservatory to bring certain types of fruit on the verge of extinction back into favor. These include the "pointed apple of Trescléoux," the "orange apricot of Provence" and "Curé" pears. Standard orchards such as this one near Gap (Hautes-Alpes) have been restored, and experimental sites have been created throughout the region.

Left

● **The joy of sailing.**
Not all of the *calanques* are protected sites. Some of them, such as this one near Marseilles (Bouches-du-Rhône), have become authentic marinas.

Right

● **The Chausey islands, the largest archipelago in Europe.**
The Chausey archipelago, which has been made into a conservation area, stretches into the Channel off the coast of the Cotentin. At low tide, the archipelago has as many islands as there are days in the year: 365. At high tide, there are only fifty-two. With a tidal range of forty-five feet, low tide opens up fifteen square miles of rocks and stones that can be strolled over on foot.

You have to see Chausey at low tide. Suddenly, the territory becomes gigantic.—*YAB*

It's a very beautiful place, very hospitable. It's also an outpost toward England, just like the Minquiers islands, which were long disputed and now belong to the English.—*PPDA*

Following spread

● **The fortress of Polignac.**
This impregnable medieval fortress was erected on a volcanic mound between the eleventh and sixteenth centuries. Sheltered behind a unique system of fortifications, the fortress' 105-foot square dungeon towers over the town of Polignac (Haute-Loire). The fortress was long closed to the public, but it was reopened in 2004, allowing enthusiasts to discover its rampart walk and its deep cisterns. Princess Constance of Polignac, the heiress to the fortress, is currently proceeding with an archaeological dig to uncover the building's foundations and rebuild it. Her plans for rebuilding the fortress have a cultural emphasis rather than a historical one, and call for an amphitheater to be included in the restored edifice.

● **The Vercors, an oasis for nature.**
Conifers and broad-leaved trees take on the steep hills of the Vercors in the northern part of the mountainous region (Isère). Some farmers in the region have recently begun cultivating environmentally sound crops based on the principle of "slow food," which implies a less intensive development. The *Villard de Lans,* a bovine species that was downgraded in 1946, has been reintroduced to the high mountain pastures. Once used for plowing, these robust cows are now appreciated for the quality of their meat and milk.

Above

● **Ewes on the wide causses of the Lozère.**
There are more sheep and goats than humans in this area. In fact, in 1850 there were as many as 300,000 sheep in the Lozère. Today, 14 percent of the working population of this still predominantly rural department is employed in agriculture, versus 4 percent on the national level. Large herds of up to 5,000 head spend the transhumance at elevations of 3,000 feet on the high limestone plateaus known as causses, beneath the peaks of the Mont Lozère (5,574 feet). In all, some 150,000 goats and ewes sustain roughly a thousand farms in the Lozère. The cattle are largely raised for their milk, which is used to produce local cheeses such as roquefort or pélardon des Cévennes.

Opposite

● **Flowers bloom on the slopes of the Lyonnais.**
Half the cherry trees currently blooming on the slopes of the Lyonnais are young trees planted over the last decade. Thanks to these new trees, the department of the Rhône has become the third-most-significant producer of cherries in France.

Left

● **Agronomic research
in the Beauce.**
The Beauce's water table contains 700 billion cubic feet of
water threatened by nitrates.
The fragility of this subter-
ranean reservoir has forced
farmers to consider new types
of crops. Tests are currently
being run to develop "cultivated
fallow land" producing perfume
plants for the "Cosmetics
Valley" in Chartres or opium
poppies for the pharmaceutical
industry. Locals are also considering introducing certain fodder plants with nodules that
are able to absorb nitrogen,
which is a major pollutant.

Right

● **Vineyards in the Val de Loire.**
The valley of the Indre, a tributary of the Loire that features
heavily in Honoré de Balzac's
1836 novel *Le Lys dans la vallée*
(The Lily of the Valley), is home
to several prosperous vineyards,
including this one near Oulches
(Indre). Wine from these vineyards is included in Interloire
production, which comprises
Anjou, Sancerre, and Touraine
wines. In total, these vineyards
occupy 153,202 acres of land and
produce over twenty *appellation
d'origine contrôlée* wines.

Previous spread

● **The wine-growing village of Heiligenstein.**
Nestled around a church at the foot of Mont Sainte-Odile, the Alsatian village of Heiligenstein (Lower Rhine) has been known for its wine production since the twelfth century. Heiligenstein's reputation rests on Klevener, a specific type of wine with a pronounced taste of the local soil. Heiligenstein Klevener was introduced here in 1742 and has had an *appellation d'origine contrôlée* (registered designation of origin) since 1945. The vineyards that provide the grapes for Klevener production cover 247 acres. Sitting at an elevation of 918 feet, the village is part of the "circuit of Alsatian wines" (105 miles) that stretches through all of the area's vineyards (29,652 acres).

Opposite

● **Les Baux-de-Provence.**
Les Baux-de-Provence (Bouches-du-Rhône) is considered one of the most beautiful villages in France. It stands on a rocky plateau in the Alpilles at an elevation of 803 feet. The entire citadel, which includes a château, a church, and several Renaissance private mansions, has been patiently renovated. The village only has five hundred year-round residents, including many artists, but it draws more than a million and a half visitors per year.

Left

● **Castillon-du-Gard.**
Castillon-du-Gard (population 1,000) is located in the heart of the Côtes du Rhône vineyard, in the Gard. Man has inhabited the hillock on which Castillon-du-Gard sits since prehistoric times. Situated near the ancient bridge known as the Pont du Gard, the commune also includes the ruins of the Roman La Gramière villa, which probably date back to the first century. The village was restored in the 1970s and continues to enchant visitors with the typically southern charm of its narrow cobblestone streets and gargoyles.

Right

● **The steeple of Sainte-Foy-l'Argentière.**
Nestled in a valley in the Lyonnais Mountains at an elevation of 1,475 feet, the town of Sainte-Foy-l'Argentière (population 1,186, in the Rhône) drew its name from the deposits of argentiferous lead mined here during the Middle Ages. Its neo-Romanesque church was built in the nineteenth century on the ruins of an old medieval chapel, and its steeple was covered in colored tiles made in the region.

Following spread

● **The celebrated cherry trees of the Vaucluse.**
Planted in tight rows along the hills of the Lubéron (seen here near Saint-Saturnin-lès-Apt), cherry trees contribute to the agricultural wealth of the Vaucluse, the leading cherry producer among French departments. The Vaucluse's orchards produce the burlat cherry, which accounts for 20 percent of France's dessert cherries. They also produce 75 percent of French cherries intended for processing for use in candied fruits made in the region of Apt, as well as in jams and flavored yogurts. Cherry growing is often associated with growing grapes such as the muscat grape, but the department has also specialized in growing melons, in Cavaillon, and apples, along the banks of the Durance.

Previous spread

● **The olive harvest in Les Baux-de-Provence.** With its two hundred and fifty thousand olive trees, the valley of Les Baux-de-Provence (Bouches-du-Rhône) is the self-proclaimed land of the olive. There, 2,200 olive growers cultivate *salonenque, verdale, grossane,* and *béruguette* olives, all of which are ingredients in Baux olive oil, an *appellation d'origine contrôlée.* Cocktail olives, olive pieces, and pickled black olives are harvested at the end of August or the beginning of September. Beginning in November, olives intended for processing are raked together, gathered in nets, and fed into the oil mills. In order to ensure the quality of the oil, it is essential that the ripe fruit does not touch the ground. The area produces 500,000 liters of olive oil per year.

Opposite

● **The château of Montsoreau.** Immortalized by the Alexandre Dumas novel *La Dame de Montsoreau* (The Lady of Montsoreau), the eponymous castle has stood on the banks of France's longest river (633 miles) since the eleventh century. Once a strategically key fortress, it is the only château of the Loire to "have its feet in the water." Reconstructed during the Renaissance by Jean II de Chambes, an advisor to King Charles VII, the château imposed itself as a "papist" stronghold against Protestant Saumur during the sixteenth century Wars of Religion. From 1994 to 2001, Montsoreau was restored at the behest of the Maine-et-Loire departmental council. Since then, the château, which is part of the Val de Loire World Heritage Site, has attracted about thirty thousand visitors a year.

The Loire is no sluggish river: it can be violently excessive and terribly capricious. Nonetheless, one gets the feeling that nothing could overcome these fortifications and this typically French way of life.—*PPDA*

Following spread

● **The ephemeral beauty of land art.** Taking advantage of the snow covering this park in the Yvelines, the artist Jacques Simon has drawn these ephemeral curves in the tradition of earth art, a contemporary art movement characterized by artists working in and with nature. This aesthetic movement first appeared in the United States in the 1960s, and aims for an on-site use of materials such as sand, wood, or soil, to create works that are left where their building blocks were found. Christo followed this type of approach when he wrapped the Pont-Neuf, in Paris, as did Jean Vérame when he painted the Tibesti Mountains in the Sahara.

Left

● **An Airbus in Toulouse.** On April 27, 2005, a prototype of the Airbus A380 successfully accomplished a test run in Toulouse-Blagnac (Haute-Garonne), thereby reaffirming the importance of Europe's leading aeronautics center. With a laden weight of 861 tons, a length of 239 feet, a 262-foot wingspan, and room for 656 passengers, this super-jumbo jet is a veritable giant of the skies. Its assembly was finished here in Toulouse, thirteen years after the project was initially conceived. The aircraft's parts were constructed in the sixteen Airbus sites throughout Europe: the wings come from Great Britain, the back of the fuselage from Hamburg (Germany), the passenger cabin from Nantes. The pieces of the puzzle were then transported to Toulouse by special truck convoys. These 1,640-foot-long convoys required hundreds of trees along their itinerary to be cut down. The birth of a competitive industrial zone based around an "Aerospace Valley" in Aquitaine and Midi-Pyrénées is now on the horizon, with the promise of forty thousand new jobs opening in the next twenty years.

Right

● **Toulouse, the beautiful Occitan.** Comfortably settled beneath its Roman tile roofs in a loop of the Garonne, Toulouse (Haute-Garonne) was already famous for the good life by A.D. 1000. Over the centuries, the city and now its suburbs (joint population of 480,000) have developed around the Romanesque basilica of Saint-Sernin. Once the private kingdom of the counts of Toulouse, the pink brick city was ceded to the French crown in 1271. There are over seventy sixteenth- and seventeenth-century private mansions in Toulouse. Thanks to Airbus, Toulouse has become the European aerospace capital. Its economic dynamism has led it to become the fourth-largest French city.

Toulouse is one of the most beautiful cities in the world. I like its total harmony. And its pink, of course, the city's dominant color, as can be seen in every shade imaginable around the place du Capitole.—*PPDA*

As I flew over the city, I couldn't get the Claude Nougaro song, "Toulouse," out of my head.—*YAB*

When you hear people sing that song at rugby matches, which happens increasingly often, it's a totally different experience from the war chants you hear in other stadiums.—*PPDA*

Page 274

● **In the Gulf of Morbihan.**
A natural inland sea off the coast of Vannes (Morbihan) in the Atlantic Ocean, the Gulf of Morbihan reportedly includes no less than 40 islands. According to legend, the gulf was formed by the tears of the fairies of Brocéliande when they were chased out of the Breton forest. As for the islands of Morbihan, they sprang from the flowers the fairies threw into the water. This picture shows how the tides toy with boats, making them rotate on their anchors as the water recedes.

Page 275

● **Belle-Ile-en-Mer.**
The largest of the Breton islands is twelve miles long and five and a half miles wide. Formed of shale, Belle-Ile-en-Mer is a veritable paradise for leisure sailors. In summer, the over-crowded pontoons of the Port du Palais force sailors to adopt this new type of anchoring in circular clusters. Though it has become a significant tourist attraction, Belle-Ile remains agriculturally productive, with regular harvests, which were first introduced here in 1766. At the turn of the twentieth century, the actress Sarah Bernhardt owned a residence here on the Pointe des Poulains.

Previous spread, above, and opposite

● **The Roissy-Charles-de-Gaulle airport.**
Construction work on the Roissy-Charles-de-Gaulle airport (Val-d'Oise) began in 1967 under Paul Andreu, the designated engineer and architect for Aéroports de Paris (ADP). Expansion of the airport has continued, module by module, to the present day, with the latest terminal, Terminal 2E, being opened in June 2003. Forty-four million people per year go through CDG's various terminals, and the airport records more than 700,000 annual aircraft movements.

Looking like a giant scarab, the airport spreads across the fields and draws countless planes to hang from its gates.—YAB

Opposite

● **Heat wave over the marshes of the Camargue.**
Situated in the Bouches-du-Rhône, the plains of the Camargue are only three feet above sea level at their highest elevation, so there is no doubt the area would be one of the first victims of global warming if the oceans were to rise. In the meanwhile, a summer of heat waves is enough to dry out and crack the Rhône Delta, leaving a pattern resembling the thorns of a strange thistle drawn in marsh salt on the sun-baked mud. This protected ecological zone is absolutely unique. Among other things, it is a sanctuary for pink flamingoes and is home to many halophyte plants such as the glasswort.

When I take aerial pictures, I'm constantly looking for patterns. In this case, I found one in the mud of the Camargue. I'm only fifteen feet above the ground and yet the landscape is totally abstract. There's no way of telling whether this picture was taken from very close up or very far away.—*YAB*

It practically looks like a drawing from antiquity. You might even think you were looking at a cracked Greek vase.—*PPDA*

Pascal said that Man felt trapped between two infinities, the infinitely big and the infinitely small. When I'm in a helicopter, I sometimes feel I can attain both: the leaves of a tree can create an illusion of terrestrial erosion, while immense crevasses can be confused with meaningless little fissures. It's no coincidence that photographs taken through a microscope often look like aerial photographs.—*YAB*

● **Hunters in the vineyards of the Loire.**
Vineyards cover 197,680 acres along the course of the Loire, ranging from the mountains of Auvergne to Saint-Nazaire, and coming to an end with the designated wine-producing country around Nantes (Loire-Atlantic). In the fall, weekend hunters scour the countryside and the vineyards along the banks of the river in hopes of flushing a partridge. About one million Frenchmen practice leisure hunting, making up the largest hunting population of the European Union, and provoking the ire of ecologists campaigning for reduced hunting seasons and extended animal protection. In truth, traditional hunting respects cynegetic resources and regulates the number of animals such as the wild boar, which is known to reproduce too quickly.

● **The Raynaude church and its Stations of the Cross.**
A few years after the sightings of the Virgin in a grotto in nearby Lourdes, Father Rousse, the curate of Mas-d'Azil in Ariège, decided to open a sanctuary on this hill at the foot of the Pyrenees. In 1863, a fourteen-chapel way to the cross was added to plans for the Raynaude church. When alms began to grow insufficient, American visitor and oil magnate John D. Rockefeller offered the funds required to finish construction. The church and its Stations of the Cross were inaugurated in 1895.

Above

● **The Scandola nature preserve.**
The Scandola nature preserve
was one of the first created, in
1975. Dominated by impressive
red porphyry peaks on the
Girolata peninsula (Corsica),
the preserve is a haven for
22,239 acres of scrub grown
thick with juniper, strawberry
trees, lavender, and heather.
Wild boars and foxes frolic here
in complete freedom. The area's
status as a nature preserve also
extends to 2,471 acres of water
rich with wonderful opportuni-
ties for boaters to discover
intact coral, admire more than
450 types of algae, and maybe
even catch a glimpse of a
grouper, a fish that has become
rare in Mediterranean waters.

Opposite

- **A semitroglodytic house
  in Cabrerets.**
  The Lot valley still contains
  semitroglodytic houses built
  into the cliffs, such as this
  house in Bout du Lieu, in
  Cabrerets (Lot). Many caves
  in this area have been inhabited since prehistoric times.
  Some of the caves are deco-
  rated with paintings, the
  astonishing history of which
  is told in Cabrerets's Pech-
  Merle Prehistorical Museum.

Opposite

● **The Sperone golf course.**
Located along the sea at the
southern tip of the Isle of
Beauty, near Bonifacio
(Corsica), the Domaine de
Sperone includes an eighteen-
hole golf course ranked sixth
among France's best courses.
Designed to extend over 192
acres of land by architect
Robert Trent Jones in 1990, the
20,032-foot course faces the
Lavezzi Islands Nature Preserve.
Nowadays, buying a property
with a view of the water in this
magnificent region surrounded
by the Corsican scrub has
become a luxury: real estate
prices here have doubled over
the past five years.

Following spread

● **Bréhat island.**
An extension of the Pointe de
l'Arcouest, Bréhat island (Côtes-
d'Armor) is surrounded by a
vast network of islets and reefs
in the English Channel. This
2.2-mile long, 0.9-mile wide
insular body consists of two
islands connected by a single
bridge. The rocky North Island,
home to the Paon lighthouse, is
by far the wilder of the two. As
for the South Island, its position in the Gulf Stream's path
has graced it with practically
Mediterranean vegetation. In
the summer, Bréhat (population
471) receives up to five thousand
visitors a day, most of whom
reach it by using the shuttle
boat that connects the island
to the Continent.

Opposite

● **Vézelay, the hill of eternity.** It is here in Vézelay, in the Yonne, that Cistercian preacher Saint Bernard of Clairvaux proclaimed the Second Crusade in 1146. With its semicircular vaulted nave and its sculpted tympanum representing the Last Judgment, the twelfth-century basilica of the Madeleine is a jewel of Romanesque art. The building was restored in the nineteenth century by Viollet-le-Duc, a lover of medieval architecture. A UNESCO World Heritage Site, Vézelay remains a capital of French spirituality.

Going to Sunday morning mass in Vézelay's small side chapel is an amazing experience. First you see these white ghosts go by. Then they begin to sing. At that point, it doesn't matter whether you're Christian or not. You're simply at the core of humanity. You go into your heart, your own heart, to look for reasons to be comforted or filled with hope. I have so much admiration for what our ancestors left us. I wonder if our generation is capable of leaving its descendants something as pure as this.—*PPDA*

Opposite

● **The wooded Beaujolais near Mont Saint-Rigaud.**
In the north of the department of the Rhône, vineyards give way to forest and the hills become accentuated, culminating in the 3,310-foot Mont Saint-Rigaud. The wooded Beaujolais, also known as the "Little Switzerland," contains many Douglas firs originating in the United States, along with deciduous trees such as oak, hornbeams, beeches, and chestnut trees. Rare animal species such as the finch and the Tengmalm owl live here in peace.

Following spread

● **The Vercors, the symbol of the resistance.**
The limestone massif of the Vercors covers about 420,070 acres in the departments of the Drôme and the Isère. It is also home to the National Historic Site of the Resistance. As early as 1940, these difficult-to-access high karstic plateaus became the refuge for victims of the Vichy government's discriminatory measures. In 1943, with the help of the area's population, the resistance organized itself to turn the Vercors into a stronghold. A year later, following the Allied landing on June 6, 1944, four thousand resistance fighters held off the German troops stationed in Grenoble under General Karl Pflaum. The fighting lasted a week, resulting in the death of six hundred resistance members and numerous civilians.

Opposite

● **An unusual view of the Saint-Nazaire construction yards.**
These powerful chains built to hold ships' anchors serve as reminders that the biggest ocean liner in the world, the British *Queen Mary 2*, was built in Saint-Nazaire's Atlantic Yards (Loire-Atlantic). The ship was christened in late 2003. It

is 1,161 feet long, stands 242 feet, of which 203 are above water, and has a tonnage of 150,000. Its motors total 154,000 horsepower, and the power generated on board could light a city of 300,000 inhabitants. The *Queen Mary 2* can sail with 2,500 passengers and 1,250 crewmembers aboard.

Below

● **Bennecourt, a Gallic archeological site.**
The poplar-lined prairies around the commune of Bennecourt (Yvelines) are rich with buried Gallic vestiges. A sanctuary dating to 200 B.C. has already been uncovered in the area.

Pages 300 and 301

● **Champagne, an agricultural patchwork.**
Among the thirteen departments that could provide for all of France's food requirements, the Marne department, in the heart of the Champagne-Ardenne region, is of the first

rank, not only for its wheat production, but also for its alfalfa, barley, high-protein peas, and its sugar beets. Hence the wide variety of cultures such as those seen here near Châlons-en-Champagne. Traditionally a producer of cereals, Champagne

also carries on the tradition of growing grapes to produce Champagne wines. Champagne production accounts for 40 percent of the department's exports and generates 30,000 jobs in the region.

Opposite

- **The ruins of Nouveau Windstein.**
  These ruined walls in the heart of the forest a few miles from Niederbronn-les-Bains (Lower Rhine) are all that remains of the old fortress of Nouveau Windstein. This fourteenth-century medieval fortress once contributed to the defense of German Alsace, but was destroyed by the French in 1676, two years before they annexed the region.

● **The Centre Beaubourg in Paris.**

Situated near the old neighborhood of Les Halles, in the 4th arrondissement, the Centre Culturel Beaubourg (Beaubourg Cultural Center, also known as Centre Georges Pompidou, in honor of the late president who commissioned its construction) has received over 150 million visitors since it opened on February 2, 1977. Built on 4.9 acres of land by international architects Renzo Piano, Richard Rogers, and Gianfranco Franchini, the building has a surface area of over a million square feet, spread over seven levels of glass and steel—15,000 tons of metal and 118,403 square feet of glass. The various service shafts secured to the facades are distinguished by color: blue for air conditioning, green for water pipes, yellow for electrical systems, and red for security (fire pumps, etc.). The renovation of the center, completed in 2000, cost approximately 88 million euros.

● **The cathedral of Rodez.**

Standing 285 feet tall, the Rodez cathedral's filigreed pink sandstone belfry rises high above the roofs of the capital of Rouergue (Aveyron). As one of the hundred or so French diocesan seats to remain open for worship, the Gothic cathedral is a reminder of France's profoundly Catholic beginnings. Yet France, which was long considered "the Church's eldest daughter," is losing its spiritual fervor. Only 10 percent of the population continues to attend mass, and the church is even having difficulty recruiting priests to ordain.

Below

● **Fishing with square dipping nets in Charente-Maritime.** This shack built on stilts in the estuary of the Gironde, in Talmont (Charente-Maritime), is used for traditional fishing with square dipping nets known as *carrelets*. Enthusiasts catch all sorts of fish in these square nets mounted on two hoops and attached to a jointed pole, including eel, mullet, white perch, and lamprey. Both saltwater and freshwater fish inhabit this estuary formed by the confluence of the Dordogne and the Garonne. The effects of the tide on the estuary can be felt for some sixty miles.

Man's immersion in nature is very discreet here; nothing to do with those off-shore nets that dump out twenty tons of fish every time they're lifted out of the water.—PPDA

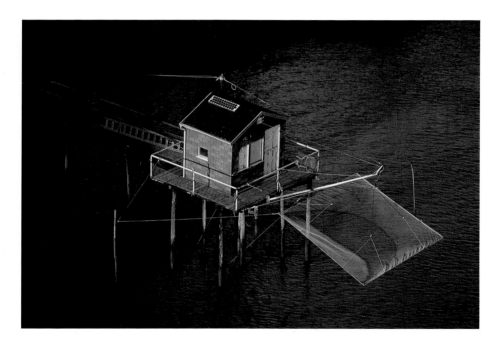

Opposite

● **Saint-Malo and its waves of tourists.** Home of some of the biggest tides in Europe, the famous corsair city (population 50,000, in Ille-et-Vilaine) has become one of the leading tourist attractions in Brittany, to the point that the summer crowds have begun to seriously bother some of the city's inhabitants. During the seventeenth and eighteenth centuries Saint-Malo was enriched by the *guerre de course* (war race), which allowed corsairs to legally seize hold of ships owned by the enemy and, particularly, the British. Partially destroyed during World War II, the city was rebuilt brick by brick, as an identical copy of its past self. Today, its ramparts and museum-château attract about two million visitors a year, most of whom tend to concentrate in rue Porcon and rue Broussais. These central byways have been turned into outdoor shopping malls by the tourist boom. Referred to as the "Mont-Saint-Michel syndrome" by the city's inhabitants, this phenomenon is detrimental to local stores, which are gradually being pushed into outlying parts of the city and are sorely missed by the downtown population once summer is over.

Page 308

● **A fog blankets Lyons.**
The Greater Lyons area (population 1,260,000, in the Rhône) is subjected to pollution from car exhausts and industrial gas emissions from the Rhône valley. In this picture, the buildings of the Croix-Rousse barely rise out of the smog weighing over the city. Yet one type of pollution, which is increasingly frequent during the summer, is invisible: ozone pollution is due to the sun's effect on automobile and industrial discharge, and is aggravated by severe heat. According to the European Commission, ozone pollution is responsible for an annual 21,400 premature deaths in Europe.

Page 309

● **A house in the forests of Alsace.**
The Alsace region includes 770,952 acres of public, national, or private forests comprising 2 percent of France's total forest area. The Alsatian forest consists of 57 percent deciduous trees (notably oak and beech) and 43 percent of conifers (fir, Scottish pine, and spruce); 8 percent of French lumber cutting takes place in Alsace's forests. Beginning in 1992, many of these forests were added to the Program for the Endorsement of Forest Certification plans, which attests that forests are being managed in keeping with current sustainable-development policies.

Opposite

● **The Chamborigaud railroad viaduct.**
Built in nineteen months by the PLM railroad company and inaugurated on August 12, 1867, the Chamborigaud viaduct stands 170 feet above the Luech valley. About ten trains on the Paris–Nîmes line going through the Cévennes continue to cross the viaduct every day. Its very sharp curve requires trains to slow to a cautious 12 mph.

Left

● **The Pont du Gard.**
Built at the beginning of the
Christian Era with stones
extracted from surrounding
quarries (some of which
weighed over six tons), the
Roman Pont du Gard stretches
895 feet over the temperamental
Gardon River. Standing 160 feet
above ground, it is the tallest
surviving antique bridge-
aqueduct. The bridge was once
used to move water between the
towns of Uzès and Nîmes, covering 31 miles at an average flow
of 706,000 cubic feet per day.
Registered as a UNESCO World
Heritage Site since 1985, the
Pont du Gard attracts more than
a million visitors per year.

Right

● **The Canal du Midi.**
Dug by twelve thousand workers from 1666 to 1681, under the
reign of Louis XIV, the Canal
du Midi is the oldest European
canal still in use. It was designed
by architect Pierre-Paul de
Riquet to run 150 miles from
Toulouse (Haute-Garonne) to
the Étang de Thau, thereby
linking the Atlantic and the
Mediterranean, via the Garonne
and its lateral canal. Registered
as a World Heritage Site in 1996,
the Canal du Midi has lost its
economic importance, but is
still widely used by small
tourist barges.

*Previous pages
and opposite*

• **Agriculture, a major source
of water consumption.**
On average, farmers use more
than half of France's water
resources to irrigate fields of
wheat and corn (such as these
wheat fields in the Beauce)
before harvest. Wheat and corn
crops require 132 gallons of
water to produce 2.2 pounds of
grain. The drought of the summer of 2005 forced seventy
French departments to reduce
their water consumption.
Knowing that a third of annual
precipitation runs off without
being used has spurred many
farmers to begin studying methods of stocking rainwater.

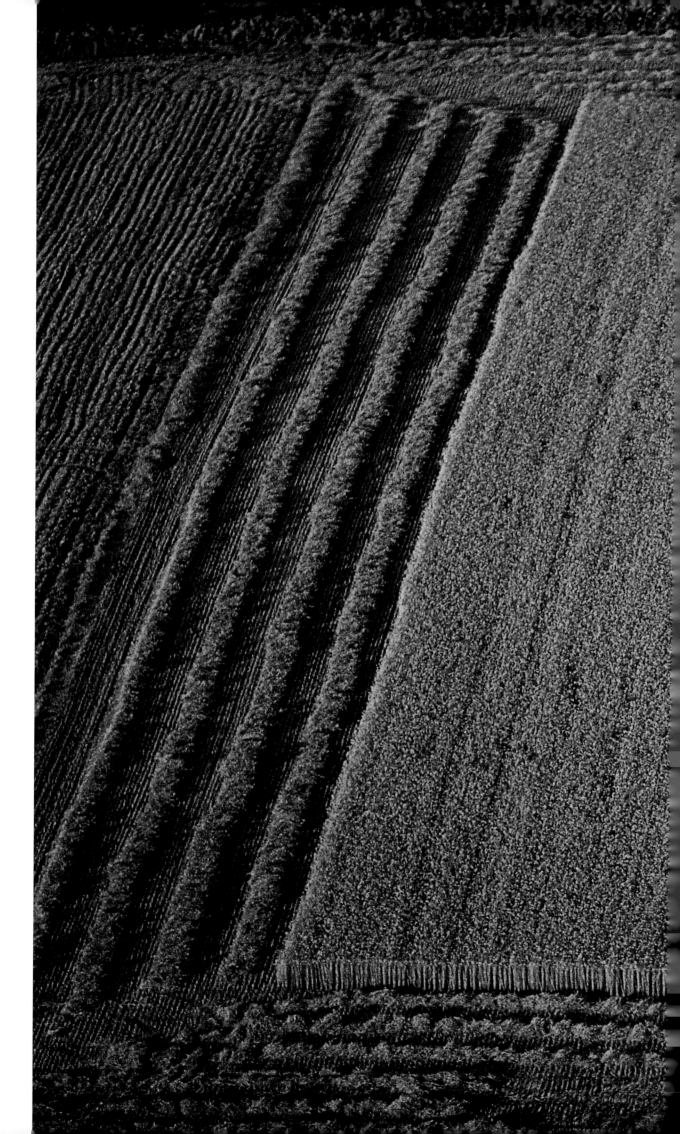

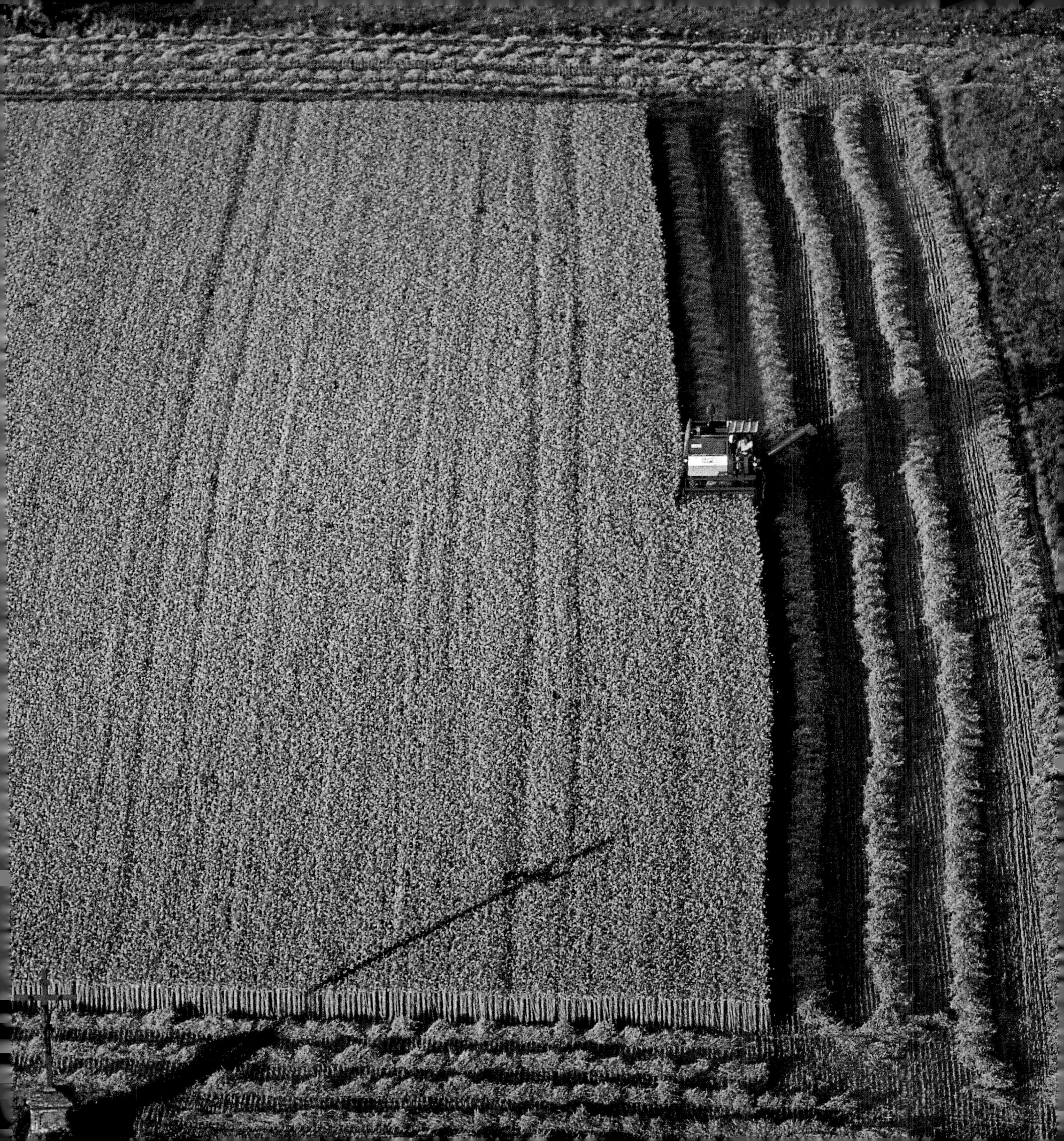

● **The Puy de Dôme is in need of protection.**
As can be determined from its Gallo-Roman temple devoted to Mercury, the Puy de Dôme has been venerated since antiquity. Today, however, it is showing signs of ecological fragility. Though sheep are clearly welcome here, the increase in tourism, with some 520,000 visitors a year, is threatening the already eroded flanks of the old volcano. Footpaths need to be restored and the hills of the massif must be replanted. Several development projects are in the works to include the Puy de Dôme in the "Great French Sites" network created in 2000 to develop sustainable tourism.

● **The clear waters of the Gulf of Murtoli in Corsica.**
The Gulf of Murtoli in Corsica has preserved its untamed, remote peacefulness. Only a few houses hang off its rocky surfaces, the water is clear, and the scrub is fragrant with the smell of mastic trees. With its beaches of fine sand providing idyllic moorage for sailboats, the Gulf of Murtoli single-handedly expresses the magic of the Isle of Beauty.

Opposite

● **The ruins of Occi, an abandoned Corsican village.**
A premature victim of rural desertification abandoned by its inhabitants in the nineteenth century, the village of Occi stands in ruins near Lumio, in Balagne (Corsica). An association backed by notables such as actress Laetitia Casta has come together to preserve the village and restore its church. Today church services are regularly held here, and a statue of Saint Nicholas is carried through the narrow streets during religious holidays. Nonetheless, cars cannot access the village. One can only reach Occi the way it has been reached for centuries: along a dirt path.

Following spread

● **The reservoir lakes of the Orient Forest.**
Three reservoir lakes covering a total of 12,355 acres in the Orient Forest Regional Nature Park (Aube) allow for the flow of the Seine and the Aube rivers to be regulated, thereby avoiding droughts and floods downriver, in areas including Paris. Winter and spring water level swells are capped by a system of floodgates that stocks excess water. In the summer and the fall the stocked water is released to supplement low water levels. Opened in 1966, the Seine reservoir lake can hold up to seven billion cubic feet of water. The Aube reservoirs have been in use since 1990, and can hold six billion cubic feet of water. The lakes are also the pride and joy of local water sports enthusiasts.

Pages 326–27

● **The Chanteloup pagoda.**
Standing on a thirty-four-acre park on the edge of the Amboise forest, the Chanteloup pagoda (Indre-et-Loire) is the only remaining trace of a château that once belonged to the duke of Choiseul, a disgraced minister of the court of Louis XV. Inspired by Chinese architecture, the pagoda was built in 1755 by Nicolas Le Camus and restored in 1910 by architect René-Édouard André. Standing 144 feet, the pagoda is composed of seven stone cupolas, one on top of the other. This unique structure is one of the rare surviving examples of the "follies" fashionable at the end of the eighteenth century.

This pagoda is an eighteenth-century "folly," a relic of a period when people had the money and time to build things that may have been gratuitous but that had the merit of being out of the ordinary.—*YAB*

Pages 328–29

● **Before and after the flood.**
The waters of the Saône, a powerful 300-mile tributary of the Rhône, swell during the November–April winter period. These rises in the water levels, which hydrologists call plains floods, are slow enough that the risks tied to flooding can be controlled. Nonetheless, the Saône rises far out of its riverbed, flooding surrounding farms and fields, such as these between Saint-Loup-de-la-Salle and Lux (Saône-et-Loire). Recently, in January 1995 and 1999 and in March 2001, the Saône region experienced several spectacular floods.

Below

● **The mechanical ship lift in Saint-Louis-Arzviller.** This mechanical ship lift located between Saint-Louis and Arzviller, on the Marne canal in the Rhine, in the Moselle region, was put into service in 1969 as a replacement for the tedious series of seventeen locks that used to cost bargemen an entire day. Barges now only take a few minutes to be raised or lowered 130 feet in a trolley-tub moving at 13 feet per second on an incline thanks to two 450-ton counterweights. There are only three of these enormous machines in the world (the other two are in Belgium and Siberia). Surprisingly, the lift can be operated by only two technicians.

Opposite

● **The Étang de Gondrexange in Lorraine.** Small artificial lakes in the Sarrebourg area of the Moselle extend from the Marne canals of the Rhine to the mines of the Sarre. Medieval monks dug most of these lakes to farm fish. One of them, the Étang de Gondrexange (148 acres), has remained a well-known fishing hole, with pike and carp wriggling through its shallow waters. It is also a hotspot for water sports, though rowing and windsurfing take precedence over motorboats, which are strictly forbidden. There has also been a relative upsurge of river tourism on the nearby canals.

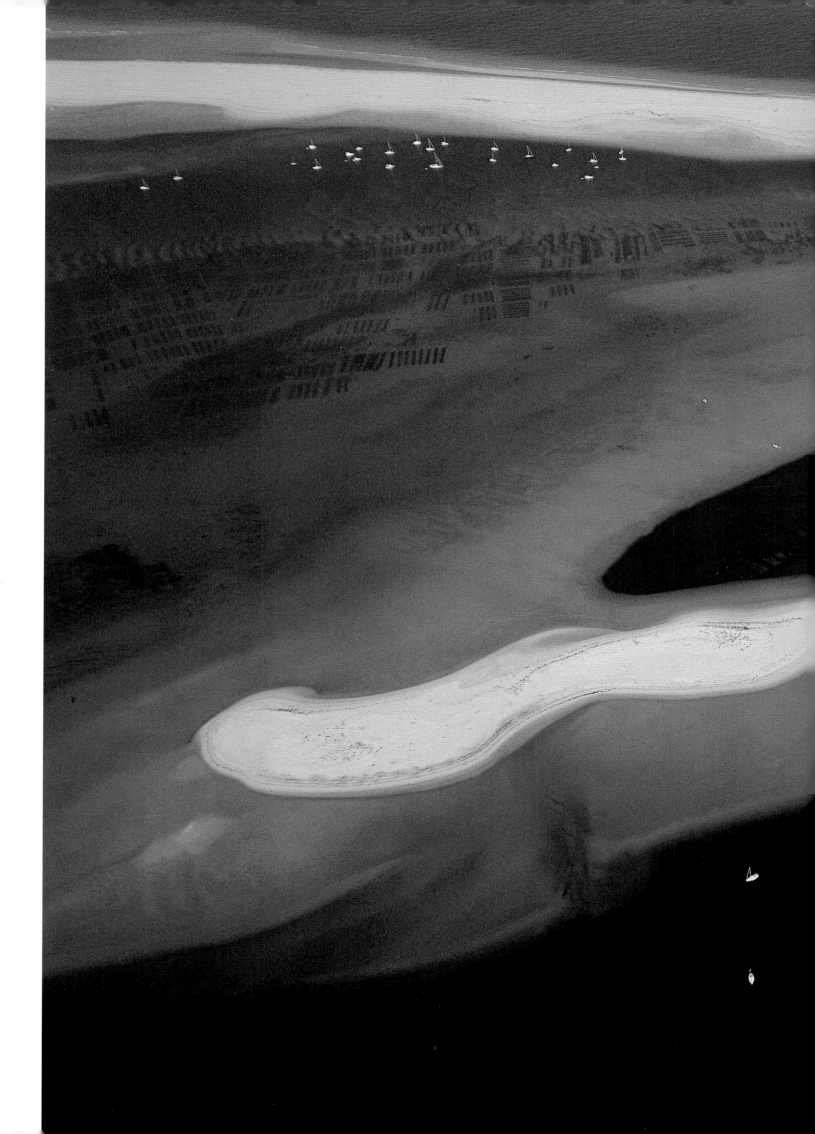

Opposite

● **The Banc d'Arguin nature preserve.**
Situated at the opening of the
Bay of Arcachon (Gironde),
between the Pilat sand dune
and the tip of Cap-Ferret, the
Banc d'Arguin sandbank
spreads its golden sands over
a length of about 2.5 miles and
a width of 1.25 miles at low tide.
The sandbank's contours are
constantly modified by the
bay's powerful currents. Classified as a nature preserve since
1972, the sandbank serves as a
stopover for many migratory
birds, including the sandwich
tern, or "sea swallow," which
comes to nest here in the spring.

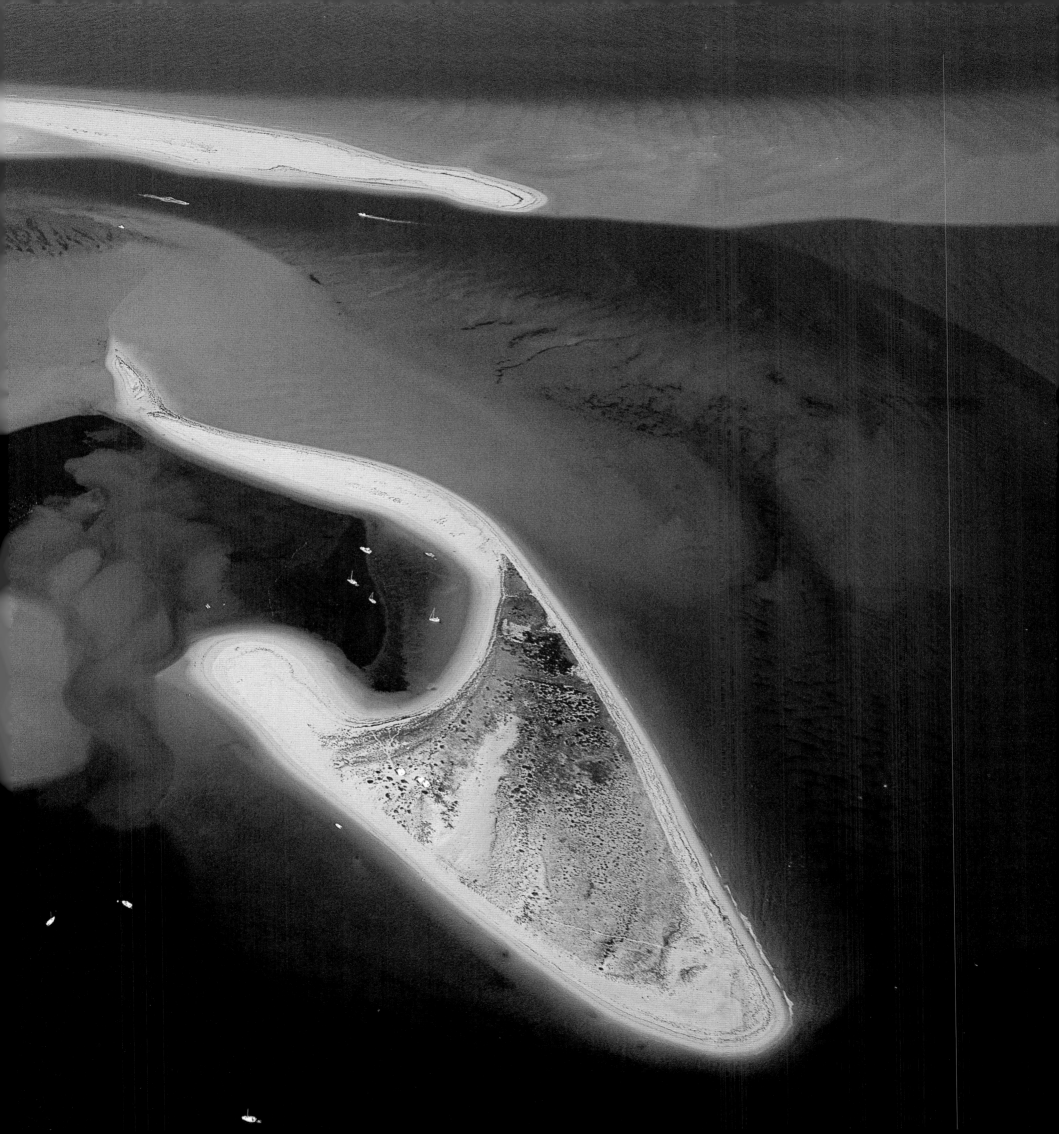

Opposite

● **The Aiguille du Midi
in the Alps.**
The Aiguille du Midi (Haute-
Savoie) rises 12,604 feet in the
heart of the Alps, and com-
mands access to the famed
Vallée Blanche. The idea of
creating a shortcut to the Mont
Blanc (15,771 feet) via an "aerial
cable car" extending from the
Chamonix valley to this high
mountain area was first
hatched in 1905. The dream

became reality in 1958, with a
route divided into two sections,
the second of which relied on
a six-thousand-foot steel cable
hanging over the void. The
Aiguille du Midi cable car
service, which was modernized
in 1991, covers a difference in
level of about ten thousand feet.
It carries five hundred thousand passengers a year, at an
average rate of six hundred
people an hour.

Opposite

● **Ten thousand hearts form one red ribbon.**
We have a humanitarian operation carried out on September 25, 2004 to thank for this symbol of a generous France. The city of Le Mans organized thousands of people to gather on a field in the Sarthe and form a human chain. Participants wore red T-shirts and caps to form a scarlet heart. The funds raised by the operation were dedicated to fighting AIDS in Mali.

To help a Malian village beleaguered by AIDS, a massive crowd came together in a field near Le Mans to form this red heart, a symbol of compassion and generosity. I am delighted to close this volume with this picture.—*YAB*

Index of captions

Acknowledgments

This book would have been impossible without the friendship and expertise extended by a vast group of people. It would be equally impossible to mention any of them without forgetting others. May all those who shared their knowledge, talent, and friendship accept our deepest thanks.

First of all, I would like to thank my "photographic family," FUJI and CANON, for the human and professional qualities displayed by their respective staffs, and for the genuine friendship we have shared these many years.

All the helicopter pilots who flew with me were crucial contributors to the search for "the right light and the right angle."
Thank you all for your patience and your talent:
Willy Gouère, Franck Arrestier, Jean-Luc Scaillierez.
As well as:
Richard Sarrazy, Alexandre Antunès, Antoine de Marsily, Francis Coz, Bernard Séguy, Gustave Nicolas, Michel Beaujard, Dominique Cortesi, Alain Morlat, Serge Rosset, Michel Anglade, Daniel Manoury, Thierry Debruyère, Gilbert Giacometti, Raphaël Leservot, and Jean Roussot.

Among the many assistants who participated in this long-term project, I would like to make particular mention of my two faithful accomplices, Françoise Jacquot and Françoise Le Roch'-Briquet, for their tireless research in the "image bank" I've been building up for fifteen years! And, of course, Isabelle Bruneau and Isabelle Lechenet.
And:
Franck Charel, Marc Lavaud, Franck Lechenet, and Frédéric Lenoir.

I would also like to mention all the staff members at prefectures and administrative departments who remained highly cooperative, even when I "hustled" them to get shooting permits in twenty-four hours.

I must single out Olivier Fontvieille, my artistic director, for accepting to put off his vacation to see this adventure through with me, as well as Malika Rehailia.

I'd also like to mention the patience and professionalism displayed by the staff of Arts Graphiques du Centre in Tours, and particularly by Éric Frette, Jean-Claude Bellenfant, Christelle Pichois, and Valérie Moreau.

Finally, I keep a special place in my heart for Isabelle Grison of Éditions de La Martinière, who valiantly fought off my doubts, accepted my demands, and helped me wrestle with many a question . . . Without forgetting Brigitte Govignon, Juliette de Trégomain, and Dominique Escartin.

The vast majority of the pictures in this book were taken on Fuji Velvia (50 ASA) film.
I principally used a CANON EOS 1N camera and CANON L series lenses.
A few photographs were taken with a PENTAX 645 N.

Yann Arthus-Bertrand's photographs, as well as those by François Jourdan and Claudius Thiriet,
are distributed by the Altitude agency, Paris, France.
www.altitude-photo.com
www.yannarthusbertrand.org

All photographs in *France from the Air* are by Yann Arthus-Bertrand except:

Pages 125, 130–31: © Claudius Thiriet/Altitude

Pages 252–53, 262, 264–65, 296–97, 310–11: © François Jourdan/Altitude

PROJECT MANAGER, ENGLISH-LANGUAGE EDITION: Céline Moulard

EDITOR, ENGLISH-LANGUAGE EDITION: Mary Christian

DESIGN COORDINATOR, ENGLISH-LANGUAGE EDITION: Shawn Dahl

JACKET DESIGN, ENGLISH-LANGUAGE EDITION: Eric J. Diloné

PRODUCTION COORDINATOR, ENGLISH-LANGUAGE EDITION: Colin Hough Trapp

BRITISH LIBRARY CATALOGUING IN PUBLICATION DATA

A catalogue record for this book is available from the British Library.

Printed and bound in Italy

10 9 8 7 6 5 4 3 2 1

HNA
harry n. abrams, inc.
a subsidiary of La Martinière Groupe

115 West 18th Street
New York, NY 10011
www.hnabooks.com

MICHELANGELO

PAINTINGS · SCULPTURES · ARCHITECTURE

BY LUDWIG GOLDSCHEIDER

COMPLETE EDITION · FOUR HUNDRED ILLUSTRATIONS

THE PHAIDON PRESS · LONDON

ALL RIGHTS RESERVED BY PHAIDON PRESS LTD

5 Cromwell Place · London SW7

first edition 1953

second edition 1954

third edition 1959

reprinted 1961

fourth edition 1962

reprinted spring 1963

reprinted autumn 1963

reprinted spring 1964

The ornament on the binding

is a reproduction of

Michelangelo's stone-mason's mark

C4864

MADE IN GREAT BRITAIN

BOOK DESIGNED BY THE AUTHOR

TEXT AND COLOUR PLATES PRINTED BY HUNT BARNARD AND CO LTD · AYLESBURY

MONOCHROME PLATES PRINTED BY CLARKE AND SHERWELL LTD · NORTHAMPTON

FOREWORD

IN the course of the last thirty years the Michelangelo literature has increased to a formidable extent. Nevertheless, the most indispensable books have not been brought up to date and we still have to rely on works which are slowly growing old and weak. For instance, we have still no substitutes for the collections of letters published by Milanesi, Gotti and Frey, with their often incorrect dating and their many gaps, while the volumes by Giovanni Poggi, the forthcoming publication of which was announced, have still to appear. Similarly, there has been no new concise work containing reproductions of all Michelangelo's paintings, sculptures and architectural works—no unpretentious yet comprehensive volume which might have replaced the one published long ago in the 'Klassiker der Kunst' series and which rendered good service to several generations of readers, but has now become unusable.

In the meantime the quantity of photographic and illustrative material available has greatly increased and the conception underlying it has changed. There exist to-day special publications reproducing all the frescoes in the Sistine and Pauline chapels, with an almost unlimited abundance of details, there are new works on the Medici chapel and the tomb of Julius, with hundreds of illustrations. For the two volumes in large format, published by the Phaidon Press during the recent war, new photographs were taken of all the sculptures and of numerous details from the frescoes. All these photographs have been used in the present comprehensive volume, yet almost a third of the reproductions are from entirely new photographs, some of them of details never published before.

As regards the reproductions of architecture and the remarks thereon, the reader must not expect to find what he would be justified in expecting in a specialized work. He will, however, find reproductions corresponding to those in the volume of the 'Klassiker der Kunst', though of better quality. Virtually all the illustrations in this volume show the buildings as they are to-day.

The textual portions of the present volume are quite straightforward and consist solely of concentrated material from which the reader may construct his own Michelangelo book. For this reason I have refrained from writing an introduction in the form of an essay expounding my own views and experience and offer the reader in its place an easily readable chronological table which he can consult from time to time if he wishes to refresh his memory of Michelangelo's life and works or of the background to some period of his career. The conception underlying the whole volume is that it should serve the reader as a constant companion to the Michelangelo literature, or, in the case of less patient readers, give them, with the choice and arrangement of the illustrations, a coherent idea of the work of one of the most prolific masters of all time.

London: Spring 1953

NOTE ON THE FOURTH EDITION

SINCE the appearance of the last revised edition of the present volume (in Spring 1959) a number of important books and articles on Michelangelo have been published, of which the following may be mentioned.

Michelangelo by Herbert von Einem (Stuttgart 1959) is at present the only monograph on the artist which incorporates all the research of the last twenty years. It is a rather slender volume, very readable, and an excellent first introduction to the Sculpture and Painting of Michelangelo. Unfortunately it is available only in German.—A very short and very charming first chapter of an English monograph on the master can be found in *The Horizon Book of the Renaissance* (New York 1961, pp. 105-111), 'The Young Michelangelo' by Kenneth Clark, the only perfect seven pages in the whole volume.—In André Chastel's *Art et Humanisme à Florence* (Paris 1959) there are many paragraphs that throw a bright light on the spiritual background of Michelangelo's life (e.g. pp. 505-21, *La tragédie de Michel Ange: le triomphe de Saturne*).—Luitpold Dussler's *Die Zeichnungen des Michelangelo* (Berlin 1959) contains more than a discussion of the drawings; and so does Professor Johannes Wilde's valuable article '*Cartonetti' by Michelangelo* (Burlington Magazine, Nov. 1959, pp. 370-81).—The fifth volume of Tolnay's monumental work on Michelangelo (*The Final Period*, Princeton 1960) deals with the late frescoes and the last Pietàs.—The three last Pietàs are also discussed at length by Alexander Perrig in *Michelangelo Buonarrotis letzte Pietà-Idee,* Berne 1960.—Chapter VIII of Armando Schiavo's *San Pietro in Vaticano* (Rome, Istituto di Studi Romani, 1960) discusses the alterations which Michelangelo's model for the cupola of St. Peter's has suffered.—The *Journal of the Society of Architectural Historians,* vol. XIX (1960, pp. 97-108) contains an article by Elizabeth MacDougall on 'Michelangelo and the Porta Pia'.—Professor James S. Ackerman's *The Architecture of Michelangelo* (two volumes, London 1961) is the long expected standard work in this field.

I have read these books and articles with great profit; but on the whole I have left the text of my book almost exactly as it was in the first edition. A few illustrations have been added. *The Vase with the Medici arms,* our pl. IV-a, was first published by Professor Charles de Tolnay in his 'Michelagniolo', Firenze, 1951, pl. 148; the *Fibula of Brutus* (p. 262), in the same author's 'Michelangelo IV': *The Tomb of Julius II,* Princeton, 1954, pl. 92. Our reproductions of these two important details are based on original photographs and not on the illustrations in Tolnay's books.

London: Spring 1962

BIOGRAPHICAL CONSPECTUS

I. CHILDHOOD · APPRENTICESHIP · BEGINNINGS

1474. The Florentine Republic, during the rule of Lorenzo de' Medici, appoints Lodovico di Lionardo Buonarroti Simoni (1446–1531) of Florence 'Podestà' (i.e. mayor and local magistrate) of Caprese and Chiusi for the period of six months. Lodovico's wife was Francesca di Neri (1455–81). Caprese is in Tuscany, about 40 miles from Florence in the district known as the Casentino, in the upper valley of the Arno.

1475–84. Michelangelo born on 6 March 1475 at Caprese, the second son of Lodovico Buonarroti. (In Florence, the name was spelled Michelangiolo; but Vasari calls him Michelagnolo, and thus the name is sometimes written in the documents. Michelangiolo di Lodovico Buonarroti-Simoni is the correct full form of the artist's name.) When Michelangelo is not yet a month old, his father's term of office expires and the family returns to Florence. Michelangelo is placed in the care of a foster-mother at Settignano (five miles east of Florence), but it is not known how long he remained there. His mother dies when he is six years old.

1485–87. In 1485 Michelangelo's father marries his second wife, Lucrezia Ubaldini (who dies in 1497). About this time Michelangelo returns to Florence to live with his father, stepmother, four brothers and an uncle in a gloomy house in the Via de' Bentaccordi, near Santa Croce. He attends a school kept by Francesco da Urbino.

1488. Michelangelo makes friends with a young painter named Francesco Granacci, who works with the brothers Ghirlandaio. On 1 April Michelangelo becomes an apprentice in Domenico and David Ghirlandaio's workshop. He makes sketches after frescoes by Giotto and Masaccio and copies drawings of the old masters and Schongauer's engraving 'The Temptation of St Anthony'.

1489. Michelangelo leaves the Ghirlandaio workshop (probably in the early part of the year) and enters Bertoldo's 'school for sculptors'. He makes clay figures and a free copy in marble, after an antique model, of the head of a Faun (since lost).

1490–91. The attention of Lorenzo de' Medici is drawn to Michelangelo's talent and he invites him to reside as a guest in his palace, where Michelangelo remains until Lorenzo's death on 8 April 1492. There Michelangelo comes into contact with several leading humanists, among them Angelo Poliziano, who inspires him to carve the relief of the Battle of Centaurs (Plate 2), Marsilio Ficino, the interpreter of Plato, and Cristoforo Landino, the commentator of Dante. Michelangelo creates his relief of the 'Madonna of the Stairs' (Plate 1). Lorenzo de' Medici appoints Michelangelo's father an excise officer.

1492–95. Lorenzo's successor, Piero de' Medici, invites Michelangelo to live in the palace again, but gives him only one commission – to make a statue of snow (January 1494). The spiritual ruler of Florence at the time is Savonarola, whose sermons Michelangelo hears. In the meantime he finishes an over-lifesize marble statue of Hercules and a wooden crucifix (both lost). Florence is threatened by the advance of the French army (entry of Charles VIII into the city, 17 November 1494) and in October 1494 Michelangelo flees to Bologna and thence to Venice; there his money runs out and he returns to Bologna. (Dürer, four years older than Michelangelo, in Venice. Death of Ghirlandaio and Memling.) Michelangelo's father loses his post. Piero de' Medici and his brother Giuliano go into exile. Florence becomes a republic. In Bologna Michelangelo sees the works of Jacopo della Quercia and himself makes three statuettes for the shrine of San Domenico (Plates 4–6). At the end of 1495 Michelangelo returns to Florence, where Lorenzo di Pierfrancesco de' Medici commissions him to carve a marble statue of the youthful St John (lost).

1496. Michelangelo makes a marble statue, in antique style, of a recumbent Cupid (lost). This statue comes into the hands of the art dealer Baldassare del Milanese in Rome, who offers it for sale as a genuine antique. Michelangelo tries in vain to regain possession of the statue, which is eventually sold to Cesare Borgia, and was later in the collection of Isabella d'Este. In June 1496 Michelangelo arrives in Rome.

II. THE YOUNG MASTER

1496–1501. Michelangelo in Rome. He makes a life-size marble statue of Cupid (or Apollo?), which he sells to Jacopo Galli (since lost); Galli also purchases his 'Bacchus' (Plate 7) and obtains for Michelangelo from Cardinal Jean de Villiers de la Groslaye the commission for a Pietà (Plate 13), which is completed in the spring of 1499. Two years later Michelangelo returns to Florence, where the situation has meanwhile become quieter. (Savonarola burned at the stake on 23 May 1498; the Republic survives until 1512.)

1501–5. Michelangelo in Florence. Contract for fifteen figures for the Piccolomini altar in Siena (5 June 1501), of which only a few were executed (Plates 28–31); contract for the marble 'David' (16 August 1501), which was not completed until 1504 (Plate 19). Contract (August 1502) for a bronze 'David', which was sent to France and has since been lost. Contract for twelve figures of Apostles for the Duomo in Florence (April 1503), of which only the 'Matthew' was begun (Plate 47). A 'Madonna with the Christ Child,' begun at the same time as the statues for the Siena altar, was not delivered in Bruges until 1506 (Plate 34). During these years Michelangelo executes three tondi of the Madonna, two of them sculptures and one a painting (Plates 43, 45, 44). Leonardo da Vinci obtains the commission for a mural painting of the 'Battle of Anghiari' in the Palazzo Vecchio, Florence, the left half of the wall being reserved for a 'Battle of Cascina' by Michelangelo, who gets no further than the cartoon; this, too, has been lost and is known to us only through copies (Plate XXIV). Raphael in Florence.

1505-8. Pope Julius II summons Michelangelo to Rome. First design for the 'Tomb of Julius'. (1506: Laocoön found in Rome.) Michelangelo feels that he is neglected in Rome and flees to Florence (17 April 1506). There he resumes work on his cartoon for the 'Battle of Cascina', on the 'Matthew' and perhaps also on designs for the Pope's tomb. In November 1506 he goes to Bologna to meet Julius (who occupies the city in the course of his war against Perugia and Bologna). Michelangelo makes a large bronze statue of the Pope, which is installed in February 1508 on the façade of San Petronio. (This bronze portrait was destroyed in 1511.) (1506: Death of Mantegna and Columbus.)

III. CEILING FRESCOES IN THE SISTINE CHAPEL · TOMB OF JULIUS

1508-12. In the spring of 1508 Michelangelo is summoned to Rome by Pope Julius to paint the ceiling of the Sistine Chapel. The first half of the ceiling is finished by September 1510. In December 1510 Michelangelo visits the Pope in Bologna, to protest against intrigues. After his return he resumes his work in the Sistine Chapel and finishes it in October 1512. One month earlier the Medici had been reinstalled in Florence by Spanish troops (12 September 1512); Giovanni de' Medici (destined to become Pope in the following year under the name of Leo X) and his brother Giuliano de' Medici (Duke of Nemours) become masters of the city. (1510: Death of Botticelli and Giorgione.)

1513-16. Julius II dies in February 1513. Michelangelo concludes a new contract with the Pope's heirs for the tomb of Julius. Two statues of 'Captives' are begun (Plates 149, 152) and work on the tomb continues until 1516. (At this time Raphael paints his last Vatican frescoes and Grünewald finishes the Isenheim Altar.)

IV. IN THE SERVICE OF THE MEDICI

1516-20. Michelangelo in Florence, in June 1516 and then again from August on, after spending the month of July in Rome, where he makes a third contract for the tomb of Julius. He becomes the patron of Sebastiano del Piombo, and helps him with drawings for the 'Raising of Lazarus' and other paintings. At this time (1516-19) the head of the Medici family in Florence is Lorenzo, Duke of Urbino, who is succeeded by Giulio de' Medici (later Pope Clement VII). Commissions to artists for the embellishment of Florence, however, are awarded by another member of the Medici family, Pope Leo X. From 1516 on Michelangelo discusses with him the improvement of the façade of San Lorenzo. Baccio d'Agnolo makes a wooden model after Michelangelo's design, but Michelangelo rejects it and makes his own model (spring 1517–winter 1517–18; cf. Plate 159). He spends most of his time in the quarries at Carrara and Pietrasanta, with occasional visits to Rome. On 19 January 1518 the contract for the façade of San Lorenzo is signed, but Michelangelo continues working in Florence on the tomb of Julius. To Leo X he offers to execute a Tomb of Dante without payment (1518, Document in the Archivio di Stato, Florence). He gives up his house in Rome and many of his cartoons are burned. In November 1518 Michelangelo begins building a house for himself and his workshop in the Via Mozza, Florence. In the summer of 1519 he begins the 'Statue of Christ' (Plate 155), commissioned as long ago as 1514, work on a first version having soon been suspended because the block of marble proved to be defective. The second version is completed in spring 1520. On 10 March the contract for the façade of San Lorenzo is cancelled. Work on the tomb of Julius continues during this year. (Leonardo dies in 1519, Raphael in 1520.)

1521-33. In 1521 Luther (who in 1517 nailed his theses to the door of the church in Wittenberg) is declared a heretic by the Diet of Worms, retires to the Wartburg and begins translating the Bible. The Reformation. (Holbein paints his 'Dead Christ', now at the Basle Museum.) In the spring of the same year Michelangelo begins work in the Medici Chapel. In November 1523 Giulio de' Medici is elected Pope (Clement VII). Alessandro de' Medici becomes ruler of Florence. In 1524 Michelangelo is still working on the models for the sculptures in the Medici Chapel. Work begun on the Biblioteca Laurenziana. In 1525 new agreement for the tomb of Julius which is now to be executed as a wall tomb, and not standing free. The 'Allegories of the Phases of the Day' for the Medici Chapel are still not quite finished. In October 1526 Michelangelo sends a new design for the tomb of Julius to Rome. In the following year Rome is occupied by imperial troops under the Connétable de Bourbon, and the Pope, a Medici, is besieged in Castel Sant'Angelo. In consequence, the Medici are driven out of Florence again. Two years later the Emperor Charles V and Pope Clement VII agree to restore Alessandro. In 1529 Michelangelo is employed mainly as a military engineer, fortifying Florence against attacks by the Medici in their attempts to return. Michelangelo lends the city a thousand scudi. He goes to Ferrara to ask the Duke for advice concerning fortifications, promises him a picture and paints 'Leda and the Swan'. The picture (afterwards lost in France) is not delivered, but presented to Mini, Michelangelo's favourite pupil. In September 1529 Michelangelo returns to Florence, but in the same month flees to Ferrara and thence to Venice. He is declared a traitor and threatened with confiscation of his property, whereupon he returns to Florence while the city is besieged. On 12 August 1530 Florence

Jonah. Detail of Plate 137.

capitulates and the imperial troops enter the city, which is handed over to Clement VII, who appoints Baccio Valori his plenipotentiary. Michelangelo remains in hiding, but is promised immunity by the Pope if he will continue his work on the Medici Chapel. In the autumn of the same year he resumes work in the Chapel and presents Baccio Valori with an 'Apollo' (Plate 210). During this disturbed period Michelangelo's father dies (not in 1534, as was at one time supposed). The reliquary loggia in San Lorenzo completed in 1532 (Plate 168). On 29 April of the same year, fourth contract for the tomb of Julius. From August 1532, Michelangelo in Rome.

V. TRANSITIONS

1533–34. Michelangelo spends the winter 1532–33 in Rome. He forms a lifelong friendship with Tommaso de' Cavalieri, to whom he dedicates many poems and drawings. He decides to settle in Rome. In June 1533 he returns for four months to Florence. At that time the 'Allegories of the Phases of the Day' still reposed on the floor of the Medici Chapel, but shortly before Michelangelo's final move to Rome, at least the statues of the two Medici Dukes had been installed in their niches. From November 1533 to June 1534 Michelangelo is in Rome, where he receives from the Pope the commission for the 'Last Judgement' and works once more on the tomb of Julius. After this he again spends three months in Florence; the benches

and the wooden ceiling of the Biblioteca Laurenziana, designed as long ago as 1526, are now completed (Plates VIII and IX). Assistants carry on the work on the Laurenziana and after many interruptions it is at last finished in 1559, when Ammanati and Vasari execute the staircase after drawings and a model by Michelangelo (Plate 166). The Medici Chapel is also left unfinished after Michelangelo's departure and the remaining work is entrusted to assistants (see, e.g., Plate IV).

In September 1534 Michelangelo moves to Rome. He never returns to Florence during the remaining thirty years of his life. The Medici remain rulers of the city; first Alessandro, and after his murder (1537), Cosimo I, both of whom are disliked by Michelangelo, who refuses all the flattering offers of Duke Cosimo.

VI. THE 'LAST JUDGEMENT'

1534–41. Two days after Michelangelo's arrival in Rome, on 25 September 1534, Pope Clement VII dies. He is succeeded by Alessandro Farnese (Paul III). Michelangelo, who wants to continue work on the tomb of Julius, is ordered by the new Pope to begin the altarpiece for the Sistine Chapel, the 'Last Judgement'. The preparatory work lasts until 1536 and the fresco is completed in 1541. Friendship with Vittoria Colonna, for whom Michelangelo makes a 'Christ on the Cross' and other religious drawings. He comes into contact with Cardinal Pole and the religious circle of the 'spirituali'. In 1538 Ignatius Loyola comes to Rome; Michelangelo's conversations with Francisco de Hollanda. (Vesalius works on his 'Anatomia'. Death of Paracelsus.)

VII. RELIGIOUS THEMES

1542–45. First fresco in the Cappella Paolina, the 'Conversion of St Paul', commissioned by Pope Paul III (Plate 243). At the same time, after forty years' work, the tomb of Julius is completed (Plate 238). On 8 January 1544 (according to the Florentine calendar, =1545), death at the age of fifteen of Cecchino Bracci, nephew and favourite of Luigi del Riccio, one of Michelangelo's friends. Michelangelo composes fifty poetic inscriptions and makes a drawing for the boy's tomb (Plate XX–a). Titian in Rome, visits Michelangelo. In November 1545 Pietro Aretino attacks Michelangelo in an open letter for his 'godlessness' and blames him for the unseemliness of the many nudes in the 'Last Judgement'. The Council of Trent begins its sittings. The Counter-Reformation.

1546. Vasari in Rome. Antonio da Sangallo dies and Michelangelo takes over the construction of the Palazzo Farnese, at the same time making the first designs for the rebuilding of the Capitol and beginning his share in the work of building St Peter's (Plates 252–256; XVIII).

1546–53. Second fresco in the Cappella Paolina, the 'Crucifixion of St Peter' (Plate 244). Work begins on the 'Florentine Pietà' (Plate 262) and on the Nicchione del Belvedere (Plate 261, about 1550). First plans for the reconstruction of San Giovanni dei Fiorentini in Rome (on which Michelangelo works until 1560). The first edition of Vasari's 'Vite' is published, including the biography of Michelangelo (1550). In the same year appear Benedetto Varchi's 'Due Lezioni' on Michelangelo as a poet. (1547: Death of Sebastiano del Piombo and of Vittoria Colonna.) In February 1550 Vasari comes to Rome and stays until the end of 1553. He sees Michelangelo working on his Florentine Pietà. Later on, after 1555, he is told that Michelangelo has smashed the Pietà to pieces.

VIII. THE LAST PHASE

1553–64. In 1553: Execution of the floor of the Biblioteca Laurenziana (Plate 162), in imitation of the carved ceiling; publication of Ascanio Condivi's 'Vita di Michelangelo'; Pieter Bruegel in Rome. At the end of 1555, death of Michelangelo's servant and assistant, Francesco Urbino, who served him for twenty-five years. Shortly after this, Michelangelo with blows of his hammer damages the 'Florentine Pietà' (Plate 262), which Tiberio Calcagni subsequently restores. Michelangelo begins the 'Palestrina Pietà' (Plate 268), which is completed by another hand. He also begins the 'Rondanini Pietà' (Plate 266), on which he himself works until his death. Production of important religious drawings, especially 'Crucifixions'. In 1558 Michelangelo makes a model for the staircase of the Laurenziana (Plates 163, 166), and begins his model for the dome of St Peter's, which he finishes in 1561 (Plate 272). About the same time Michelangelo works on the project for the transformation of the Thermae of Diocletian into the church of Santa Maria degli Angeli (Plate XVII), the designs for the outer side of the Porta Pia (Plate 270) and for the Sforza Chapel in Santa Maria Maggiore (Plate XX–b). By order of Pope Paul IV, some nudities in the 'Last Judgement' are painted over by Daniele da Volterra (1559–60). On 12 February 1564 Daniele da Volterra watches the master working all day long on a 'Pietà'. Two days later Michelangelo falls ill and, though feverish, wanders about in the open air, telling his assistant Calcagni that he can find no rest. The following day, still more feverish, he remains by the fireside. After only two days in bed, he dies on 18 February 1564, in the presence of Tommaso de' Cavalieri, Daniele da Volterra and a number of doctors and friends. The body is taken to the church of the Santi Apostoli and the Pope wishes it to be buried in St Peter's, but Michelangelo's nephew and heir, Leonardo Buonarroti, removes the body to Florence. The dead master arrives there on 10 March and is buried in Santa Croce, but the solemn commemoration is not held until 14 July, in San Lorenzo. More than a hundred artists are present but not Duke Cosimo de' Medici) and the funeral oration is spoken by Benedetto Varchi. (Shakespeare was born a few weeks after Michelangelo's death.)

MADONNA DONI. Florence, Uffizi

CATALOGUE

MADONNA OF THE STAIRS. Plate 1. Marble relief, 22 × 15¾ in. Executed c. 1491, when the artist was about sixteen years old. First mentioned by Vasari in the second edition of his *Lives* (1568) and described by him as being not quite one (Florentine) ell[1] in height (see Paola Barocchi, *Vasari: Michelangelo,* 1962, vol. II, notes 92–94). According to Vasari, it then belonged to Leonardo Buonarroti, Michelangelo's nephew. It subsequently came into the possession of the Medici, who in 1617 presented it to the Casa Buonarroti. Since Vasari's day its relationship to reliefs by Donatello has often been stressed, notably by Bode. The attribution to Michelangelo has, without adequate reason, been doubted by Charles Holroyd (1903) and Ernst Benkard (1933). H. Brinckmann (in *Barockskulptur*, Berlin, 1919, p. 18) suggested that the relief ought to be dated 1494; R. Longhi (in *Paragone*, 1958, No. 101, p. 61 f.) dated it after the Pietà of S. Pietro; this idea of a late dating was adopted by J. Pope-Hennessy (in *Italian High Renaissance and Baroque Sculpture,* Catalogue, p. 1, London, 1963).

BATTLE OF CENTAURS. Plate 2 (3). Marble relief, 33¼ × 35⅝ in. Vasari (1568) calls it 'a battle between Hercules and the Centaurs', while Condivi (1553) describes it as 'the Rape of Dejanira and the battle of Centaurs'. According to Condivi, the idea of this relief was suggested to Michelangelo by Poliziano (died 1494), the tutor of Lorenzo il Magnifico's sons. The poet and humanist Poliziano may have derived his knowledge of the subject from Boccaccio's *Genealogia* or from the collection of legends attributed to Hyginus. The details in this relief are not very clear; it has neither been agreed which of the figures are Centaurs and which are human, nor which are the men and which the women. Wölfflin maintained that there was not a single female figure in the relief, whereas Symonds believed that the central figure was female. According to Justi, however, this central figure is the Centaur Eurytion, while Knapp thinks it is either Hercules or Theseus.[2] The representation is modelled on sarcophagus fronts of the Roman Imperial period, and Bertoldo's equestrian relief has rightly been compared with it. Michelangelo seems to have been very fond of his Centaur relief, which he executed when he was seventeen (his fondness for it is confirmed by Condivi); in any case he kept it all his life, and it then passed into the possession of his family.

THE THREE BOLOGNA STATUETTES. Plates 4–6. Marble; Proculus, 22 in.; Petronius, 25 in.; the Angel, 20¼ in. high, with base. Condivi mentions only the *Petronius* and the *Angel holding a candlestick* and says that Michelangelo received 18 ducats for the Saint and 12 for the angel. According to C. Gnudi (1942) and Bertini (1945), the *Petronius* was begun by Niccolò dell' Arca and finished by Michelangelo, who left the back of the statue as he found it. This opinion is based on a statement by Lodovico da Prelormo (1572), but Tolnay declared the statuette to be 'entirely by the hand of the Master'. The *Proculus,* 'the most interesting of the three figures' (Johannes Wilde), is first mentioned, together with the other two, by Leandro Alberti in his '*De divi Dominici obitu et sepultura*' (1535). 'Foratti questions the authenticity of the Proculus, which it is true one would not be sorry to see eliminated from Michelangelo's œuvre, but on the other hand it is too well authenticated by Fra Lodovico da Prelormo and Leandro Alberti to justify its arbitrary rejection' (Panofsky). In addition to Foratti, Wölfflin and Frey have declared themselves against the attribution of the Proculus to Michelangelo; Thode, Mackowsky and Bode have given excellent reasons in favour of its authenticity. According to contemporary reports, the statue was knocked down and broken in 1572 while it was being cleaned; the shanks were broken off and it is still easy to see where they were stuck on again. Thode thought: 'In my opinion there can be no doubt that in the Proculus we have a self-portrait of the nineteen-year-old artist.' – Michelangelo's angel is the male counterpart of the delicate female angel by Niccolò dell' Arca, who executed the rest of the decoration over the shrine of St Dominic. Justi summed up the figures: 'The three Bologna statuettes – the fruits of one year's sojourn in the city – are probably the most insignificant and least satisfactory works which have been handed down to us under Michelangelo's name, but it must be admitted that they are only too well authenticated.' On the other hand, Stendhal says in their favour: 'These figures are remarkable, one sees quite clearly that this great artist began by imitating nature in the most painstaking way and that he knew how to render all her charm and *morbidezza*.'

BACCHUS. Plate 7 (8–12). Marble, 80 in. high, including base. According to Condivi, executed for the Roman banker Jacopo Galli in his house. Commissioned in 1496; intended for erection in a garden. The Bacchus and Satyr are hewn out of one block. Vasari was the first to notice the hermaphroditic element in the figure: 'A marvellous blending of both sexes – combining the slenderness of a youth with the round fullness of a woman'; to which Condivi adds: 'The eyes are dim and lewd.' The pathological character of the figure has often repelled critics. Brinckmann calls it 'the coarsest work by Michelangelo which we possess'; Mackowsky describes the 'vice in a beaming youthful countenance' as an aesthetic error. Stendhal remarks: 'Michelangelo divined the antique, in so far as it expresses strength, but the face is coarse and without charm.' Similarly the poet Shelley wrote: 'The countenance of this figure is the most revolting mistake of the spirit and meaning of Bacchus. It looks drunken, brutal and narrow-minded, and has an expression of dissoluteness the most revolting.' He finds fault with the stiffness of the legs; quite wrongly, for they are naturalistic rendering of the semi-paralysed movements of the

---

[1] A Florentine ell = 23 in.
[2] There is a detailed study of the subject-matter in Tolnay, I 133. Wickhoff suggested that the correct title should be: 'The Marriage of Deidameia and Battle between Centaurs and Lapithae'. When I examined the relief, I counted six Centaurs: the central figure (horse's legs just visible); top left, a figure holding a woman by the hair; the figure in the right corner of the front row; the fallen figure in the centre foreground; the figure above, with his arms round a woman's waist; towards the right, a strangler.

MICHAEL·AͤGLVS·BONARͭVS·FL®ENT·FAͨEBAͭ

Michelangelo's signature on the Pietà at St Peter's

drunken god. All critics note the artistic perfection of the sculpture and the Christian element in this pagan theme.

PIETÀ (Madonna della Febbre). Plate 13 (14–18). Marble, 69 in. high. The only work by Michelangelo bearing his genuine signature. The group was commissioned by Cardinal Jean de Villiers de la Groslaye (died 1499), French Ambassador to the Holy See. The contract was made on 27 August 1498, the price agreed upon being 450 ducats. The chief work of Michelangelo's youthful period. The subject was a complete novelty for Italy – at least as far as sculpture is concerned,[3] and many of Michelangelo's contemporaries considered it heretical; an orthodox writer in 1549 describes it as a 'Lutheran notion'. Michelangelo's Pietà originally stood in the Petronilla chapel, the so-called French chapel of the old church of St Peter's; after the demolition of the latter about 1535, it was installed in the new St Peter's, at first in the Cappella della Febbre, the 'fever chapel'. Since 1749 it has been in the Cappella del Crocifisso (Cappella della Pietà). Four fingers of the Madonna's left hand were broken off and replaced in 1736.

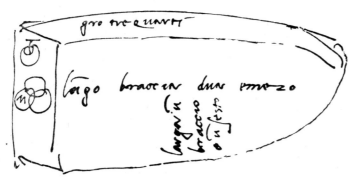

Michelangelo's sketch of a marble block with measurements and his stone-mason's mark. (Pen and ink drawing. Formerly Collection Stefan Zweig.)

DAVID ('The Giant'). Plate 19 (20–26). Marble, 16 ft. 10½ in. high, including base. The contract between the Operai of the Cathedral and Michelangelo is dated 16 August 1501, with a term of delivery of two years and a fee which was subsequently raised to 400 ducats. On 25 January 1504 a conference of artists was held, to decide where the David should be erected; among the participants were Leonardo da Vinci, Botticelli, Filippino Lippi, Perugino and Piero di Cosimo. It was resolved that Donatello's Judith should be removed from the entrance to the Palazzo Vecchio, in order to make room for Michelangelo's David. On 8 September 1504 the erection in front of the Palazzo Vecchio was completed. In 1873 the statue was removed to the Accademia and in 1910 a marble replica was placed in front of the Palazzo Vecchio. Michelangelo was given a block of marble out of which Agostino di Duccio, or perhaps Baccellino, had attempted to hew a David. 'So Michelangelo made a wax model of a youthful David holding the sling, which might serve as the emblem of the palace' (Vasari). When the Medici were driven out of Florence on 26 April 1527, the statue was damaged by a bench thrown out of one of the palace windows and the left arm was shattered. The three pieces were found by Salviati and Vasari and in 1543, by order of Duke Cosimo, they were replaced. Burckhardt finds fault with the 'preoccupation with the model' seen in this statue and with the 'mistake' of trying to represent the figure of an adolescent in colossal proportions. 'Only grown persons can be conveniently enlarged. . . . When seen through a diminishing glass, the David gains uncommonly in beauty and life; to be sure with exception of the head, which seems to have been designed for quite a different mood.' On the other hand Justi writes: 'His most perfect statue of a nude man, considered from a purely technical and plastic standpoint as life in marble.'

FIVE STATUES OF THE PICCOLOMINI ALTAR, SIENA CATHEDRAL. Plates 27–33. Marble, each about 50 in. high. Cardinal Francesco Piccolomini, later Pope Pius III, ordered the altar from the Lombard sculptor Andrea Bregno, who erected it in 1481–5. Sixteen statues were to decorate this altar, and in 1501 (when Bregno was eighty), the Cardinal approached Pietro Torrigiano, who began the figure of St Francis (Plate 28), but did not finish it. In the same year the commission was offered to Michelangelo, who first finished Torrigiano's St Francis, and then, between June 1501 and October 1504, delivered four more statues (Plates 29, 30, 31, 32). The contract was renewed in 1504. Valentiner believes that the Bruges Madonna (Plate 34) was originally intended for the upper central niche of this altar. St Peter and St Paul were of course meant as counterpieces, and in 1944 they were placed accordingly: St Peter in the lower right niche, St Paul in the lower left niche. St Francis, previously in the place of St Paul, was moved to the upper left niche. St Gregory and St Pius, also counterpieces, have always rightly been placed in the middle niches. Burckhardt (1891). Thode (1908), J. Wilde (1932), Toesca (1934), F. Kriegbaum (1941), Valentiner (1942), and A. Bertini (1945) have accepted the statues as Michelangelo's own work. Tolnay (1947 and 1951) insists that the execution is due mainly to Baccio da Montelupo.[4] According to Kriegbaum, the St Paul (Plate 27) is a self-portrait of Michelangelo (who at that time was about twenty-seven).

---

[3] There is a clear relationship, not confined merely to the choice of subject, to the Lamentation of Christ by Jacopo del Sellaio (1442–93), now in the Berlin Museum (Cat. No. 1055), especially as regards the pathetic opening of the Madonna's hand and the pendent right arm of the Christ.

[4] On plates 26 and 27 the heads of *David* and *St Paul* have been juxtaposed in order to show that there are indeed technical differences in these two sculptures, which are generally dated from the same period. This is particularly obvious in the treatment of the pupils and the corners of the mouths: the drill has been used to a great extent in the statue of St Paul, with a similar result as in late Roman statues, leaving the holes made by the drill undisguised.

THE BRUGES MADONNA. Plate 34 (35-42). Marble, 50½ in. high, including base. The earliest mention of this work occurs in Albrecht Dürer's diary of his journey to the Netherlands, on 7 April 1521: 'I saw the alabaster Madonna in Our Lady's Church that Michelangelo of Rome made.' (Alabaster here means white marble, and 'Our Lady's Church' means Notre-Dame.) Condivi, who never saw the work, which Francesco del Pugliese brought to Bruges in 1506, describes it as a bronze,[5] and says that the Bruges merchant Mouscron[6] paid 100 ducats for it.[7] The French sculptor David d'Angers claimed to have discerned the hand of an assistant; Wölfflin was of the same opinion. Pieraccini, in his guide to the Tribuna del David (Prato, 1883) includes it among the 'doubtful works'. The back and side views (Plates 36-39) show that an assistant, perhaps Baccio da Montelupo, did some work, at least on the drapery and the socle of rough stones on which the Virgin is seated. Apparently the group is designed to be placed rather high. In the present position the head of the Child seems too large.[8]

THE ROUND MADONNA RELIEF IN LONDON. Plate 43. Marble, 46¼ in. Also known as the Taddei Madonna, after its first owner, Taddeo Taddei. Thode and Wölfflin think that the Pitti Madonna is the older, but Knapp, Kriegbaum and others consider the Taddei tondo to be the older. The relief is held to be unfinished and a number of opinions concerning its sketchiness were collected by Justi (II, p. 190). Walter Pater wrote of it: 'Michelangelo secures that ideality of expression which in Greek sculpture depends on a delicate system of abstraction, and in early Italian sculpture on lowness of relief, by an incompleteness, which is surely not always undesigned, and which trusts to the spectator to complete the half-emergent form.' Within Michelangelo's œuvre these two round reliefs represent his 'small sculptures'. Justi stresses the 'genre-like' treatment of the Taddei Madonna and the fact that it was 'intended for a room in a bourgeois home'. The boy on the left is characterized as the Baptist by the christening bowl at his hip; the bird in his hands which startles the Christ Child is a goldfinch, a symbol of the Passion. (The goldfinch is supposed to be fond of feeding on thorns and thus recalls Christ's Crown of Thorns. Cf. Herbert Friedmann, *The Symbolic Goldfinch*, New York, 1946.) The Taddei Madonna was bought in 1822 by Sir George Beaumont in Rome, and after his death, and the death of his wife, it was presented to the Royal Academy (1830).[9]

THE HOLY FAMILY. Plate 44. Wood, resin and tempera.[10] Diameter 47¼ in. Known as the 'Doni Madonna', after Angelo Doni, who commissioned the work. The only certain easel painting by Michelangelo, but at the same time the least esteemed of his paintings. Even Doni seems to have been dissatisfied with it, for Vasari tells us of a long dispute about the fee. The picture was subsequently taken out of its original frame and a tondo by Lorenzo di Credi was put in its place.[11] Stendhal thought that the task was unworthy of Michelangelo: 'A Hercules at the spinning wheel'. Critics of the late nineteenth century were unanimous in their disapproval of the Doni Madonna. 'With sentiments of this kind nobody ought to paint a Holy Family', was Burckhardt's opinion, and he also discovered 'deliberate difficulties' in it. Justi did not hesitate to say: 'The play of the arrangement of the limbs ruins the impression; the idyll of parental felicity becomes a gymnastic exercise.' Nevertheless, the picture is a miracle of draughtsmanship and powerful composition, merits which perhaps only painters are capable of appreciating. The colours would have aroused the enthusiasm of Ingres. The work contains the germ of everything which makes the ceiling of the Sistine Chapel unique, even the superabundance of muscles. This Madonna is a sister of the Delphic Sibyl; the youth half concealed by Joseph's shoulder is a forerunner of one of the nudes of the Sistine ceiling.

THE ROUND MADONNA RELIEF IN FLORENCE. Plate 45 (46). Marble, 33½ in. Also known as the Pitti Madonna, after Bartolommeo Pitti, who commissioned it. Executed at about the same time as the other two round Madonnas, the *Taddei Madonna* in London (Plate 43) and the tempera painting, the *Doni Madonna* in Florence (Plate 44). Justi stresses the intimate character of the work and the fact that it was intended 'for the

---

[5] Vasari calls it a 'bronze tondo'. Considering that Condivi wrote under Michelangelo's eyes, one cannot simply assume that he also made a mistake. Valentiner (*Art Quarterly*, 1942) showed the possibility that the Bruges Madonna was originally intended for the Piccolomini altar, and therefore it is not impossible that Mouscron bought from Michelangelo also a bronze tondo, perhaps similar in style to the two marble tondi, Plates 43 and 45. Benedetto Varchi, in his funeral oration for Michelangelo (which he spoke in front of all the academicians of Florence) counted up the master's works in bronze and also mentioned 'una vergine Maria col Bambino in collo maravigliosissima, mandata in Fiandra da alcuni mercatanti de' Mascheroni'.

[6] Alexander Mouscron had warehouses in Florence and Rome. He dealt in English clothing materials.

[7] A fee of 100 ducats would have been rather little for an almost life-size marble group. Michelangelo received 450 ducats for the Pietà ordered in 1498 by Cardinal de la Groslaye, and 400 for his David in 1502, which did not include the cost of the marble. A few years later, when Michelangelo was working on the Sistine ceiling frescoes, living very economically and having no travelling expenses, he mentioned in a letter to his father that he was spending 20 ducats a month.

[8] In Rembrandt's atelier there was a cast of the Child Jesus of the Bruges group (in the inventory of 1656 it figures as 'a child, by Michelangelo'). This cast of Rembrandt's is reproduced in a painting by Jan Lievens (Hans Schneider, *Lievens*, Haarlem 1932, Plate 14; Louvre). Another cast of the Child appears in Wallerant Vaillant's painting *The Young Artist*, of about 1670 (London, National Gallery, No. 3591). During the last war Hitler took the *Bruges Madonna* to Alt-Aussee in Austria, with the intention to present it to the Linz museum.

[9] When the auctioneer Claridge of Curzon Street, London, exhibited the relief (not for sale) in 1829, he stated in his advertisement that the sculpture was 'bearing the date 1504'. This date, perhaps written on the back, has now disappeared. (W. T. Whitley, *Art in England 1821-37*, London 1930, p. 202.) Our Plate 43 shows the correct position of the relief, which differs from the position in which it is now placed at the R.A. The engraving by William Young Ottley, 1828, already shows the correct position and Knapp and Kriegbaum have also pointed out that the exergue should be horizontal.

[10] Heath Wilson, Ricci and Carl Justi maintain that the picture is painted in oil, but technically this is incorrect. We have here the usual Italian mixed technique of the period, with powerful outline drawing on a plaster ground, a thin layer of green earth, in covering resin, and a graduated heightening in white with tempera; the over-painting is done with transparent resin, except in the flesh parts, which are painted in pure tempera.

[11] The painting and frame were not brought together again until 1905 (Poggi, *Kunstchronik* XVIII, p. 299 f., and E. Bock, *Florentinische und Venezianische Bilderrahmen*, Munich, 1902, p. 78). The frame bears the arms of Angelo Doni and Maddalena Strozzi. It is supposed that the painting was commissioned on the occasion of their wedding, about 1503-4. Cf. Appendix, Plate xv.

home' and 'not for oratories or tombs'. At one time the relief was considered to be 'unfinished', but to modern eyes this does not seem to be the case.

ST MATTHEW. Plate 47 (48). Marble, 8 ft. 11 in. Unfinished. Begun immediately after the David, a contract having been signed on 24 April 1503 with the Arte della Lana in Florence for twelve Apostles for the Cathedral. In the winter of 1504–5 Michelangelo was working mainly on his battle cartoon; in March 1505 he was summoned to Rome by Julius II, with whom he made a five-year contract for the tomb. After this, on 18 December 1505, the contract for the Apostles was cancelled. Four months later, when Michelangelo fled from Rome to Florence, he appears to have resumed work on the St Matthew (April–November 1506). At the end of November 1506 he joined the Pope in Bologna and began work on the large bronze portrait (since lost). The St Matthew thus remained unfinished.[12] It was kept in the Opera del Duomo until 1834, when it was removed to the Accademia in Florence. Wölfflin and Justi think that most of the work on the statue was done about 1504; Thode and Macowksky, about 1506. Ollendorf has drawn attention to a certain influence of the Laocoön, which was discovered in 1506, especially in the expression and poise of the head. Grünwald has established that the antique 'Pasquino' was used as a model.

THE CEILING FRESCOES IN THE SISTINE CHAPEL. Plates 49–144. The ceiling painting, as reproduced in Plate 50, measures 45 × 128 ft.

Fresco-painting (fresco buono) is painting on damp lime wash. In this process the lime serves to bind together the pigments and also to provide the white colouring. Only a limited number of colours can be used and these become lighter when dry. The painter applies as much of the plaster as will serve for one day's work; if the plaster were allowed to stand for more than a day, a film of lime would be formed on which the painting would appear patchy. In Michelangelo's frescoes the edges of each application can be clearly discerned and we can thus determine how much he painted every day. In his time the ground was composed of two parts marble sand to one part plaster. To this ground of sand and plaster, which was dampened the night before, and applied in several layers, was added a damp covering of marble dust and plaster. The previously prepared drawing, or cartoon, was cut into pieces, each of which represented a day's work. The section of the

drawing was then fastened on to the fresco ground and the outlines were traced with an iron stylus. (These traced contours, which were not always followed exactly in the execution of the painting, can be clearly discerned in some of our reproductions, e.g. Plate 62.) The fresco took about six weeks to dry. After drying, the ceiling paintings of the Sistine Chapel were partly gone over *a secco* in size-colour. The colouring does not greatly differ from that of the 'Doni Madonna', but in the course of the four years' work Michelangelo tended more and more towards the use of subdued grey, grisaille-like tones. The modelling, especially that of the flesh parts, is lead-grey; the high lights have the full strength of the white lime. Grey, grey-violet, grey-brown, grey-green, olive-green, yellow, cerise, orange-red and even pure black are used; the colours achieve their strongest effects in the shadows, in the half light they are broken with grey and in the full light with yellow.

The project of re-painting the ceiling of the Sistine Chapel was conceived by Pope Julius II in 1506. The contract with Michelangelo was concluded on 10 May 1508. Scaffolding was erected a month later and on 27 July the ceiling was covered with plaster as a ground for the frescoes. Numerous assistants took part in the work, among them Francesco Granacci, but they seem to have carried out only labourer's work. According to Biagetti and Redig de Campos, the work of assistants can be seen not only in the ornamental parts, but also in single figures of the *Flood*, the earliest of the frescoes. The standing mother with her children is quoted as an example of where the sharp outlines are said to show the hand of a helper who slavishly followed the master's cartoon. This assumption, however, is not easy to prove. Giuliano da Sangallo gave Michelangelo technical advice, especially as to the means of avoiding 'efflorescence' – the formation of mould on damp plaster. Before Michelangelo overpainted it, the face of the vaulting of the chapel had been painted to form a blue sky with gold stars. According to his original plan, the central portion was to be filled with grotesques and the twelve Apostles were to be painted between the empty spandrels.[13] Gradually the plan was extended until it became the final version, including the spandrels and lunettes, with Prophets and Sibyls instead of the Apostles; three hundred figures were executed, as against the twelve of the first project. Between the autumn of 1508 and September 1510 the eastern half of the ceiling was completed. This is the part beginning at the entrance and running from Noah's Drunkenness to the Creation of Eve, with the nude figures of youths, Prophets and Sibyls as far as Ezekiel and the Cumaean Sibyl. Between January and August 1511 the western half of the ceiling was painted.[14] On 14 August 1511 the ceiling frescoes were unveiled and on 31 October 1512 the first Mass was celebrated in the chapel.

---

[12] In his life of Andrea Ferruci da Fiesole, Vasari says: '*Andrea was employed by the wardens of Santa Maria del Fiore to make the statue of an Apostle, four ells high* [about 7 ft. 10 in.]. *This was at the time when Cardinal Giulio de' Medici was ruling in Florence. At the same time* [1512–15] *four similar figures were allotted to four different masters: one to Benedetto* [Rovezzano, 1512], *one to Jacopo Sansovino* [c. 1513], *a third to Baccio Bandinelli* [1514–15] *and a fourth to Michelangelo Buonarroti.*' The contract with Andrea Ferrucci for a statue of St Andrew the Apostle is extant, dated 13 October 1512. Was there a second contract with Michelangelo for an Apostle statue at about the same date? (Cf. *Vasari*, ed. Milanesi, 1879, vol. IV, pp. 478, 479 – note 2, and 532.) I accept the usual dating 1504–06, but only with some doubt, as the *St Matthew* agrees in style much more with the statue of Moses and could therefore be connected with a hypothetical second commission for Apostle statues in about 1512. Moreover, the only extant drawing by Michelangelo for the statue of an Apostle (BB.1521r.) shows a figure which recalls rather the statues of the Piccolomini altar and is quite different from the *St Matthew* in the Florence Academy.

[13] The simple decoration of a starry sky was painted (twenty-five years before Michelangelo came to the Sistine Chapel) by Pier-Matteo Serdenti d'Amelia. This decoration was destroyed when Michelangelo began his work. In a letter to Giovanni Francesco Fattucci, of December 1523, Michelangelo says: 'My first design included the twelve Apostles between the lunettes, and for the rest a certain arrangement of compartments filled with ornaments, such as is customary.'

[14] The Ancestors of Christ, in the lunettes and the spandrels above them (Plates 103–124), were painted after the finishing of the last Histories and the unveiling, i.e. between October 1511 and October 1512; the cartoons had been finished by the beginning of 1511.

THE LIBYAN SIBYL. Sistine Chapel Ceiling

The two destroyed lunette paintings. Engravings, after now lost sixteenth-century drawings, by William Ottley

The impression produced on Michelangelo's contemporaries by these frescoes was enormous and it has been maintained through four centuries. Goethe wrote in 1786: 'No one who has not seen the Sistine Chapel can have a clear idea of what a human being can achieve. . . . The master's inner security and strength, his greatness is beyond all description. . . . At the moment I am so engrossed by Michelangelo that even Nature makes no appeal to me, for my vision is so small compared with his. If there were only some means of fixing such pictures in one's soul! But at least I shall bring with me all the engravings and drawings after his works that I can find.' In England the fame of Michelangelo had already been exalted in the Academy lectures given by Reynolds (1769–91) and Henry Fuseli (1801). Reynolds called his style 'the language of the gods', while Fuseli said: 'A beggar rose from his hand the patriarch of poverty; his women are moulds of generation; his infants teem with the man; his men are a race of giants.' Another painter, Benjamin Haydon, objected to this exaggeration (*Encyclopædia Britannica*, 7th edition, 1838): 'His women may be moulds of generation, but certainly not of love.' And he attacked vigorously Michelangelo's monumental style: 'When you see an outline like iron, that is the grand style. When hands are twisted, heads distorted, one leg up, the other so far removed from the body, that you may question if it will return, that is the grand style. . . . Every figure of his looks as if he was insulted and preparing to return a blow. If they sleep they seem as if they would kick; if they move when they are awake, they seem as if all their muscles are cracking.'
The general view of the ceiling (Plate 50) shows the whole of the paintings except for the lunettes, which extend downwards on the walls. The three triple central portions contain the actual narrative (Plates 51–59). Stendhal already recognized that 'spiritually we must separate these compartments from everything that surrounds them and consider them as separate paintings'. They narrate the three origins of the world and mankind: the first Trinity, the origin of the World: the division of light from darkness, the creation of the stars, the separation of water from land and with the latter the creation of animals and plants (Plates 51–53).[15] The second Trinity, the origin of mankind: the creation of man and woman, the Fall, the expulsion from the Garden of Eden into the

wilderness of this world (Plates 54–56).[16] The third Trinity, the origin of Sin: the Flood, Noah's sacrifice and his covenant with God, the drunkenness of Noah and the continuing of Sin (Plates 58, 57, 59).[17] This ends the narrative of the middle compartments – the tale of mankind living in sin and awaiting redemption. Round these nine pictures are the twenty youths bearing garlands, who with their vigorous movements emphasize the same idea as the captives on the tomb of Julius, namely the vain efforts of mankind while still unsaved (Plates 72–91). The chorus of seers, Prophets and Sibyls, likewise points to salvation (Plates 127–144). The four subjects in the triangular spaces at the corners deal with temporal salvation, the deliverance from earthly distress, the miraculous deliverances of Israel (Plates 66–69). The victory of a boy and the victory of women are represented, the victory of weakness over strength and of the grace of God over violence. We see the triumphs of David, Judith and Esther; but the most significant of these pictures is the fourth, the 'Brazen Serpent'. 'And as

[15] Plate 41 reproduces what Vasari calls 'The Dividing of the Waters from the Land' and Condivi 'The Creation of the Denizens of the Waters'. Konrad Lange (*Rep. f. Kunstwissenschaft* XLII, 1919, p. 1 f.) and Adolfo Venturi (*L'Arte* XXII, 1919, p. 85 f.) accept in a way Vasari's interpretation, but Erwin Panofsky (col. 41–4) supports Condivi's theory. – Lange and Venturi, however, call the fresco 'The Separation of Sky and Water' because there is no earth to be seen in it. The Bible describes thus the third day of the Creation: 'Let the waters that are under the heaven be gathered together into one place, and let the dry land appear.' Which means that at the beginning of the third day the earth was not yet visible, just as on the second day.
[16] In Plate 60 the right arm of God is stretched out creating Adam, while his left arm is round the shoulders of a young woman and his left hand rests on a child. According to an ingenious explanation of J. P. Richter, the one figure is Eve, as she appears before her creation in God's mind, the other figure is the Christ child (*Thode*, II, p. 323; *Tolnay*, II, p. 35).
[17] The sequence of the narrative is altered in the ceiling paintings because Michelangelo wanted to use the large central compartment for the 'Flood' with its numerous figures. – Condivi, and following him Vasari in the second edition of his work, calls the first compartment not 'Noah's Sacrifice', but the 'Sacrifice of Cain and Abel'. This sacrifice was the cause of Abel's murder, the first sin upon earth; and if we are to assume that Condivi was right, then the sequence of the three pictures would be correct.
The theme of the Deluge was chosen by Savonarola for his Lenten sermon of 1494 on the Ark of Noah: 'Ecce ego abducam aquas super terram – behold, I, even I, do bring a flood of waters upon the earth'; in this sermon Savonarola foretold the divine wrath and the fall of Florence. Pico della Mirandola relates that he trembled in every limb and that his hair stood on end when he heard this stern warning; Michelangelo must have heard the sermon too, for he did not leave Florence until October of that year.

Moses lifted up the serpent in the wilderness, even so must the Son of man be lifted up: That whosoever believeth in him should not perish, but have eternal life' (Gospel according to St John, iii, 14, 15). This prefiguration of the Redeemer's coming is connected with the pictures of the Ancestors of Christ in the other spandrels and lunettes (Plates 103–126).

The first two lunettes, painted above the altar, were destroyed by Michelangelo himself, when he walled them up (1535) in order to paint the 'Last Judgement' on this wall. (See the illustrations on p. 13.)

The Sistine ceiling frescoes have of course suffered during the more than four hundred years of their existence. As early as 1547 they are mentioned as being in a poor state in a letter from Paolo Giovio to Vasari. About 1570 parts were restored, especially 'The Sacrifice of Noah', of which a piece had fallen off. The female figure in the left foreground was completely repainted by the restorer Domenico Carnevali. Further restorations were carried out in 1625 and 1712. On 28 June 1797 the blast of an explosion in the gun powder magazine of the nearby Castel Sant' Angelo damaged a part of the *Flood* and the decorative parts around it. Extensive restorations followed. A drawing at Windsor Castle (Plate 74), a copy by a pupil of Michelangelo, reproduces one Nude Youth almost completely destroyed by that explosion. The latest restorations were carried out in 1903–6, and 1935–8.

THE TOMB OF POPE JULIUS. Plates 145–154; 238–240; X, XI. First contract and first design, March 1505; it was stipulated that there should be forty statues, delivery within five years, against payment of 10,000 ducats. In April Michelangelo went to the quarries at Carrara; in December he returned to Rome and set up a workshop in Piazza San Pietro. 'If only my blocks of marble would arrive from Carrara!' he wrote to his father on 31 January 1506. 'In this matter I think I have the greatest ill-fortune. . . . A few days ago a vessel arrived which had been all but sunk owing to contrary winds, and when I had succeeded in unloading it there came a flood which swamped everything in such a way that I could not begin work.' The work thus began without the blessing of the stars and elements. Condivi called the story of its execution 'The Tragedy of the Tomb'. On 17 April 1506 Michelangelo fled from Rome, feeling that he was not properly appreciated by the Pope and that he had been grievously offended. From Florence he wrote on 2 May 1506 to Giuliano da Sangallo: 'If I had stayed in Rome any longer, it would have been indeed a question not of the Pope's tomb, but of my own. That was the reason for my sudden departure.' But a few days later Roselli wrote to Michelangelo that people in Rome were saying that Michelangelo was frightened by the idea of having to execute the frescoes in the Sistine Chapel and that this was the reason for his flight. In Florence Michelangelo may have resumed work on his battle cartoon; the tomb seems to have been forgotten. The Pope had important political plans; he was thinking of war and of reconquering for the Church her lost territories. On 23 August 1506 he left Rome and on 11 November he entered Bologna without encountering resistance. He at once summoned Michelangelo thither, in order that he might cast his statue in bronze for the reconquered city. Michelangelo went to Bologna 'with the rope round his neck', as he himself expressed it; but the tomb seems to have been forgotten again. From 1508 to 1512 Michelangelo worked in Rome on the frescoes for the ceiling of the Sistine Chapel. After finishing them, he wanted to resume work on the tomb, but no agreement could be reached. In October 1512 Michelangelo wrote to his father: 'I am still doing no work and am waiting for the Pope to tell me what to do.' On 21 February Julius II died and on 6 May a second contract was concluded with the executor of his will. Michelangelo undertook to complete the tomb in seven years and not to accept any other work in the meantime; he was to receive 1300 ducats in addition to the 3500 he had already had from Pope Julius. He submitted a revised design. Between 1513 and 1516 the *Moses* and the two *Captives* were executed (Plates 145–154). Michelangelo had a workshop at the Macello dei Corvi and employed Florentine stonemasons. In July 1516 a third contract was made and a modified design submitted, but there was a fresh interruption owing to work on the designs for the façade of San Lorenzo. The following years were spent in unproductive work in Florence and in journeys to the marble quarries of Carrara, Pietrasanta and Seravezza. In 1520 the contract for the façade of San Lorenzo was definitely cancelled, but work on the Medici tombs was begun. In 1525, while working on the Libreria, he first had the idea of completing the Julius monument as a wall-tomb. But no decision was reached, although Michelangelo submitted a new design in October 1526. He went on working on the Medici tombs. The year 1529 was spent in work as an architect of fortifications. On 29 April 1532, after prolonged negotiations, a fourth contract was drawn up, but then came the execution of the *Last Judgement* and after its completion in 1542 the work on the tomb of Julius, which had long been relegated to assistants, was entrusted entirely to Raffaello da Montelupo and Pietro Urbano. 'I wish I had learned in my youth to make matches,' wrote Michelangelo in this year, 'then I should not be in such a state of agitation. . . . I do not want to go on living under this burden. . . . Only death or the Pope can release me from it. I have wasted all my youth, chained to this tomb.' In the fifth contract (20 August 1542) everything was granted that Michelangelo had requested in his petition to Pope Paul III. 'Master Michelangelo Buonarroti,' begins this document, 'undertook a long time ago to execute a tomb for Pope Julius.' . . . 'Master Michelangelo,' it says later, 'shall be authorized to entrust three of the six statues destined for this tomb to a good and esteemed master . . . and the other three, among them the Moses, shall be by his own hand. But as Master Michelangelo has given the three statues named, which are already far advanced, namely the Madonna with the Child on her arm in a standing posture, and a Prophet and a Sibyl, both seated, to the Florentine Raffaello da Montelupo . . . there remained for him to complete with his own hand only the other three statues, namely the Moses and the two Captives, which are all three almost finished. But as the two Captives mentioned were begun when the work was planned on a far larger scale [a much larger number of statues had been contemplated, but by the contract of April 1532 the number was reduced], they are no longer suited to this project. . . . Wherefore Master Michelangelo began work on two other statues, which are to stand on either side of Moses, namely the Contemplative and the Active Life, which are fairly well advanced, so that they can easily be completed by other masters.' At that time Michelangelo had undertaken a work for Pope Paul III, the frescoes in 'his chapel', that is to say the Cappella Paolina, a work which, as he himself says, 'required a whole man free from care'. In February 1545 the monument was finally erected. 'It can now be seen in San Pietro in Vincoli',[18] wrote Condivi in 1553. 'not, as in the first design, with four façades, but with *one* front, this being one of the smaller ones, not standing free, but against the wall. But although the work has been so patched up and reduced, it is still the worthiest monument to be found in Rome and perhaps in the whole world, on account of the three figures thereon which are by the master's own hand.' (Plates 145, 239, 240).

The lower storey of the architecture is the work of Antonio del Pontasieve (1513-14). The four herms are by Jacomo del Duca (who, about twenty years later, helped Michelangelo with the Porta Pia). The upper storey of the architecture is the work of Urbino (Francisco di Bernardino d'Amadore), whose assistant Giovanni de' Marchesi is probably responsible for the four ugly heads underneath the candelabra. The contract between Michelangelo and Urbino is dated 21 August 1541. The Pope's coat-of-arms is by Donato Benti (1543). The four figures on the upper storey are the work of two independent assistants (see caption of Plate 238). About the Sibyl and the Prophet by Montelupo we may believe what Vasari says: 'Raffaello da Montelupo fell ill while engaged upon the work, he could not devote his usual care and diligence to it, so that he lost in reputation and Michelangelo was dissatisfied.' The Madonna was begun by Sandro Fancelli (called Scherano da Settignano), but also finished by Montelupo. Urbino had perhaps a share in Boscoli's statue of the Pope. (See also Appendix, Plates X, XI and XIV-a.)

MOSES. Part of the tomb of Julius. Plate 145 (146-148). Marble, 100 in. high. According to Thode, it was begun in 1506, but Knapp maintains that a consignment of marble from Carrara of 24 June 1508[19] was intended for the Moses as well as for the two Captives now in the Louvre. Vasari, however, states explicitly: 'While Michelangelo was engaged on this work, the remaining blocks of marble destined for the tomb arrived from Carrara and were unloaded at the Ripa'; at that time the Pope had 'his head full of Bologna matters'; this must therefore have been in 1506. Between the beginning of this work and its completion came the execution of the figures of Prophets on the ceiling of the Sistine Chapel, Joel and Jeremiah. 'When Michelangelo had finished the Moses,' writes Vasari in 1568, 'there was no other work to be seen, whether ancient or modern, which could rival it.' He praises especially the painteresque treatment of the hair – 'one might almost believe that the chisel had become a brush'. Stendhal (1817) says: 'Those who have not seen this statue, cannot realize the full power of sculpture,' but he also mentions the 'profound disparagement' which had been the statue's lot and quotes the sculptor Falconet, who declared that the Moses was more like a galley-slave than a divinely inspired lawgiver, and the painter Fuseli, who discovered in it a resemblance to a satyr or a 'goat's face'. About this time Goethe kept a small bronze copy of the Moses on his writing desk. The costume is imitated from antique statues of barbarians (an attempt at historical accuracy). 'The rest is entirely in the antique style,' says Condivi.

THE HEROIC AND THE DYING CAPTIVES. Belonging to the Julius tomb. Plates 149-154. Marble, 7 ft. 1 in. and 7 ft. 6½ in. These two statues were not used for the tomb of Julius, because, as we learn from Michelangelo himself, they could not be fitted into the reduced design. In 1544, while the tomb was being erected, the master was lying ill in the palace of Roberto Strozzi. The latter, a cousin of Caterina de' Medici and a great-grandson of Lorenzo il Magnifico, was the owner of banking houses in Rome and Lyons and had influence at the French court. He conspired against Grand-Duke Cosimo de' Medici and shared with Michelangelo the ambition of restoring Florence to its republican freedom. In 1544 Michelangelo presented him with the two statues, and six years later Strozzi gave them to King Henri II of France, who in turn presented them to the Connétable Anne de Montmorency for his castle of Écouen; in 1632 they belonged to Cardinal Richelieu; in 1794 they became state property and so passed to the Louvre. The Heroic Captive shows a deep crack, which goes across the face and down to the left shoulder (retouched in most reproductions). The antique prototypes of these Captives were not the statues of fettered barbarians, but the Hellenistic representations of Marsyas, which survived in mediaeval figures of St Sebastian. Ever since Condivi's time captious attempts have been made to discover the allegorical significance of the Captives; almost every possible suggestion has been made, down to the 'personification of the mass for the dead'. Condivi writes (in 1553): 'Between the niches there should have been herms, to which, on cube-shaped projections, other statues were bound like captives. These represented the liberal arts and in the same way painting, sculpture and architecture, each statue with its attributes, making them easily recognizable. This was intended to signify that all the noble arts had died at the same time as Pope Julius.' Oscar Ollendorf has interpreted the Captives in the platonic sense, Werner Weisbach as triumphal symbols. A political interpretation, which has not found support, was given by Vasari: 'These Captives represent the provinces which the Pope subjugated and incorporated in the Papal State.' If we ignore all these conjectures, and also those of Justi, Thode, Brockhaus, Borinski and Laux, if we wish to see nothing except what the works themselves reveal to our eyes, these Captives become easily comprehensible, eternally human symbols: captives

---

[18] Instead of in St Peter's, as was originally planned.
[19] The accompanying letter to Michelangelo mentions 'the large statue', 'two statues' and the 'statue of His Holiness', in other words four blocks hewn in the rough. Laux (*Juliusmonument*, 1943, p. 158) assumes a much later date for the Moses: after 1515 or even after 1519. See the contract of 1542 (here p. 14) where the Moses statue is called 'almost finished'. This means that parts of the statue were probably retouched in the time from 1542 to 1545.

of life, of dreams and of death, struggling against the bonds of fate and relentless nature, Titans who wrestle in vain or relapse into redeeming unconsciousness. In this sense these eternally vanquished beings become the counterparts of the temporal conquerors, the Victories (see Plate 207).

THE RISEN CHRIST. Plates 155-157. Marble, 6 ft. 10 in. high. Commissioned on 14 June 1514 by Metello Vari and two other Romans, in return for a fee of 200 ducats. A black vein was found in the marble, which disfigured the face, and Michelangelo had to begin again. This first version, since lost, was seen by Aldovrandi in 1556 in Vari's courtyard. Owing to this defect in the marble, work was broken off in 1516; on 21 December 1518 the new block of marble from Carrara had not yet arrived. At that time Michelangelo wrote to Lionardo Sellaio in Rome: 'I am also being pressed by Signor Metello Vari concerning his statue, which is in Pisa[20] and should arrive by one of the first vessels. I have never answered him and shall not write to you again until I have begun the work; for I am dying of grief and against my will appear to myself as a swindler.' The barges conveying marble from Carrara had been held up in Pisa owing to the drying-up of the Arno. The second version of the Christ was created in Florence between the beginning of 1519 and April 1520. Michelangelo's assistant Pietro Urbano was sent to Rome to erect the statue in Santa Maria sopra Minerva and to finish it there. On 6 September 1520, Sebastiano del Piombo wrote in a letter to Michelangelo: 'I must tell you that Pietro Urbano has ruined everything that he has worked upon. Especially the toes of the right, completely visible foot, which he has mutilated, also he has shortened the fingers of the hands, especially those of the right hand holding the Cross, so that Frizzi says that they look as if they had been made by a baker of cracknels. . . . Also one can see clearly what he has been up to with the beard; my apprentice could have done it more cleverly. . . . Then, too, he has knocked one of the nostrils about – a little more, and only God himself could have put this nose right! Pietro thinks he is a great master – poor man, he will never learn what it means to make such figures – for the knees of this statue are worth more than the whole of Rome.' Federigo Frizzi subsequently repaired and completed the statue. Nevertheless, Michelangelo proposed to his customer Vari that he should make a new statue, that is to say a third version, for he would hardly have made a replica. But Vari, who had been waiting for this work for seven years, wanted no improvements: 'It shows the loftiness of your mind, that you wish to replace a work which could not be better by one that is better.' On 27 December 1521 the statue was unveiled; on 12 January Sebastiano del Piombo wrote to Michelangelo: 'The statue makes a very good impression. All the same, I have said and caused to be said, in all places where it seemed to me fitting, that the execution is not by your hand.'

A SMALL CHAPEL IN CASTEL SANT'ANGELO. Plate 158. This chapel, dedicated to Cosmas and Damian, the patron saints of the Medici, shows the Medici arms on the interior, while outside there is the coat-of-arms of Pope Leo X (1513-21). Erected before Michelangelo moved to Florence in 1516.

WOODEN MODEL FOR THE FAÇADE OF SAN LORENZO. Plate 159. 7 ft. high and 9 ft. 4 in. wide. In 1513 Giovanni de' Medici, a son of Lorenzo il Magnifico, became Pope (Leo X, died in 1521) and in 1523 Giulio de' Medici (Clement VII, died in 1534), a son of the Giovanni who had been murdered in the Pazzi conspiracy of 1478. Under these two Medici Popes Michelangelo received commissions for several works which were meant to do honour to the Medici family. These works were: the façade of San Lorenzo; the transformation of the loggia of the Medici palace; a small aedicula in Castel Sant'Angelo; the Biblioteca Laurenziana; and the Sepulchral Chapel of the Medici. On the designs for the Lorenzo façade Michelangelo worked from 1516 onwards; he even made a small terracotta model which has been lost; then he entrusted to Baccio d'Agnolo the task of making a wooden model after his designs (cf. Plate 159);[21] which did not satisfy him, however, and finally, from August to December 1517, he made another model (with the help of Pietro Urbano) which included wax sketches of the statues and probably also of the reliefs. This model has also been lost. (See Ackerman, *The Architecture of Michelangelo*, 1961, Catalogue, p. 9f. and fig. 5a.) The contract for the Lorenzo façade was concluded on 19 January 1518 and cancelled on 10 March 1520, a few months before the inception of the Medici tombs.

A WINDOW OF THE MEDICI PALACE IN FLORENCE. Plate 160. While Michelangelo was working on his models for the Lorenzo façade, or perhaps after this plan had been abandoned and before the work on the Medici tombs began, Pope Leo X decided to transform the ground-floor loggia of the Medici palace into a hall. 'Michelangelo,' says Vasari, 'made a model for two kneeling windows (finestre inginocchiate) of the Medici palace . . . and directed the making of perforated copper jalousies (gelosie di rame straforato), executed by the goldsmith Piloto.' Piloto worked with Michelangelo in 1520-4, when he made the polyhedric ball with the cross for the dome of the Sagrestia Nuova, the Medici Chapel. Piloto's 'copper jalousies' were later replaced by iron grills; or else, they have perhaps never been on those windows, as Vasari gives contradictory information in the Life of Giovanni da Udine: 'Cosimo il Vecchio had made on his palace a loggia for the citizens to meet. . . . This loggia was now closed, following a design by Michelangelo, and was made in the form of a chamber with *two kneeling windows with iron bars* the first of the kind erected outside palaces.'

THE BIBLIOTECA LAURENZIANA. Plates 161-167; Plates VIII, IX, XII-f. Commissioned by Pope Clement VII. Michelangelo made the first drawings for it in

---

[20] He means, of course, the block hewn in the rough.

[21] Plate 159 is identified by A. Schiavo and V. Mariani with d'Agnolo's work; but Tolnay (1951, p. 166) sees in it 'una riduzione del modello del contratto', which must mean a reduced version of Pietro Urbano's model, which he made in December 1517 under the eyes of Michelangelo and took to Rome to show it to the Pope. Prof. Wilde describes this wooden model as 'a free replica of the original' and suspects that it is the work of Giovanantonio Dosio.

anuary 1524. In the same year the design for the carved eiling was also made, but this was finished only *ca.* ten ears later by Battista del Tasso and Antonio Carota see Plate IX–b). In 1559, when Ammanati finished the taircase of the Laurenziana (with Vasari's help), Duke Cosimo I de' Medici asked him whether it were not possible to acquire Michelangelo's original design for the carved ceiling. The floor, which repeats the design of the ceiling, was made by Tribolo (together with Sante Buglioni and others), the carved benches by Battista del Cinque and Ciappino, probably also from sketches by Michelangelo. (See Plates VIII and IX.)

THE 'PERGAMO' OF SAN LORENZO. Plate 168. This sacrarium was ordered by Pope Clement VII in order to store there the relics collected by Lorenzo de' Medici. Michelangelo made his first design for it in February 1526, but the work was not finished before the winter of 1532–3. It is erected over the main entrance to the church and faces the altar. Over the left pilaster appear the three Medici rings, while under the loggia – over the door of the church – there is the coat-of-arms of Clement VII, in the shape of a horse's skull, also designed by Michelangelo.

THE FUNERARY CHAPEL FOR THE MEDICI FAMILY. Plates 169–205; 213–215; III–VII, XIII–b, XIV–c. Commissioned by Cardinal Giulio de'Medici, afterwards Pope Clement VII. Originally, in 1520, planned as a free-standing edifice with four tombs, for Lorenzo il Magnifico, Giuliano the Elder, Giuliano Duke of Nemours (died 1516), son of Lorenzo il Magnifico, and Lorenzo Duke of Urbino (died 1519), grandson of Lorenzo il Magnifico; then as mural decoration with two sarcophagi on each wall; then with the addition of a double tomb for the two Medici Popes, Leo X and Clement VII; executed after 1524 in its final form, which underwent various modifications during the work. The figure of the Madonna (Plate 200), which had been projected from the first, was to have been placed on the tomb of Lorenzo il Magnifico and his brother. The final solution was that the papal tomb and those for the Magnifici were omitted, and the project was limited to two separate tombs for the Dukes. In March 1521 the construction of the chapel was begun and the cupola was in position by January 1524 (see Plates VII and XIII). The *Madonna* was begun in the same year and should have been ready by the winter of 1531–2, but was still unfinished in the autumn of 1534, when Michelangelo went to Rome to paint the *Last Judgement* in the Sistine Chapel. Of the four recumbent figures the first to be begun was the *Aurora* (Plate 180), the dates of execution being: *Aurora*, 1524–31; *Crepuscolo* (Plate 179), 1524–31; *Notte* (Plate 183), 1526–31; *Giorno* (Plate 184), 1526–34, unfinished; statue of *Lorenzo* (Plate 173), 1524–34; statue of *Giuliano* (Plate 174), 1526–34. In addition to these, four river-gods were planned, which were to have reclined by the sarcophagi; an over-lifesize clay model for one of these is now at the Accademia in Florence (Plate 204). Participation of assistants: Tribolo began the 'Earth' for the tomb of Lorenzo, but neither the model nor the abbozzo of the statue has been preserved; Montelupo carved, after Michelangelo's model, the *Damian* (holding a pill-

box) while Montorsoli, who also helped to finish the Giuliano, executed independently the *Cosmas* on the other side of the Madonna (Plates IV–c, d). The *Crouching Boy* (Plate 213) was, according to a hypothesis advanced by Popp, intended, together with three similar unexecuted pieces, to crown the entablature. Various attempts have been made to interpret the allegorical meaning of the monument: Borinski saw in it allusions to Dante; Steinmann, to a carnival song; Brockhaus, to Ambrosian hymns; all three of them thus suggest a literary derivation. Tolnay gives an elaborate explanation, according to which the whole chapel was a synthesized representation of the universe, divided into its three zones – Hell, Earth and the Heavenly Spheres. Jacob Burckhardt's opinion of the chapel (1855) was: 'Architecture and sculpture are conceived together in such a way, as if the master had previously modelled both out of one and the same clay.' On the other hand the French painter Henri Regnault declared (1867): 'The statues are in a bad setting. This architecture, which is attributed to Michelangelo, made me quite wild. It is common and without charm, and it reduces and destroys the figures. Those little mausoleums, those tiny pillars and windows which surround the divine figures of the Thinker and Giuliano, made me turn livid with rage.'
The frontispiece shows that Michelangelo made use of marble of various colours. The body of the 'Notte' is almost white, the body of 'Giorno' almost brown; the sarcophagus is yellowish, etc.

LORENZO AND GIULIANO DE' MEDICI. Belonging to the Medici tombs. Marble, 5 ft. 10 in. and 5 ft. 8 in. high. Plates 173–178; 190–192; 194–195. Vasari mentions the collaboration of Montorsoli in the execution of both statues; according to Steinmann, his participation was limited to the helmets, armour and other details. Michelangelo made no effort to achieve portrait-like fidelity in the statues of the two dukes; to the Florentines, who missed this lifelikeness and were puzzled by the purely idealistic conception, Michelangelo proudly answered that in a thousand years' time nobody would know what the two Medicis had really looked like. Lorenzo represents the vita contemplativa, Giuliano the vita activa, as already suggested by J. Richardson in 1722.

THE FOUR PHASES OF THE DAY. Belonging to the Medici tombs. Plates 169–170.
Crepuscolo, length of the marble block, 6 ft. 4¾ in.; Plate 179.
Aurora, length of the marble block, 6 ft. 8 in.; Plate 180.
Notte, length of the marble block, 6 ft. 4¾ in.; Plate 183.
Giorno, length of the marble block, 6 ft. 8¾ in.; Plate 184.
Stendhal (in *Histoire de la peinture en Italie*, 1817) says: 'The statues in San Lorenzo are partly unfinished. This deficiency is rather an advantage in view of Michelangelo's powerful style.' Stendhal was also the first to draw attention to the resemblances to the 'Belvedere Torso'. 'In both the male figures', he says while discussing the *Giorno* and the *Crepuscolo*, 'one finds striking reminiscences of the Belvedere Torso, but transformed by Michelangelo's genius.' Burckhardt writes: 'In these four statues the master has proclaimed his boldest ideas on the limits and aim of his art. . . . For his successors this was the straight road to ruin.' Vasari wrote: 'And what can I

say of the Night, this statue which is not only a great and rare work of art, but is also unique? Who, in any period, has ever seen a statue, whether ancient or modern, of such a high degree of culture? One can well understand that it was this Night which completely obscured all those artists who for a time sought, not to surpass, but to equal Michelangelo.' Daniele da Volterra made copies of all the figures in the Medici Chapel, and Tintoretto, El Greco and Rubens, among others, drew inspiration from them.

MADONNA AND CHILD. Belonging to the Medici tombs. Plates 200–203. Marble, 7 ft. 5⅜ in. Burckhardt says of it: 'It is hardly more than hewn in the rough. . . . Owing to a fault in the marble or a slip on the part of the artist, the right arm did not turn out as it should have done and was therefore adjusted behind as we see it to-day. Probably this affected the rest of the statue, which for that reason was completed only schematically and inadequately.' But to this Carl Justi added: 'We live in an age of revision of all values, of a fundamental transformation of the world of culture: and thus it happens that the most criticized of Michelangelo's marble figures, which previously was almost ignored, is now the most praised, as the most powerful expression of his style.'

RIVER-GOD. Modelled in clay and oakum, over wood. 5 ft. 10 in. long. Plates 204–205. On 24 October 1525 Michelangelo wrote to Fattucci in Rome: 'The four rough-hewn statues[22] are not yet ready and there is still much work to do on them. The four others, representing rivers, have not yet been begun, as I have not yet got the marble blocks in my house, although they have arrived in Florence.' The four rivers were conceived as allegorical figures for the bases of the two sarcophagi in the Medici Chapel, but the work does not seem to have progressed further than clay models of the two river gods for the sarcophagus of Lorenzo, of which only one, much damaged, has been preserved (which would probably have been placed beneath the Aurora). Plate 204 shows approximately the correct position, Plate 205 the same figure in a wrong position, as exhibited now.

CLAY MODEL FOR A 'VICTORY' GROUP. Plate 206. 16½ in. high. It is often called 'Hercules and Cacus' or 'Samson slaying a Philistine', but according to Springer, Wilde and Laux (Michelangelos Juliusmonument, Berlin, 1943, pp. 54 and 411) it belongs, like the group in the Palazzo Vecchio (Plate 207), to the tomb of Julius and is a model for a group which was not executed. See also Appendix, Plate XXIII. (But cf. E. Panofsky, Studies in Iconology, New York, 1939, pp. 231 f.) The illustrations in Bode's Denkmäler der Renaissance-Sculptur in Toscana (pl. 531) and in Klassiker der Kunst (pl. 166) show this model without heads and without the right arm of the standing figure, which were only added in 1927, but not quite correctly. There is a copy in wax in the Victoria and Albert Museum, London, that ought to be compared.

THE VICTORY. Probably intended for the tomb of Julius.[23] Plate 207 (208, 209). Marble, 8 ft. 7½ in. high.

Knapp thinks the group was destined for the façade of San Lorenzo; Brinckmann, too, thinks that it was not intended for the tomb of Julius and sees in it an allegory of the platonic Eros; on the other hand, Schottmüller, Wilde and Panofsky, are against this theory. Justi gave it a political interpretation, as symbolizing the overthrowing of liberty in Florence; he describes the group as 'probably the most puzzling work which Michelangelo has bequeathed to posterity'. Mackowsky suspects the collaboration of assistants on account of the 'exaggerated modelling' and dates it about the same time as the Apollo, which was executed after 1530, thus assigning it to the same period as Justi.[24] A terminus post quem is given by the fact that the marble of this statue comes from the quarries of Serravezza which were not worked before the year 1518. A resemblance between the features of the vanquished figure and those of Michelangelo was noted by the older writers (Symonds, I, 89); by assuming that some young minion of Michelangelo was the model for the beautiful figure of the victor, it was easy to arrive at an erotic interpretation.[25] The group was left unfinished in Michelangelo's Florentine workshop. The head is now in parts polished, which may have been done by some assistant; the pupil is incised in the right eye, but not in the left, which is also probably due to the same assistant. After Michelangelo's death the statue was in the hands of Daniele da Volterra, who proposed to put it, together with other sculptures, on the Master's tomb. R. Wittkower (in Burlington Magazine, 1941, p. 133) suggested that the head of the Victor is the work of Vincenzo Danti; Tolnay called this 'a not very convincing opinion'.

APOLLO. Plates 210 (211, 212). Marble, 4 ft. 10¼ in. high, including base. In 1527 the Medici were driven out for the second time, but the Emperor Charles V joined forces with Pope Clement VII and laid siege to Florence, (Michelangelo was then responsible for the fortifications.) The city fell after eleven months (on 12 August 1530). Vasari relates: 'After the capitulation of Florence, Baccio Valori, as the Pope's plenipotentiary, was ordered to arrest some of the most prominent party leaders among the burghers. The court sent to Michelangelo's house to seek him, but, foreseeing this, he had taken refuge in the house of a friend near-by.' The Pope ordered that he should be found and promised him immunity from punishment if he would resume work on the chapel of the Medici family. 'When Michelangelo felt himself thus reassured, he sought first to win the favour of Baccio Valori. He made for him from a block of marble, three ells high [about five foot nine inches], a figure representing an Apollo, who is drawing an arrow from his quiver. This statue, which was not quite finished, now stands

---

[22] Presumably the Madonna, Lorenzo, Aurora and Crepuscolo.
[23] On this point see the detailed exposition by Karl August Laux, Michelangelos Juliusmonument, Berlin 1943, p. 46 f., and note 18 on p. 411.

[24] See Johannes Wilde, Michelangelo, The Group of Victory, Oxford 1945.
[25] There is a late echo of this Victory group in the 'Apotheosis of Prince Eugen' by Balthasar Permoser, 1721, in which the 'Vanquished' is actually an authentic self-portrait of the artist (reproduced by Ludwig Goldscheider in 500 Self-portraits, 1936, Plate 295). Michelangelo's group is reminiscent in its composition of Donatello's 'Judith and Holofernes', to which it may also be akin in its meaning as representing the victory of innocence over the power of sin. Male figures of 'Victory' were to be placed on the Julius monument opposite female figures of identical meaning (cf. Plate I-a), representing the chosen few who, notwithstanding their weakness, have been vouchsafed great victories and triumphs over evil, whereas the 'Slaves' symbolize the common crowd overcome by sin.

in the chamber of the Duke of Florence.' Popp describes the statue as a niche figure for the Magnifici tomb and does not believe that it is the statue intended for Valori. She calls it 'David', which is in accordance with the Inventory of 1553, when the statue was in the collection of Duke Cosimo I de' Medici. The bulge beneath the right foot should not be interpreted as the head of Goliath, but might very well be the head of the python slain by Apollo, or just a stone.

THE CROUCHING BOY. According to Popp, intended for the Medici tombs. Plates 213–215. Marble, 22 in. high. Its authenticity is entirely unsupported and therefore doubtful.[26] Hewn out of a cubic block, with maximum utilization of the volume. (I have included this sculpture among the authentic works because I believe that it was begun by Michelangelo himself, although probably continued by Tribolo.[27] One could say what Sebastiano del Piombo said about the Minerva Christ: 'However, I am telling everybody that the execution is not by Michelangelo's hand.') The statue is not quite finished. L. Brown, an Englishman, bought the statue in 1787 from the Medici collection in Florence, and sold it to the Academy in St Petersburg; in 1851 it was transferred to the Hermitage.

THE FOUR UNFINISHED CAPTIVES. Intended for the tomb of Julius. Plates 216–225. Marble. Youthful Captive, 8 ft. 6¾ in; Atlas, 9 ft. 1½ in.; Bearded Captive, 8 ft. 8¼ in.; Awakening Captive, 9 ft. Inserted by Grand Duke Cosimo de' Medici, who received them from Michelangelo's nephew, into artificial stalactites in a grotto at the entrance to the Boboli gardens in Florence, whence they were transferred to the Accademia in 1908. Mackowsky made a technical study of these four figures, for he believed them to be 'more suitable than any other work of the master's for deducing valuable conclusions as to Michelangelo's methods'. He declares that Michelangelo did not transfer a finished model to marble following the schematic method of point-setting, but that he hewed into the block from one side in the manner of relief. Justi arrived at the same conclusion, quoting the descriptions of Michelangelo's methods by Vasari and Cellini and referring to the five unfinished statues: the St Matthew and the four Captives from the Boboli gardens. Justi speaks of an 'extraction of the statue out of the block from the front. . . . Anyone who knew nothing of its genesis would think that the St Matthew was an unfinished relief. Here we have the front half of a figure, the parts seen in profile or frontally having been carried to different degrees of completion; the other, rear portion, is still hidden in the untouched, quadrilateral block. . . . But it was intended that this apparent half-relief should become a statue in the round.' Mackowsky speaks of the tools used: 'Nowhere can we find traces of the

drill;[28] the whole of the work was done with punch and claw-chisel. In consequence the surface shows parallel strokes which remind us of hatching in a drawing.' F. Baumgart, in *Bolletino d'arte*, XXVIII, 1934, pp. 353–5, compared the technique of the St Matthew with that of the 'Unfinished Captives' and pointed out that the block of Matthew was hewn into from the front, while the block of the 'Awakening Giant' was begun to be carved at one of the four upright edges, in such a way that *two* sides of the block were used for the figure. The same method was used for the *Atlas*, both statues being intended as corner figures. (On Michelangelo's technique compared with that of the Greek sculptors, see: *Vasari on Technique*, ed. Baldwin Brown, London, 1907, p. 193; Stanley Casson, *The Technique of Early Greek Sculpture*, Oxford, 1933, pp. 128, 186.) The sculptor Adolf von Hildebrand denied that the four unfinished Captives in Florence were the work of Michelangelo's own hand (in *Michelangelos spätere Plastik*, in *Gesammelte Aufsätze*, Strasbourg, 1916). Kriegbaum was of the same opinion and assumed that one or several assistants worked here from large models by the master. Panofsky (in *Studies in Iconology*, New York, 1939, p. 218) thinks a date as late as 1532–4 possible for the execution of the 'Unfinished Captives'. Tolnay dates the 'Unfinished Captives' after 1534,[29] but Kriegbaum and Laux (*Juliusmonument*, p. 420, Note 59) again pleaded for the earlier date, namely about 1519, Wilde about 1520.

CLAY MODEL FOR A CAPTIVE. (Casa Buonarroti No. 524.) Terra secca, 8⅝ in. high. Plate 226.

CLAY MODEL FOR A CAPTIVE. (L. Fagan, *The Art of Michelangelo . . . in the British Museum*, London 1883, p. 163.) Terracotta, painted green by a later hand. 11⅝ in. high. Plate 227. Until 1859 in the Casa Buonarroti in Florence.

THE LAST JUDGEMENT. Plates 228–237; XXX. The largest fresco in Rome, painted area 48 by 44 ft. Three frescoes by Perugino and two lunette paintings by Michelangelo were removed to make way for it. The windows in the altar wall were blocked up with bricks[30] and an inner wall of dried bricks was erected; between the wall of the chapel and this inner wall a space for ventilation was left. The wall for the fresco was built sloping, in such a way that it overhung at the top by about half a Florentine 'braccia' (about a foot), thus preventing the accumulation of dust. The ground for oil painting (mortar mixed with resin), which had been applied by Sebastiano del Piombo, was removed by Michelangelo, who painted in fresco on a ground of damp lime and mortar. He executed the whole work personally, being assisted only by an ordinary colour-

---

[26] Since these words were first printed (1939) two critics have doubted the authenticity of the statue: Kriegbaum (1940), who with good reasons attributes the execution to Tribolo, and Wittkower (1944), who suggests Pierino da Vinci.

[27] I reproduce the front view of the *Crouching Boy* intentionally facing the "Young Giant" in order to show the similarities of style, which are particulary striking in the joints (e.g. the knees). I suspect that Tribolo collaborated on both of these sculptures.

[28] The drill was used by Michelangelo in his early period, particularly in the 'Drunken Bacchus' and the 'Pietà of St Peter's' (see Plates 10–12 and 15), but also in the two earliest *Captives* (Plates 149, 152).

[29] *Michelagniolo*, Florence 1951, p. 249: 'between September 1534 and April 1536'. In *The Tomb of Julius II* (*Michelangelo*, vol. IV, Princeton 1954, p. 113 f.) Tolnay corrected his dating to '1532–1534'. Michelangelo's move to Rome in 1534 may be regarded as a certain *terminus ante quem*, for he left these unfinished statues behind in his Florentine workshop.

[30] The preparations for the fresco lasted a year, from the spring of 1535 to the spring of 1536 (*Steinmann*, II, p. 766 f.). The cartoon was finished in September 1535.

grinder. He began the work after 10 April 1536 (according to Biagetti towards the end of June or early in July), the upper portion being finished by 15 December 1540, and the complete painting was unveiled on 31 October 1541 (twenty-nine years after the unveiling of the ceiling paintings). We are told that Pope Paul III, overcome by the sight, broke into prayer with the words: 'Lord, charge me not with my sins when Thou shalt come on the Day of Judgement.' The fresco is arranged in three zones. The top one is the Kingdom of Heaven, with Christ as Judge of the World enthroned in the centre and the Virgin next to him; around him is an inner circle of Apostles in the right half of the arch, and Patriarchs in the left. Two Martyrs finish off the lower end of this circle. Above, in the lunettes, we see hosts of angels, with the instruments of Christ's Passion, the Cross, and the pillar at which He was scourged. In the other circle we have Prophets, Confessors and Martyrs on the right, and the Hebrew women, holy virgins and Sibyls on the left. – The middle zone is the realm of those who have been judged: on the left the ascent of the elect, on the right the fall of the damned, while in the centre the messengers of the Lord blow their trumpets. – The lowest zone is the realm of Charon and the demons; the Resurrection of the Dead and the arrival in Hell fill the portion immediately above the altar. – Justi described the 'Last Judgement' as 'Michelangelo's last word in formative art'. Weisbach saw in it the perfection of the 'heroic' style, while Dvořák recognized it as the 'source of a new style', and wrote: 'From the time of the *Last Judgement* the whole of Italian art becomes Michelangelesque, not only in its various forms, but in its entire trend of thought, which is filled with a new conception of ideal timelessness, of spatial universality, and with a hitherto unknown spiritual pathos. When we say that Michelangelo became the destiny of Italian art, this is true of none of his works so much as of the *Last Judgement*, and if we wished to give an exhaustive study of its influence we should have to enumerate all the works produced in Italy, and in part to the north of the Alps as well, from the day it was painted to the end of Baroque art.' In contrast to the enormous impression which it made on contemporary painters was the zealous hostility of theologians and men of letters, who were filled with the spirit of the Counter-Reformation. Two opinions have become popular and almost anecdotal, those of the papal master of ceremonies, Biagio da Cesena, and of Pietro Aretino. Biagio, who saw the upper portion of the fresco in 1540, called it a 'stufa d'ignudi', a bathing establishment. In 1537 Michelangelo wrote to Aretino: 'I regret that I cannot avail myself of your ideas, but the painting has already progressed too far. . . . As for your resolution not to come again to Rome, you should not break it for the sake of seeing my painting. That would be indeed too much. Adieu.' Eight years later came Aretino's attack, in the form of a long 'open' letter. He compared his courtesans' dialogue 'Nanna' with Michelangelo's 'Last Judgement', and claimed that he had displayed more modesty than Michelangelo; he accused the painter of being irreverent. 'Such things might be painted in a voluptuous bathroom, but not in the choir of the highest chapel. . . . Our souls are benefited little by art, but by piety.' Michelangelo is supposed to have

inserted the portraits of both these critics in his 'Last Judgement', Aretino being represented as Bartholomew[31] with the skin of the flayed martyr, which itself bears a self-portrait of Michelangelo (Plate 233). According to Vasari, he caricatured Biagio in the figure of Minos, the supreme judge of hell (Plate 232); the ears resemble a donkey's; Biagio complained to the Pope, who answered him, as witty as Boccaccio, that to rescue him from hell was outside his province; if he had been in Purgatory, that would have been a different matter, but 'ibi nulla est redemptio'. Nevertheless Biagio's opinion finally prevailed, and at a session of the Council of Trent on 3 December 1563, the representation of unsuitable subjects in churches was forbidden. Under Popes Paul IV (1559) and Gregory XIII Michelangelo's fresco was in danger of being completely destroyed. Most of the nudities were painted over, firstly by Michelangelo's pupil Daniele da Volterra, who thereby won for himself the nickname of 'il brachettone' or the 'breeches-maker'. St Catherine and the Bad Thief show particularly heavy overpainting. Under Pius V (1572) further draperies were added and at that time El Greco offered to replace the whole painting by one of his own, which 'would be decent and pious and no less well painted than Michelangelo's'. Further overpaintings were undertaken in 1625, 1712 and 1762. 'The state in which the gigantic work has come down to us is one of such mutilation that it is impossible to form an opinion as to its artistic qualities' (Thode). Copies by Marcello Venusti (1549, Appendix Plate XXX) and by Robert le Voyer (1570, Montpellier Museum), and a large engraving by Beatrizet (1562, in eleven parts) show the figures in the painting before the alterations.

THE CONTEMPLATIVE AND THE ACTIVE LIFE (Rachel and Leah). Belonging to the tomb of Julius. Plates 238–240. Marble, 6 ft. 7½ in. and 6 ft. 10 in. high. Mainly by Michelangelo's hand, but finished and polished by assistants. On 20 July 1542 Michelangelo proposed that these figures, which he had already begun, should be substituted for the Captives, as the latter no longer fitted the niches (see above, THE TOMB OF JULIUS, p. 14). According to Vasari, Michelangelo executed the statues in 'less than the span of a year'. Vasari also says that one of the figures is Leah, symbol of the active life, and the other Rachel, symbol of the contemplative life. Condivi does not mention Rachel and Leah, but calls the figures simply the Active and the Contemplative Life.[32] He adds: 'In this Michelangelo, always a zealous student of Dante, is following the latter, to whom in his Purgatorio the Countess Matilda appeared in a flowery meadow as the personification of the active life.' (Dante *Purgatorio*, XXVII, 94 f.; XXVIII, 37 f.; XXXIII, 118 f.)

---

[31] The *Last Judgement* was finished four years before Aretino wrote his aggressive letter. Therefore the tradition that Bartholomew is his portrait appears doubtful.
[32] Michelangelo himself, in his memorandum of 20 July 1542 to Pope Paul III, calls them the Contemplative and the Active Life, not Rachel and Leah. The Active and the Contemplative Life play a prominent part in the *Disputationes Camaldulenses* by Cristoforo Landino (written about 1468). The protagonists of these conversations are Leone Battista Alberti, Lorenzo il Magnifico, his brother Giuliano de' Medici and others. These conversations circulated in manuscript form in Florence and must certainly have been known to Michelangelo.

BRUTUS. Plate 241 (242). Marble, 29½ in. high without socle. On the pedestal the distich: *Dum Bruti effigiem sculptor de marmore ducit, In mentem sceleris venit et abstinuit.* (While the sculptor was hewing the effigy of Brutus out of the marble, he came upon the spirit of crime and desisted.) According to tradition this inscription was composed by the Venetian humanist Pietro Bembo (1470–1547). Vasari maintains that the inspiration came from Donato Giannotti and that the work was commissioned by Cardinal Ridolfi. In his *Dialogues*, written in 1545, Giannotti makes Michelangelo speak of Brutus: 'He who slays a tyrant, does not kill a man, but a beast in human form. For since all tyrants are devoid of that love which all men must have for their neighbours, so too they are without human feelings and therefore no men, but beasts.' Knapp remains faithful to the old political interpretation and sees in the bust a reference to the murder of Duke Alessandro de' Medici by Lorenzino. According to Vasari, Michelangelo gave the bust of Brutus to Tiberio Calcagni, in order that he might finish it – 'he himself having only executed the features of the Brutus with fine strokes of the claw-chisel'. On this point Carl Justi wrote: 'The head of Brutus remained at the stage of a sketch; only the draperies were elaborated; this trite and insignificant work is neither by the hand nor in the style of the master.' Grünwald has investigated Calcagni's share; the retouching concerns mainly the robe and the neck, but in addition to this the chin and mouth and a part of the hair have been gone over roughly with a flat chisel, an instrument which Michelangelo used only in his very early work. Attention has frequently been drawn to the resemblance to busts of Roman emperors, but this resemblance is due to the toga and the shape of the bust, which were Calcagni's work. Calcagni (1532–65) first came to Michelangelo's studio in 1556; at that time the bust was still unfinished. (See also illustration on p. 262.)

THE CONVERSION OF ST PAUL and THE CRUCIFIXION OF ST PETER. Plates 243, 244 (245–251; XXIX). Each fresco measures 20 ft. 6 in. by 21 ft. 8 in. Finished by Michelangelo when he was seventy-five years old. Badly preserved, restored and over-painted; Plate XXIX in the Appendix gives an indication of the state of preservation of the two frescoes, as the photos were taken while the paintings were stripped before the restorer retouched and over-painted them again. Most retouchings in the first fresco are, however, by Michelangelo himself. This painting, finished in 1545, was damaged by fire in the same year (see Michelangelo's letter to Luigi del Riccio; *Lettere*, ed. G. Milanesi, p. 513). Both frescoes were restored in 1933 and 1955; the restorer's work shows mainly in the landscape.

Lomazzo (in his *Idea del tempio della pittura*, Milan, 1590, p. 53) was the first critic who had any appreciation for these two frescoes. He explains that they show Michelangelo's third and greatest style (the first style being that of the Prophets and Sibyls, and the second that of the Last Judgement). The Paolina frescoes had no appeal for the writers of the eighteenth and nineteenth centuries (although William Blake copied one of the figures), but in our time Dvořák, D. Frey, Neumeyer, Baumgart, Biagetti, Redig de Campos, and H. von Einem, have established a revaluation of Michelangelo's last paintings.

THE PIAZZA OF THE CAPITOL IN ROME. Plates 252–255. Michelangelo's original plan is known from du Pérac's etching (Plate 252). The outside staircase of the Palazzo Senatorio was begun in 1544, and at the same time the façade of the building was partially altered after designs by Tommaso Cavalieri, but in 1578–1583 the new bell tower was erected and in 1598–1612 the façade was completely rebuilt. Michelangelo was therefore responsible only for the outside stairway of the central building. The Palazzo dei Conservatori was finished in 1568 according to the Master's designs, but Jacomo del Duca, at a later date, enlarged the central window and transformed it into a balcony. The Museo Capitolino (on our left when we are facing the Senatorial Palace) is an exact copy of the Palazzo dei Conservatori and was erected under Pope Innocent X (1644–55). The elliptical pavement in the Capitol Square (exactly the same pattern as appears in Michelangelo's design of 1546, Plate 252) was finished only in 1940 (Plate XII–e). The chronology of the reconstruction of the Piazza of the Capitol is complicated and still in dispute. Cf. Herbert Siebenhüner, *Das Kapitol in Rom, Idee und Gestalt*, Munich 1954; and the review by Prof. James S. Ackerman in *The Art Bulletin*, March 1956 (vol. 38–1), pp. 53–57.

PALAZZO FARNESE. Plates 256–260. Begun by Antonio da Sangallo the Younger, who died in 1546 and left the work unfinished. Michelangelo was appointed by Pope Paul III (Alessandro Farnese) to continue this work. He was responsible for the balcony and the large coat-of-arms, the windows of the upper storey, the cornice, and the upper storey of the courtyard. The balustrade of the balcony was added by Antonio Cipolla about 1866; earlier engravings show the central window without balustrade. It can be proved, however, that this

The façade of the Palazzo Farnese in the eighteenth century. Engraving, 1765

shape was intended by Michelangelo himself; the reverse of a Farnese medal, representing the Farnese Palace, shows the central window in the shape of a balcony. This medal was coined in 1548. An engraving by N. Beatrizet, dated 1549, gives an identical view.[33] The two smaller coats-of-arms are later additions (as can be seen from the engraving reproduced here). Vignola (who died 1573) and Giacomo della Porta finished the building in 1589.

---

[33] Both views are based on the model, or on drawings.

IL GRAN NICCHIONE DEL BELVEDERE (the Large Niche of the Belvedere in the Vatican). Plate 261. The lower storey was designed by Bramante (begun 1503) and had a stairway with semi-circular steps, the inside concave, the outside convex. Pope Julius III (1550-5) commissioned Michelangelo to replace Bramante's stairway by another one with a double flight of stairs, similar to that of the Palazzo dei Senatori (Plate 255). It has come down to us in an adulterated form; the balustrade and the fountain with the mask were added about 1700, whereas the antique peacocks and the pine-cone were brought there as early as 1618.

Michelangelo conceived the idea of transforming the exedra into a large niche, which means that the two upper storeys were added according to his designs; but the work was carried out in the time of Pius IV by Pirro Ligorio (1562), who was responsible for the super-structure and the colonnade. A drawing in the Uffizi (see Plate XVI-a) shows the appearance of the Nicchione in Michelangelo's time; an engraving by Brambilla shows it soon after Michelangelo's death, before the outside stairs were altered (see Plate XVI-b).

THE FLORENTINE PIETÀ (Entombment). Plate 262 (263, 264). Marble 7 ft. 8 in. Mentioned by Vasari in his first edition, it must thus have been begun before 1550. Probably in 1550, the French traveller Blaise de Vigenère saw Michelangelo working on it: 'I saw Michelangelo at work. He had passed his sixtieth year and although he was not very strong, yet in a quarter of an hour he caused more splinters to fall from a very hard block of marble than three young masons in three or four times as long. No one can believe it who has not seen it with his own eyes. And he attacked the work with such energy and fire that I thought it would fly into pieces. With one blow he brought down fragments three or four fingers in breadth, and so exactly at the point marked, that if only a little more marble had fallen, he would have risked spoiling the whole work.' From Condivi we learn that Michelangelo was still working on this group in 1553. In his second edition Vasari says: 'At this time (1556) Michelangelo worked on it almost every day as a pastime. At last he broke the stone, probably because it contained veins of emery and was so hard that the chisel struck sparks from it; perhaps also because his criticism of his own work was so severe that nothing he did satisfied him. For this reason, to tell the truth, there are few finished works by him from his late period, when he had reached the highest maturity of his artistic power of creation. His finished sculptures all date from his early period.' Vasari tells us later that Michelangelo gave the broken Pietà to Francesco Bandini, who wanted to have it finished by Tiberio Calcagni, but the latter died in 1565. When one sees what he did, one can only say that his death was a good thing for the *Pietà*. He is responsible for the highly polished and minutely chiselled Magdalen, which must have been very beautiful before; he was also responsible for the polishing of the trunk of the Christ and the sharp folds of the shroud. Note that Christ's left leg is missing. Vasari proposed that the Pietà should be placed on Michelangelo's tomb, as was the master's own intention, but this was not done. For a long time the group was left in the open air in a vineyard on Monte Cavallo, "nel giardino del Signore Cardinal Bandini". In 1664 it had already been transferred to Florence, first to San Lorenzo, and in 1722 it was placed behind the high altar of the cathedral. Finally, in 1933, it found its place in a chapel of the north choir.

THE RONDANINI PIETÀ. Plate 265 (266, 267). Marble, 6 ft. 3⅝ in. high (the elliptical base is 2 ft. 2 in. wide and 1 ft. 11 in. deep). On 12 February 1564, six days before his death, Michelangelo worked all day long standing in front of this group, as we learn from a letter of Daniele da Volterra to the nephew of the Master, Leonardo Buonarroti.

Michelangelo began the group probably by the end of 1556, when he abandoned the Florentine Pietà, and then revised it again – perhaps seven years later. The legs of the Christ and the free right arm are relics of the first version. The Rondanini Pietà was left as a legacy to Michelangelo's servant Antonio del Franzese. It is not known when the Pietà was brought to the Palazzo Rondanini. Goethe, who lived opposite the Palazzo Rondanini in Rome from November 1786 to April 1788, does not mention the work, although he knew the Rondanini collection well and had a cast made of a mask of Medusa which belonged to it. In 1952 the sculpture was bought from Conte Sanseverino by the City of Milan for 125 million Lire (about $180,000) and placed in the Castello Sforzesco.

THE PALESTRINA PIETÀ. Plate 268 (269). 8 ft. 2½ in. high. Burckhardt mentions it in the first edition of his *Cicerone* (1855), but refrains from giving his opinion on it. Wölfflin (1898), in his book *Die klassische Kunst* refers to the 'abbozzo in the castle of Palestrina', but this Pietà was first published by A. Grenier (in *Gazette des Beaux-Arts*, 1907). Wallerstein, Thode, Mackowsky, Davies, Toesca, d'Ancona and Redig de Campos maintained that it is authentic. On the other hand Schottmüller writes: 'The group is certainly close to Michelangelo's conception in his late period, but it has not the quality of the works executed by his own hand.' Anny Popp attributed the group to an 'imitator of Michelangelo', Ulrich Middeldorf thought of Pierino da Vinci. But the authenticity of the Palestrina Pietà has again been defended by A. Perrig (*Michelangelo Buonarrotis letzte Pietà-Idee*, Berne, 1960, pp. 94 f.). The work is not free from later revision by other hands. The marble used for this sculpture is a piece of ancient Roman cornice. In my opinion this Pietà was begun by Michelangelo and continued by another hand; two stages of this later revision can be detected. The head, right arm and legs of the Christ seem to me to be entirely by Michelangelo.

THE PORTA PIA IN ROME. Plate 270 (271; XIV-b). Commissioned by Pope Pius IV from Michelangelo in 1561. A number of assistants were employed; Jacomo del Duca, the most important amongst them, sculptured the mask on the keystone after Michelangelo's design, and also (with the help of Luca) the coat-of-arms.

In the time of Pius IX it was damaged by lightning and then replaced by a 'torretta' designed by Virginio Vespignani (1853). An engraving published in 1568 shows the Porta Pia finished with the top-piece over the centre being of a simple, triangular shape.

ST PETER'S IN ROME. Plates 272–279. The year 1546 was an important point in Michelangelo's life as an architect. In this year he began his work on the Palazzo Farnese, the re-planning of the Capitol square, and the work on a clay model of the dome of St Peter's. On 1 January 1547 he was entrusted by Pope Paul III with the superintendence of the building of St Peter's, and so he became the successor of Bramante, Raphael, Giuliano and Antonio da Sangallo. On the whole Michelangelo returned to Bramante's plan and removed as much as possible of Sangallo's constructions. But he completed only the drum of the dome, and after his death Vignola, Giacomo della Porta and Domenico Fontana com-pleted the dome after a large wooden model (Plate 272; XIX) which Giovanni Franzese had made from designs and under the eyes of the Master. This model measures one-fifteenth of the actual dome, namely 17 ft. 8 in. high and 12 ft. 8 in. wide. Vasari says: 'The completion of the model caused great satisfaction not only to Michel-angelo's friends but to all Rome.' But the baroque façade, which Carlo Maderna built for the church (1607–14), and Bernini's colonnades have deviated so much from Michelangelo's intentions that (as Knapp pointed out) one can only feel what Michelangelo con-templated if one looks at the back of the church from a great distance and sees the large dome against a clear sky.

St. Peter's, eleven years after Michelangelo's death. Detail of an engraving by Giambattista Cavalieri, 1575.
(The drum completed, but still without the dome.)

ADDITIONAL NOTES. – Professor Edgar Wind (in *Italian Renaissance Studies*, edited by E. F. Jacob, London, 1960, pp. 312 ff.) has renamed some of the Bronze medallions in a convincing way (our Plate Nos. 94–102). No. 94: *The Chastisement of Heliodorus*; No. 96: *Alexander the Great before the Priest of Jerusalem*; No. 102: *The Death of Nicanor*. (Edgar Wind's illustrations 22, 18, 20.) About the *Heliodorus* see also Frits Lugt, "Man and Angel", in Gazette des Beaux-Arts, XXV, June 1944, p. 345.

According to Lugt, *The Expulsion of Heliodorus* symbolizes a victory of Julius II, the expulsion of the French from Italy. Concerning the dating of our Plate 255, see James S. Ackerman, *The Architecture of Michelangelo, Catalogue*, London, 1961, p. 50. 'The inscription on the base of the statue recording the removal and consecration is dated 1538.' A drawing in the Escorial Sketchbook by Francisco de Hollanda of c. 1539–40 shows already the equestrian statue on the base which Michelangelo designed.

BIBLIOGRAPHY

The following list is intentionally kept concise, in order to help the student to find the most important titles first. There is a complete Michelangelo Bibliography in Vols. I and VIII of the *Römische Forschungen* of the Biblioteca Hertziana in Rome: *Michelangelo-Bibliographie* by E. Steinmann and R. Wittkower (1927), and a continuation by H. W. Schmidt in E. Steinmann's *Michelangelo im Spiegel seiner Zeit* (1930). For publications after 1930, see *Art Index*, New York, 1929 f., and Cherubelli, *Supplemento alla bibliografia michelangiolesca, 1931-42* (in 'Michelangelo Buonarroti nel IV centenario del Giudizio Universale'), Florence, 1942; a few additions in E. Aeschlimann, *bibliografia del Libro d'arte italiano 1940-52*, Rome, 1952. Bibliography from 1942 to the present in *Zeitschrift für Kunstgeschichte*, Munich; for literature after 1952 the *Annuario bibliografico* (Bibl. dell' Istituto nazionale d'archeologia e storia dell' arte, Rome).

I. THE OLD BIOGRAPHIES · DOCUMENTS · LETTERS

The two versions of the Michelangelo biography by Vasari (1550 and 1568) and the biography by Condivi are contained in a critical edition by Karl Frey, *Le vite di Michelagniolo Buonarroti scritte da Giorgio Vasari e da Ascanio Condivi*, Berlin, 1887. The first Vasari biography is separately available in a reprint by Corrado Ricci (Milan, 1927). There are three recent reprints of the Condivi biography, the best by Paolo d'Ancona (Milan, 1928). Many of the documents are to be found in Aurelio Gotti, *Vita di Michelangelo*, Florence, 1876; others in G. Gaye, *Carteggio inedito d'artisti*, 3 vols., Florence, 1839–40. – The only edition of Michelangelo's letters is still G. Milanesi, *Le lettere di Michelangelo Buonarroti*, Florence, 1875; the same editor collected Michelangelo's correspondence with Sebastiano del Piombo (*Les Correspondants de Michel-Ange*, I, Paris, 1890), whereas K. Frey gives a selection from all the letters addressed to the master in *Sammlung ausgewählter Briefe an Michelagniolo Buonarroti*, Berlin, 1899. The standard edition of Michelangelo's poetry is edited by K. Frey, Berlin, 1897. – There are several editions of the *Dialogues* of Francisco de Hollanda and those of Donato Giannotti. There is an English translation of Francisco de Hollanda's dialogues by Aubrey F. G. Bell, Oxford, 1928; the Portuguese text, with a German translation, was edited by Joaquim de Vasconcellos, Vienna, 1899 ('Quellenschriften', new series, vol. IX). There are several English translations of the biographies by Vasari and Condivi, and also selections from the Letters. Paola Barocchi's edition of *Giorgio Vasari, La Vita di Michelangelo* (Milan, 1962), 5 vols., with ca. 3000 pages of commentary and bibliography, is of the greatest help to any student.

II. THE LIFE AND WORK OF MICHELANGELO

Of the six volumes of Henry Thode's *Michelangelo* (Berlin, 1902–13) only vols. IV and V will prove of great value to the reader of the present book. They are published separately as 'Kritische Untersuchungen, I–II'. The sixth volume contains a catalogue of the drawings and a short list of the models. – A good survey of Michelangelo's œuvre is available in Charles de Tolnay's article in *Thieme-Becker's Künstlerlexikon*, vol. XXIV, Leipzig, 1930; another one, by Pietro Toesca, in *Enciclopedia Italiana*, vol. XXIII, pp. 165–191, Rome, 1934. – There is a corpus of illustrations, edited by F. Knapp in 'Klassiker der Kunst', vol. VII, Stuttgart, 1924, contain-ing too much and too little; and a fat volume by Charles de Tolnay, Florence, 1951, also incomplete; for instance, of the twelve Prophets and Sibyls of the Sistine Ceiling, this volume shows only four, and of the twenty nude Youths only two. Though not complete, the book is of great value owing to some illustrative material not available elsewhere. – The best edition of the *Sculptures* is by F. Kriegbaum, Berlin, 1940. – For a full list of separate essays, see the Bibliographies above; the best of those essays are only published in German, as Carl Justi's *Beiträge*, Berlin, 1900 and 1909; A. Grünwald's *Florentiner Studien*, Dresden, 1920; and Adolf Hildebrand's *Gesammelte Aufsätze*, Strasbourg, 1915. There is no really good biography of Michelangelo available in English, as the popular book by Romain Rolland (Paris, 1914), of which there is a translation, is rather misleading (see E. Panofsky, *Michelangelo-Literatur*, 1914–22, in 'Jahrbuch für Kunstgeschichte', I, Vienna, 1923) and J. A. Symonds's often reprinted *Life and Works of Michelangelo Buonarroti* (London, 1893) is definitely out of date. Herman Grimm's *Life of Michelangelo*, although first published a hundred years ago, is perhaps more satisfactory; there exists a good English translation of this book.

III. THE EARLY WORKS OF MICHELANGELO

Charles de Tolnay's *The Youth of Michelangelo*, 2nd ed., Princeton, 1947, containing full bibliographical references; some more in Aldo Bertini's *Michelangelo fino alla Sistina*, 2nd ed., Turin, 1945. The Piccolomini statuettes were re-assessed by Friedrich Kriegbaum, *Le Statue di Michelangelo nell' Altare dei Piccolomini a Siena* (in 'Michelangelo Buonarroti nel IV centenario del Giudizio Universale'), Florence, 1942; and by W. R. Valentiner, *Michelangelo's Statues on the Piccolomini Altar in Siena* (in 'Art Quarterly', 1942; reprinted in *Studies of Italian Renaissance Sculpture*, London, 1950).

IV. THE SISTINE CEILING FRESCOES

Ernst Steinmann, *Die Sixtinische Kapelle*, Vol. II, Munich, 1905. (On pp. 687 f. the Documents, edited by H. Pogatscher.) – Charles de Tolnay, *The Sistine Ceiling*, Princeton, 1945. (With references to further literature – by Wölfflin, Justi, Panofsky, Biagetti, etc.) – F. Hartt, *Lignum vitae in medio Paradisi*, in 'The Art Bulletin', XXXII, 1950, pp. 115–218.

V. THE TOMB OF POPE JULIUS II

Karl August Laux, *Michelangelos Juliusmonument*, Berlin, 1943. On the ornamental reliefs: Frida Schottmüller, *Michelangelo und das Ornament*, in 'Vienna Yearbook', 1928. Ch. de Tolnay, *The Tomb of Julius II*, Princeton, 1954.

VI. THE MEDICI CHAPEL

F. Burger, *Geschichte des florentinischen Grabmals von den ältesten Zeiten bis Michelangelo*, Strasbourg, 1904. – H. Brockhaus, *Michelangelo und die Medici-Kapelle*, Leipzig, 1909. – A. E. Popp, *Die Medici-Kapelle Michelangelos*, Munich, 1922. – Charles de Tolnay, *The Medici Chapel*, Princeton, 1948. – Erwin Panofsky, *The Neoplatonic Movement and Michelangelo*, in 'Studies in Iconology', New York, 1939, pp. 129–230. – Ernst Steinmann, *Das Geheimnis der Medicigräber Michelangelos*, Leipzig, 1907.

VII. THE LAST JUDGEMENT AND THE PAOLINA FRESCOES

D. Redig de Campos and B. Biagetti, *Il Giudizio Universale*, 2 vols., Rome, 1943. – F. Baumgart and B. Biagetti, *Die Fresken des Michelangelo in der Cappella Paolina*, Città del Vaticano, 1934. – (Same, Italian edition, Coll. 'Monumenti Vaticani di Archeologia e d'Arte', Roma, 1934.) – V. Mariani, *Gli affreschi di Michelangelo nella Cappella Paolina*, Rome, 1931 and 1932. – D. Redig de Campos, *Affreschi della Cappella Paolina in Vaticano*, Milan, 1950. – Karl Borinski, *Das Altargemälde der Sixtina* (The Last Judgement), in 'Die Rätsel Michelangelos', Munich, 1908, pp. 281–330. – D. Redig de Campos, *Fonti di Giudizio di Michelangelo* in 'Raffaello e Michelangelo, Studi di storia e d'arte', Rome, 1946. – *Studi e provvidenze per gli affreschi di Michelangelo nelle Cappelle Sistina e Paolina*. Notizie... di B. Nogara e B. Biagetti, in 'Rendiconti della Pontificia Accademia Romana di Archeologia', IX, 1934, pp. 167–199. – B. Biagetti, *Technica e Stato di conservazione del Giudizio*, in 'Rendiconti', XVIII, 1941–2, pp. 29–46. – Charles de Tolnay, *Michelangelo*, V, The Final Period, Princeton, 1960.

VIII. ARCHITECTURE

Heinrich von Geymüller, *Michelagnolo Buon. als Architekt* ('Architektur der Renaissance in Toskana', Vol. VIII), Munich, 1904. – Armando Schiavo, *Michelangelo Architetto*, Roma, 1949; and *La vita e le opere architettoniche di Michelangelo*, 1953. – C. Ricci, *Baukunst und dekorative Plastik der Hoch- und Spät-Renaissance in Italien*, Stuttgart, 1923 (340 Plates). – 'Geschichte der Neueren Baukunst', vol. I: Jacob Burckhardt, *Geschichte der Renaissance in Italien*, 5th edition, Esslingen, 1912. – A. E. Brinckmann, *Die Baukunst des 17. und 18. Jahrhunderts in den romanischen Ländern*, Berlin, 1915–19. – Jacques Veysset, *Le Palais Farnese*, Rome, 1948. – On the cornice of the Palazzo Farnese, S. Meller in 'Prussian Yearbook', XXX, 1909, p. 1 f. – On *Santa Maria degli Angeli*, Pasquinelli, Rome, 1932 and 1935. – Dagobert Frey, *Michelangelo-Studien*, Vienna, 1920 (on the 'Nicchione di Belvedere', and other essays). – Dagobert Frey, *Eine unbeachtete Zeichnung nach dem Modell Michelangelos für die Fassade von San Lorenzo*, in 'Kunstchronik', Dec. 1922, p. 226 f. – R. Wittkower, *Zur Peterskuppel Michelangelos*, in 'Zeitschrift für Kunstgeschichte', II, 1933, p. 348 f. – The same author on *the Biblioteca Laurenziana*, in 'Art Bulletin', XVI, 1934,

p. 123 f. – Charles de Tolnay, on *the façade of San Lorenzo*, in 'Gazette des Beaux-Arts', XI, 1934, p. 24 f. – The same author, on *the Libreria Laurenziana*, ib. XIV, 1935, p. 81 f. – The same author, in 'Prussian Yearbook', LI, 1930, p. 3 f., and LIII, 1932, p. 231 f.: *Beiträge zu den späten architektonischen Projekten Michelangelos*. – B. M. Apolloni, *Opere architettonice di Michelangelo a Firenze*, Rome 1936. – V. Fasolo, *La Cappella Sforza di Michelangelo*, in 'Architettura e Arti Decorative', III, 1924, p. 433 f. – A. Michaelis, *Michelangelos Plan zum Kapitol*, in 'Zeitschrift für bildende Kunst', 1891, new series, II, p. 184 f. – Dagobert Frey's essay on the model of the Cupola of St Peter's in his *Michelangelo-Studien*, Vienna, 1920, pp. 91–136, can only be used together with the corrections noted in Erwin Panofsky's *Die Michelangelo-Literatur seit 1914*, in 'Jahrbuch für Kunstgeschichte', I, Vienna, 1923, col. 18–21. – See also Hans Rose (in H. Wölfflin's 'Renaissance und Barock', fourth edition, Munich, 1926), *Der Kuppelbau*, pp. 291–310. – Valerio Mariani, *Michelangelo e la Facciata di S. Pietro*, Rome, 1943. – Adolfo Venturi, *L'architettura del Cinquecento* ('Storia dell'arte italiana', vol. XI, parte II), Milan, 1939.

IX. THE LATE WORKS

H. von Einem, *Bemerkungen zur Florentiner Pietà*, in 'Prussian Yearbook', LXI, 1940, p. 77 f. – Ch. de Tolnay, *The Rondanini Pietà* in 'Burlington Magazine', LXV, 1934, p. 146. – F. Baumgart, *Die Pietà Rondanini*, in 'Prussian Yearbook', LVI, 1935, p. 47 f. – Ch. de Tolnay, *Michelangelo*, V. The Final Period, Princeton, 1960.

X. THE MODELS IN WAX AND CLAY

A. E. Popp, *Die Medicikapelle*, discusses the Edinburgh models. The same author in *Burlington Magazine*, LXIX, 1936, p. 202 f., on the terracotta torso in the British Museum. – F. Burger, *Studien zu Michelangelo*, 1907, p. 40 f. and J. Meier-Graefe, *Michelangelo: Die Terrakotten aus der Sammlung Hähnel*, 1924, discuss the Dresden models. – On the pieces in the British Museum, see Sir Charles Holmes, *Burlington Magazine*, XI, 1907, p. 189. – The best information on the models in the Victoria & Albert Museum is given by Sir Eric Maclagan in the 1932 catalogue, p. 127 f.; also in *Burlington Magazine*, XLIV, 1924, p. 4 f.; a few particulars in Brinckmann, *Barock-Bozzetti*. – Several terracotta models are catalogued in Cornelius von Fabriczy's *Kritisches Verzeichnis toskanischer Holz- und Tonstatuen bis zum Beginn des Cinquecento* in 'Prussian Yearbook', 1909, Beiheft, pp. 38–46. – The two terracotta models in the Pietri collection are discussed by Odoardo H. Giglioli, *Due Bozzetti inediti di Michelangelo*, Florence; and *Documenti di due bozzetti inedite*, Lugano, 1951 (with contributions by L. Planiscig, E. Sandberg-Vavalà, a.o.). – The terrasecca sketch for a battle group ('Hercules and Cacus') in the Casa Buonarroti is discussed by J. Wilde in 'Dedalo', VIII, 1928, p. 653 f. and in 'Vienna Yearbook', 1928, p. 199 f. – H. Thode, *Michelangelo: Kritische Untersuchungen über seine Werke*, III (Vol. VI of the whole work), Berlin, 1913, pp. 265–286, gives an (incomplete) catalogue of all the models attributed to Michelangelo. – L. Goldscheider, *Michelangelo's Bozzetti for Statues in the Medici Chapel*, London, 1957, and *A Survey of Michelangelo's Models in Wax and Clay*, London, 1962.

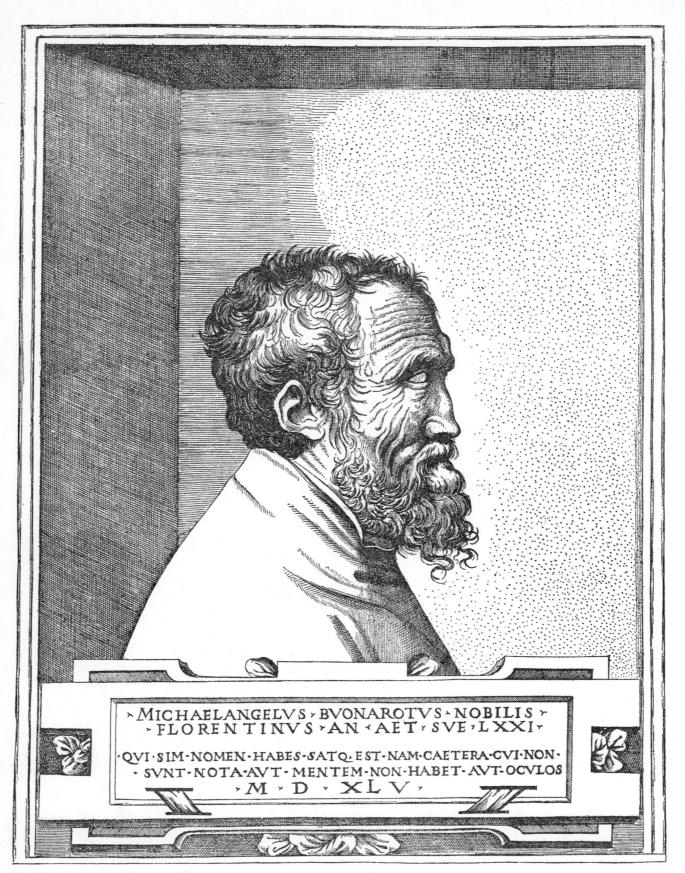

MICHAELANGELVS · BVONAROTVS · NOBILIS ·
· FLORENTINVS · AN · AET · SVE · LXXI ·

· QVI · SIM · NOMEN · HABES · SATQ · EST · NAM · CAETERA · CVI · NON ·
· SVNT · NOTA · AVT · MENTEM · NON · HABET · AVT · OCVLOS ·
M · D · XLV ·

Engraving, attributed to Giulio Bonasone, 1545.

THE PLATES

1. MADONNA OF THE STAIRS. About 1491. Florence, Casa Buonarroti

2. BATTLE OF THE CENTAURS. About 1492. Florence, Casa Buonarroti

3. BATTLE OF THE CENTAURS. Detail of Plate 2

4-5. SAINT PROCULUS AND SAINT PETRONIUS. 1494-1495. Bologna, San Domenico

6. ANGEL WITH CANDLESTICK. 1494–1495. Bologna, San Domenico

7. BACCHUS. 1496–1497. Florence,
Museo Nazionale del Bargello

8. SATYR. Detail of Plate 7

9. BACCHUS. Front view (see Plate 7)

10. HEAD OF BACCHUS. Detail of Plate 9

11. HEAD ON THE LION'S PELT. Detail of Plate 8

12. SATYR EATING GRAPES. Detail of Plate 7

13. PIETÀ. 1498–1499. Rome, St. Peter's

14. HEAD OF THE MADONNA. Detail of Plate 13

15. HEAD OF CHRIST. Detail of Plate 13

16. HEAD OF THE MADONNA. Detail of Plate 13

17. THE LEFT HAND OF CHRIST. Detail of Plate 13

18. THE LEGS OF CHRIST. Detail of Plate 13

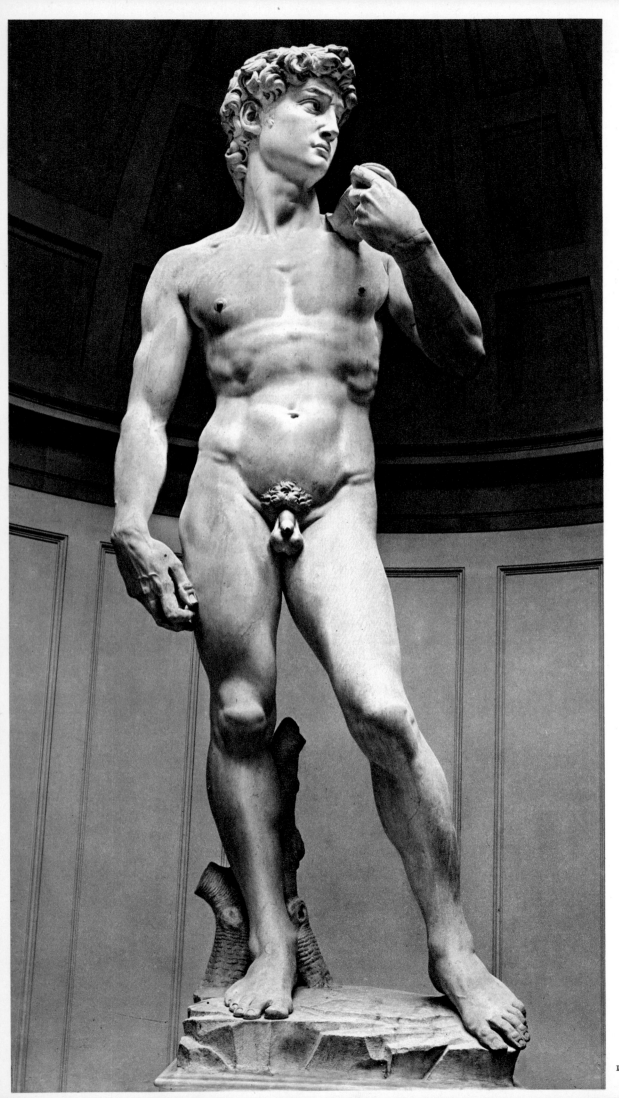

19. DAVID. 1501–1504.
Florence, Accademia

20. HEAD OF DAVID. Detail of Plate 19

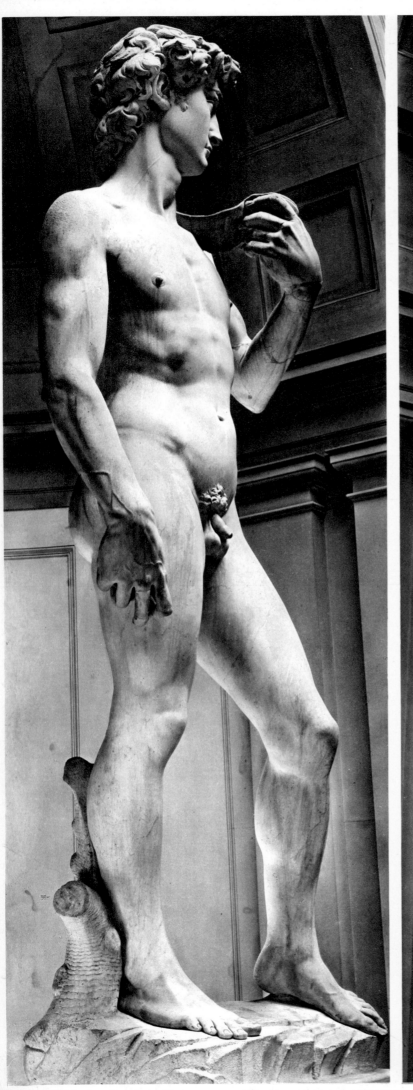
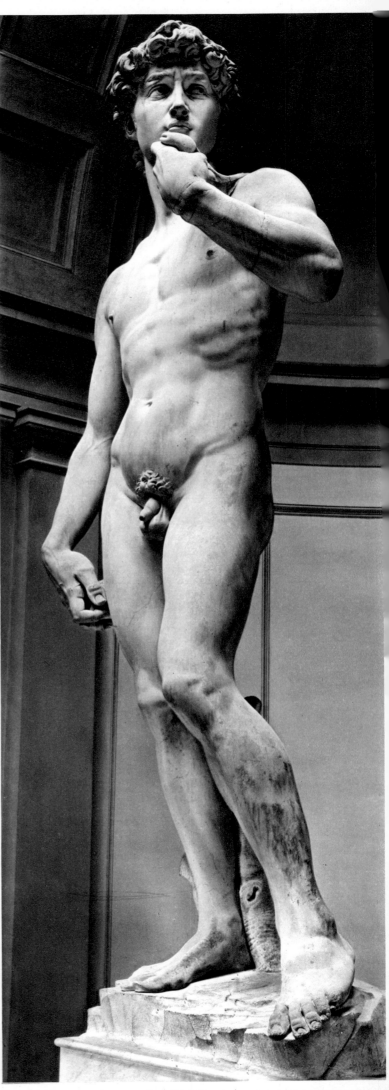

21-23. DAVID. 1501-1504.
Florence, Accademia

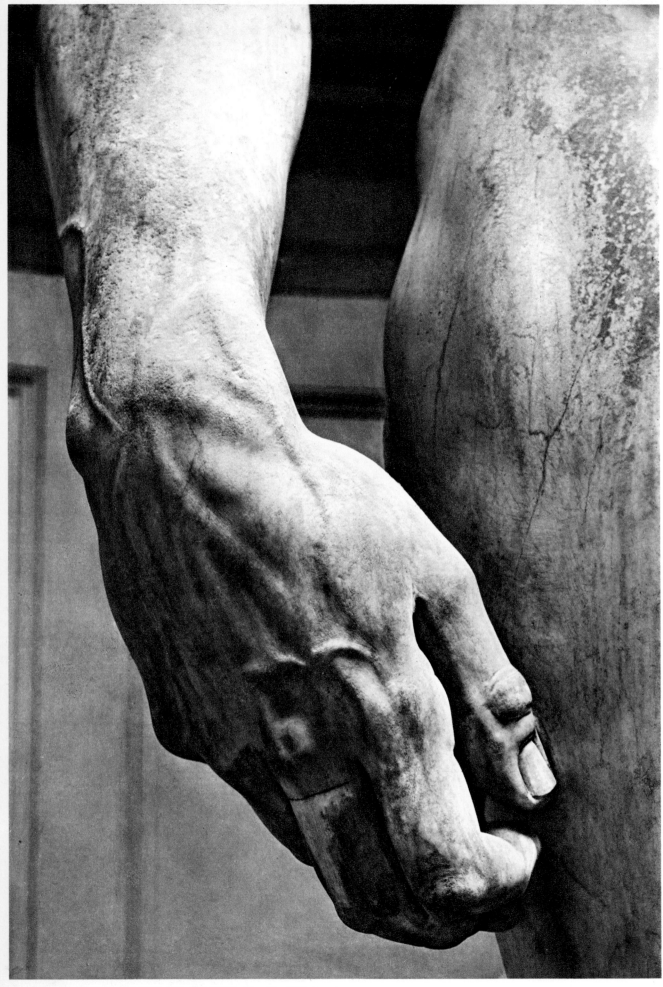

24. THE RIGHT HAND OF DAVID. Detail of Plate 19

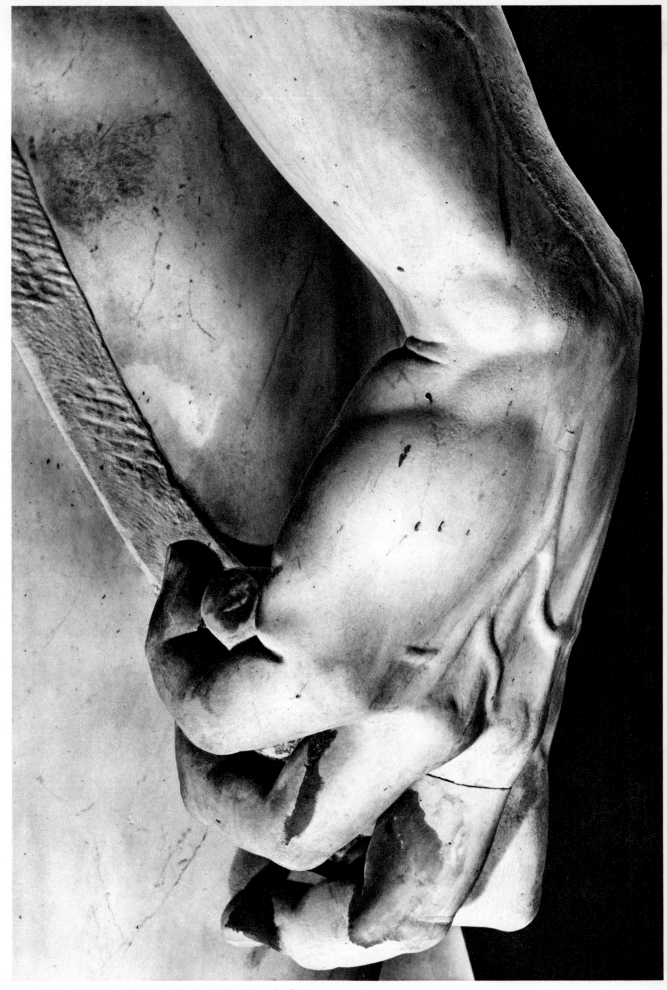

25. THE RIGHT HAND OF DAVID. Detail of Plate 19

26. HEAD OF DAVID. Detail of Plate 22

27. HEAD OF SAINT PAUL. Detail of Plate 33

28-31. FOUR STATUES OF THE PICCOLOMINI ALTAR IN THE SIENA CATHEDRAL. 1501–1504.
Saint Francis—Saint Peter—Gregory the Great—Pope Pius I

32-33. SAINT PAUL. Piccolomini Altar, Siena Cathedral. 1501-1504

34. THE MOUSCRON MADONNA. About 1504. Bruges, Notre-Dame

35. THE INFANT JESUS. Detail of Plate 34

36–39. FOUR VIEWS OF THE MADONNA OF BRUGES (cf. Plate 34)

40. HEAD OF THE MADONNA OF BRUGES. Detail of Plate 37

41. HEAD OF THE MADONNA OF BRUGES. Detail of Plate 34

42. HEAD OF THE INFANT JESUS. Detail of Plate 34

43. MADONNA TADDEI. About 1504. London, Royal Academy

44. MADONNA DONI. About 1504. Florence, Uffizi

45. MADONNA PITTI. About 1505. Florence, Museo Nazionale del Bargello

46. HEAD OF THE INFANT JESUS. Detail of Plate 45

47. SAINT MATTHEW. About 1505–1506 (?).
Florence, Accademia

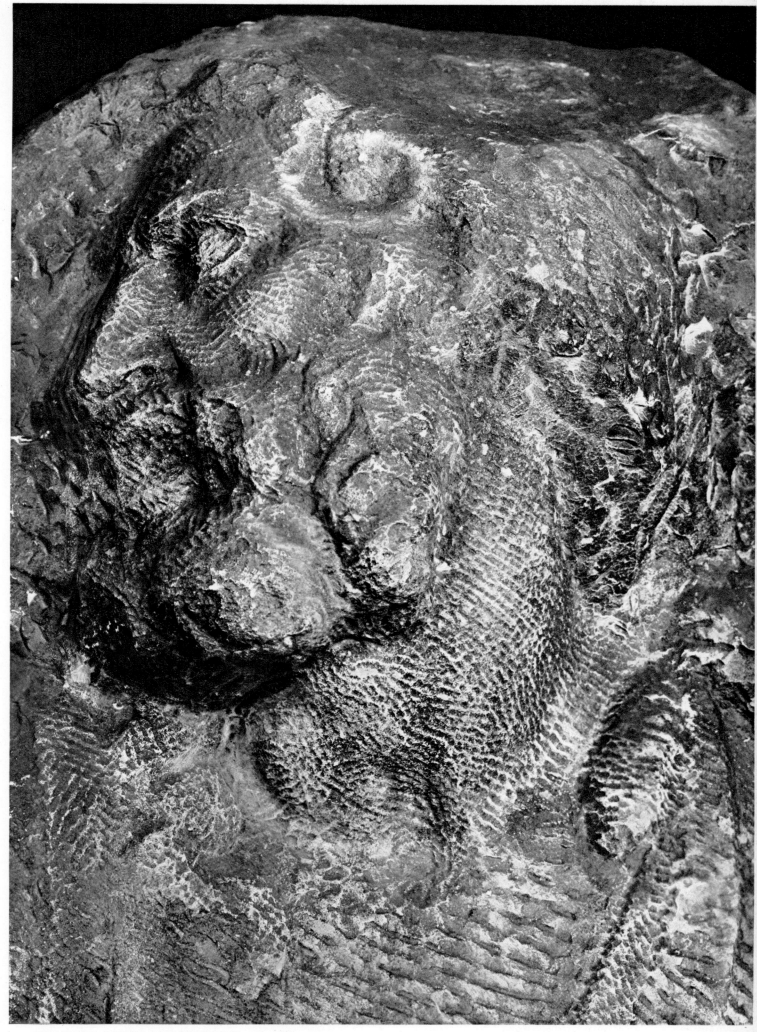

48. HEAD OF SAINT MATTHEW. Detail of Plate 47

49. INTERIOR OF THE SISTINE CHAPEL. Vatican Palace, Rome

51. GOD DIVIDING THE LIGHT FROM THE DARKNESS. 1511. Section of the Sistine Chapel Ceiling

52. CREATION OF SUN AND MOON, AND CREATION OF THE PLANTS. 1511. Section of the Sistine Chapel Ceiling

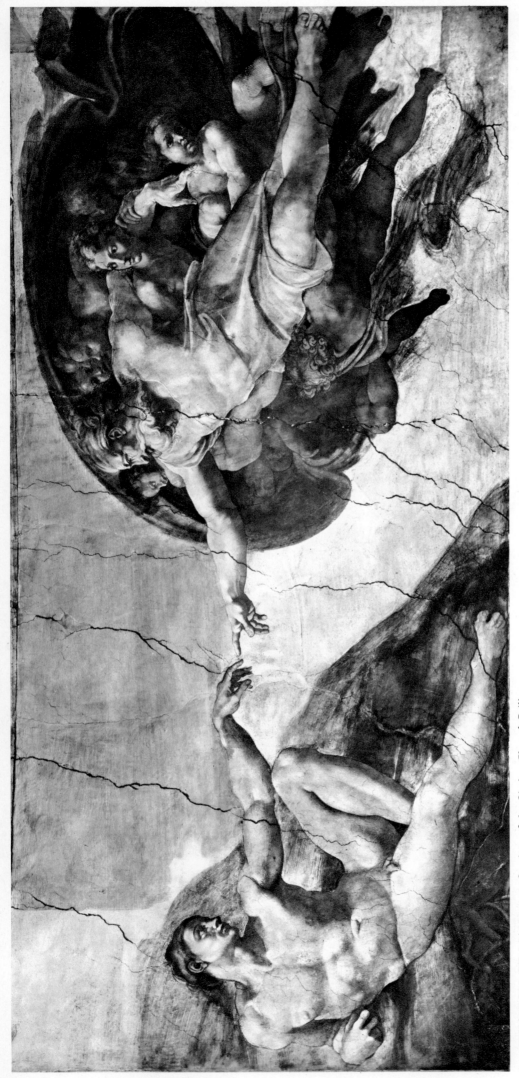

54. CREATION OF MAN. 1511. Section of the Sistine Chapel Ceiling

56. THE FALL OF MAN AND THE EXPULSION FROM THE GARDEN OF EDEN. 1509–1510. Section of the Sistine Chapel Ceiling

58. THE GREAT FLOOD. 1508–1509. Section of the Sistine Chapel Ceiling

59. THE DRUNKENNESS OF NOAH. 1508–1509. Section of the Sistine Chapel Ceiling

60. JEHOVAH. Detail of Plate 54

61. ADAM. Detail of Plate 54

62. HEAD OF ADAM. Detail of Plate 54

63. IMAGE OF EVE. Detail of Plate 54

64. HEAD AND RIGHT ARM OF JEHOVAH. Detail of Plate 53

65. ADAM AND EVE. Detail of Plate 56

66–67. THE MIRACULOUS SALVATIONS OF ISRAEL: David's Victory over Goliath—Judith and Holofernes. 1509.
Corner-spandrels, Sistine Chapel Ceiling

68–69. THE MIRACULOUS SALVATIONS OF ISRAEL: The Brazen Serpent—Esther and Haman. 1511.
Corner-spandrels, Sistine Chapel Ceiling

70. THE BRAZEN SERPENT. Detail of Plate 68

71. HAMAN CRUCIFIED. Detail of Plate 69

72. NUDE YOUTH. 1508–1509. Sistine Chapel Ceiling

73. NUDE YOUTH. 1508–1509. Sistine Chapel Ceiling

74-91. NUDE YOUTHS. 1508-1510. Sistine Chapel Ceiling

92. **CORNER DECORATION** above the Brazen Serpent spandrel: Bronze-coloured nude and grey putti. 1511. Sistine Chapel Ceiling

93-94. THE BRONZE-COLOURED MEDALLIONS BETWEEN THE IGNUDI. 1510-1512. Sistine Chapel Ceiling.
(I) The Death of Uriah

95–100. THE BRONZE-COLOURED MEDALLIONS BETWEEN THE IGNUDI. 1510–1512. Sistine Chapel Ceiling.
(II) The Destruction of the Statue of Baal—(III) King David before Nathan—(IV) The Ascension of Elijah—
(V) The Death of Absalom—(VI) The Sacrifice of Isaac—(VII) Abner being killed by Joab

101-102. THE BRONZE-COLOURED MEDALLIONS BETWEEN THE IGNUDI. 1510-1512. Sistine Chapel Ceiling.
(VIII) The Death of Joram—(IX) The Destruction of the Worshippers of Baal

103–104. THE ANCESTORS OF CHRIST: Salmon, Roboam. 1511–1512. Spandrels of the Sistine Chapel Ceiling

105–106. THE ANCESTORS OF CHRIST: Ozias, Zorobabel. 1511–1512. Spandrels of the Sistine Chapel Ceiling

107-108. THE ANCESTORS OF CHRIST: Josias, Ezechias. 1511-1512. Spandrels of the Sistine Chapel Ceiling

109–110. THE ANCESTORS OF CHRIST: Asa, Jesse. 1511–1512. Spandrels of the Sistine Chapel Ceiling

111. THE ANCESTORS OF CHRIST. 1511–1512. A window in the Sistine Chapel, the lunette painted by Michelangelo

112-123. THE ANCESTORS OF CHRIST. 1511-1512. Lunettes in the Sistine Chapel

124. THE ANCESTORS OF CHRIST. 1511–1512. A window in the Sistine Chapel, the lunette painted by Michelangelo

125. "ABIAS". Detail of Plate 113

126. "ABIAS". Detail of Plate 113

127. THE ERYTHRAEAN SIBYL. 1509. Sistine Chapel Ceiling

128. THE DELPHIC SIBYL. 1509. Sistine Chapel Ceiling

129. THE LIBYAN SIBYL. 1511. Sistine Chapel Ceiling

130. HEAD OF THE LIBYAN SIBYL. Detail of Plate 129

131. THE CUMAEAN SIBYL. 1510. Sistine Chapel Ceiling

132. THE CUMAEAN SIBYL. Sistine Chapel Ceiling

133. THE PERSIAN SIBYL. Sistine Chapel Ceiling

134. THE PERSIAN SIBYL. 1511. Sistine Chapel Ceiling

135. JOËL. 1509. Sistine Chapel Ceiling

136. EZEKIEL. 1509–1510. Sistine Chapel Ceiling

137. JONAH. 1511. Sistine Chapel Ceiling

138. DANIEL. 1511. Sistine Chapel Ceiling

139. JEREMIAH. 1511. Sistine Chapel Ceiling

140. HEAD OF JEREMIAH. Detail of Plate 139

141. ZECHARIAH. 1509. Sistine Chapel Ceiling

142. ZECHARIAH. Sistine Chapel Ceiling

143. ISAIAH. Sistine Chapel Ceiling

144. ISAIAH. 1509. Sistine Chapel Ceiling

145. MOSES. 1513–1516. Rome, San Pietro in Vincoli (cf. Plate 238)

146. HEAD OF MOSES. Detail of Plate 145

147. THE RIGHT HAND OF MOSES. Detail of Plate 145

148. THE LEFT HAND OF MOSES. Detail of Plate 145

149-150. THE HEROIC CAPTIVE. 1514-1516. Paris, Louvre

151. HEAD OF THE HEROIC CAPTIVE. Detail of Plate 150

152-153. THE DYING CAPTIVE. 1514-1516. Paris, Louvre

154. HEAD OF THE DYING CAPTIVE. Detail of Plate 153

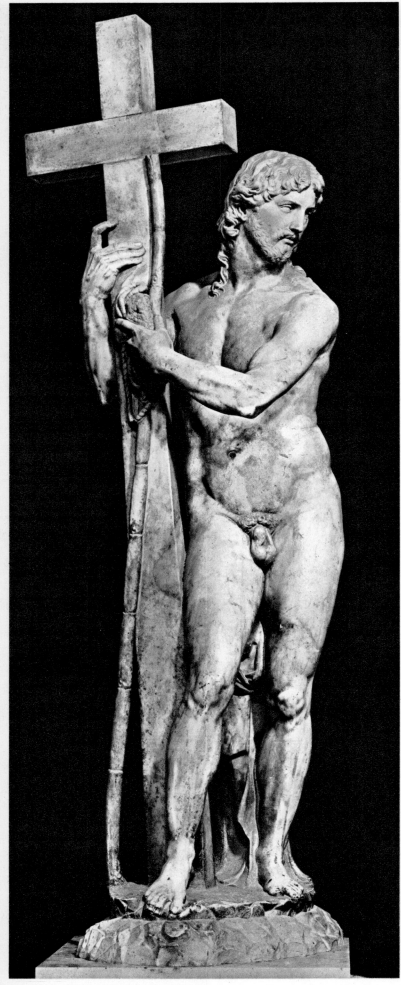

155-156. THE RISEN CHRIST. 1519-1520. Rome, Santa Maria sopra Minerva

157. HEAD OF CHRIST. Detail of Plate 156

158. MARBLE FRONT OF A SMALL CHAPEL, CASTEL SANT'ANGELO, ROME. About 1513–1516

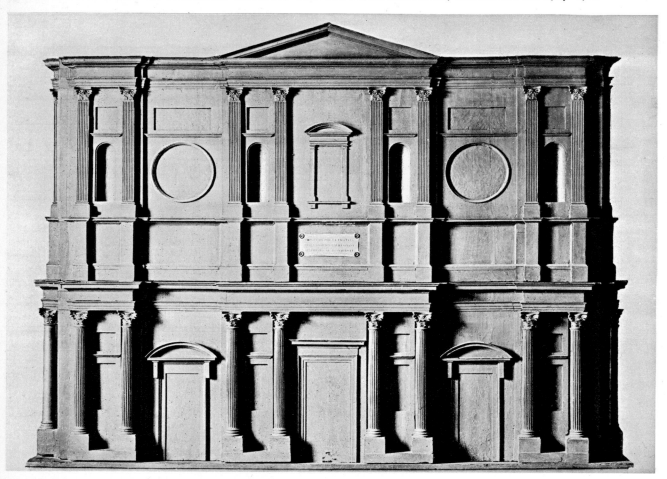

159. WOODEN MODEL FOR THE FAÇADE OF SAN LORENZO. 1518. Florence, Casa Buonarroti

160. WINDOW OF THE MEDICI PALACE, FLORENCE. About 1517–1520

161. ROW OF WINDOWS ON THE OUTSIDE OF THE BIBLIOTECA LAURENZIANA, FLORENCE. About 1524

162. READING ROOM IN THE BIBLIOTECA LAURENZIANA, FLORENCE. About 1524–1534. View without desks and tables. (cf. Appendix Plates VIII–IX)

163. THE VESTIBULE OF THE BIBLIOTECA LAURENZIANA, FLORENCE. About 1524–1526

164-165. DOOR IN THE VESTIBULE AND DOOR IN THE READING ROOM OF THE BIBLIOTECA LAURENZIANA.

166. STAIRCASE LEADING TO THE READING ROOM OF THE BIBLIOTECA LAURENZIANA. About 1524-1526. Completed 1559 by Ammanati and Vasari

167. VESTIBULE OF THE BIBLIOTECA LAURENZIANA, FLORENCE. About 1524–1526

168. THE "PERGAMO" OF SAN LORENZO, FLORENCE. 1526–1532

169–170. THE MEDICI CHAPEL. Florence, San Lorenzo, Sagrestia Nuova. 1520–1534

171. TOMB OF LORENZO
DE' MEDICI

172. TOMB OF GIULIANO
DE' MEDICI

173. LORENZO DE' MEDICI, DUKE OF URBINO. Detail of Plate 171. Florence, Medici Chapel

174. GIULIANO DE' MEDICI, DUKE OF NEMOURS. Detail of Plate 172. Florence, Medici Chapel

175. BACK VIEW OF LORENZO DE' MEDICI (cf. Plate 173)

176. BACK VIEW OF GIULIANO DE' MEDICI (cf. Plate 174)

177. HEAD OF GIULIANO DE' MEDICI. Detail of Plate 174

178. HEAD OF LORENZO DE' MEDICI. Detail of Plate 173

179. CREPUSCOLO (Evening). Detail of Plate 171

180. AURORA (Dawn). Detail of Plate 171

181. CREPUSCOLO. Detail of Plate 179

182. AURORA. Detail of Plate 180

183. NOTTE (Night). Detail of Plate 172

184. GIORNO (Day). Detail of Plate 172

185. GIORNO. Detail of Plate 184

186. THE OWL OF LA NOTTE. Detail of Plate 183

187. NOTTE. Detail of Plate 183

188. MASK OF LA NOTTE. Detail of Plate 183

189. THE LEFT HAND OF GIORNO. Detail of Plate 185

190. MONEY BOX WITH BAT'S HEAD, UNDER THE LEFT ELBOW OF LORENZO DE' MEDICI. Detail of Plate 173

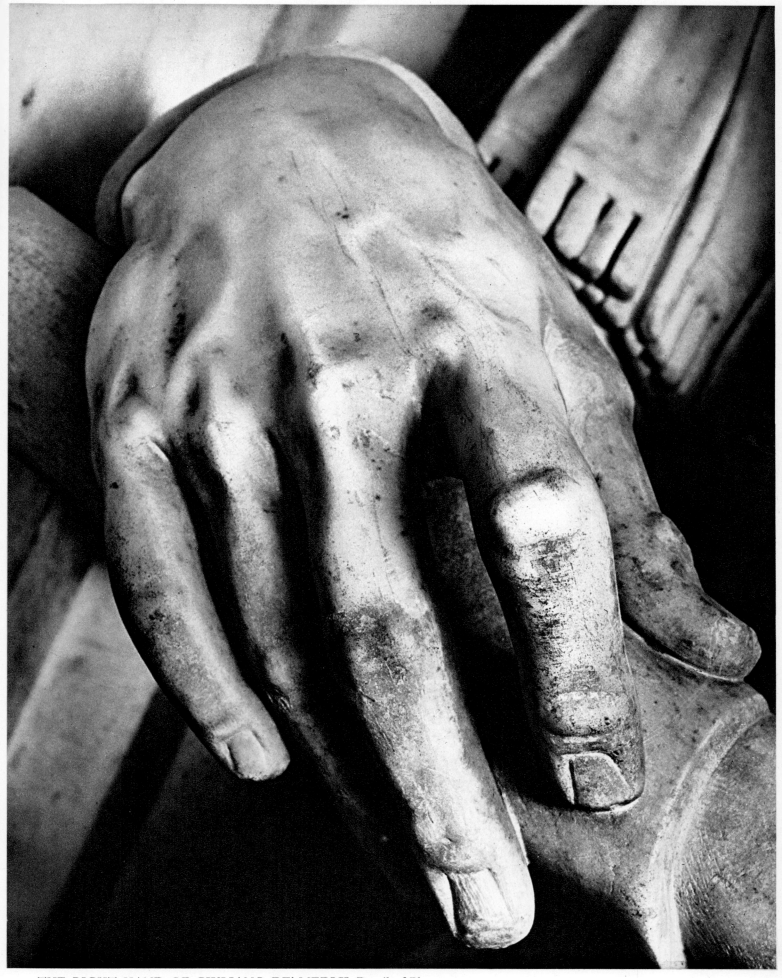

191. THE RIGHT HAND OF GIULIANO DE' MEDICI. Detail of Plate 174

192. ORNAMENTS ON THE SIDE OF THE SARCOPHAGUS OF GIULIANO. Marble relief. Detail of Plate 170

193. FRIEZE OF MASKS BEHIND "NOTTE". Marble relief. Detail of Plate 183

194–195. MASKS. Ornaments on the front and back of the cuirass of Giuliano de' Medici. Details of Plates 174 and 176

196. BACK VIEW OF "GIORNO" (cf. Plate 184)

197. BACK VIEW OF "AURORA" (cf. Plate 180)

198. BACK VIEW OF "NOTTE" (cf. Plate 183)

199. BACK VIEW OF "CREPUSCOLO" (cf. Plate 179)

200. THE MEDICI MADONNA. 1524–1534. Detail of Plate 169. Florence, Medici Chapel

201. BACK VIEW OF THE MEDICI MADONNA

202. SIDE VIEW OF THE MEDICI MADONNA

203. HEAD OF THE MEDICI MADONNA

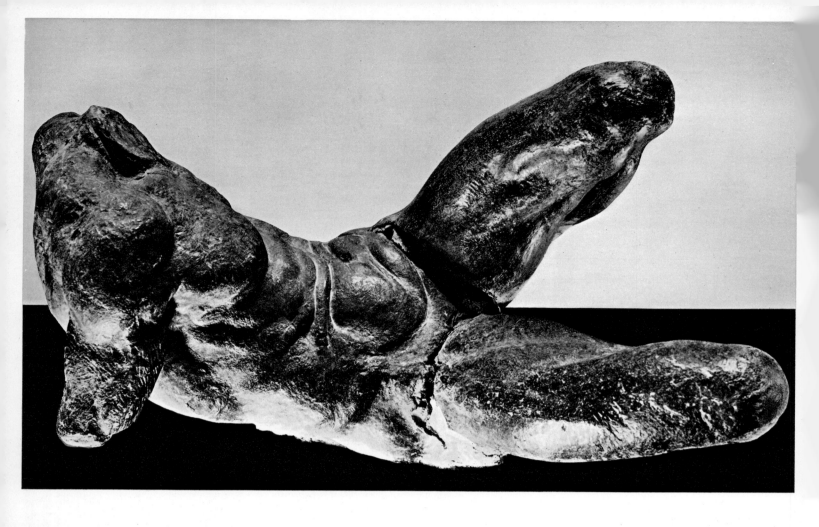

204–205. CLAY MODEL FOR A RIVER GOD. About 1525. Florence, Accademia

206. CLAY MODEL FOR A VICTORY GROUP. About 1525–1528. Florence, Casa Buonarroti

207–208. VICTORY. 1525–1530. Florence, Palazzo Vecchio

209. HEAD OF THE VICTOR. Detail of Plate 208

210–211. APOLLO. About 1530. Florence, Museo Nazionale del Bargello

212. APOLLO. About 1530. Florence, Museo Nazionale del Bargello

213. CROUCHING BOY. About 1530. Leningrad, Hermitage

214. CROUCHING BOY. About 1530. Leningrad, Hermitage

215. CROUCHING BOY. About 1530. Leningrad, Hermitage

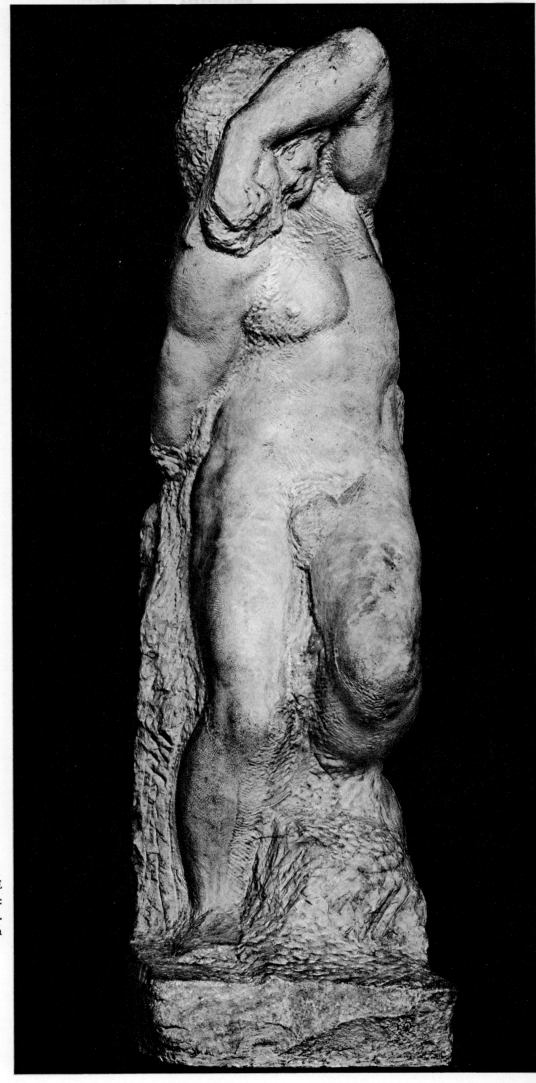

216. FIRST CAPTIVE
FROM THE BOBOLI GARDENS:
"THE YOUNG GIANT".
About 1530–1533. Florence, Accademia

217-218. FIRST CAPTIVE FROM THE BOBOLI GARDENS: "THE YOUNG GIANT". 1530-1533. Florence, Accademia

219–220. SECOND CAPTIVE FROM THE BOBOLI GARDENS: "THE SO-CALLED ATLAS". 1530–1533. Florence, Accademia

221–222. THIRD CAPTIVE FROM THE BOBOLI GARDENS: "THE BEARDED GIANT". 1530–1533. Florence, Accademia

223. HEAD OF THE BEARDED GIANT. Detail of Plate 221

224–225. FOURTH CAPTIVE FROM THE BOBOLI GARDENS: "THE AWAKENING GIANT". 1530–1533. Florence, Accademia

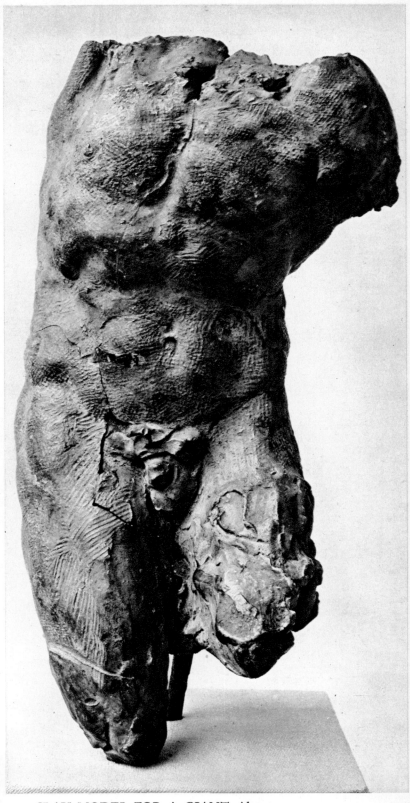

226. CLAY MODEL FOR A GIANT. About 1530.
Florence, Casa Buonarroti

227. CLAY MODEL FOR A GIANT. About 1530.
London, British Museum

228. THE LAST JUDGEMENT. 1536–1541. Rome, Sistine Chapel

229. CHRIST AS JUDGE AND THE HOLY VIRGIN. Detail of Plate 228

230. FALL OF THE DAMNED. Detail of Plate 228

231. ANGELS SOUNDING THE TRUMPETS OF DOOM. Detail of Plate 228

232. MINOS, PRINCE OF HELL (Portrait of the Master of Ceremonies, Biagio da Cesena). Detail of Plate 228

233. SAINT BARTHOLOMEW (Pietro Aretino holding the skin of Michelangelo). Detail of Plate 228

234. MICHELANGELO'S SELF-PORTRAIT. Detail of Plate 233

235. ASCENDING FIGURE. Detail of Plate 228

236. A DEVIL. Detail of Plate 228

237. DEATH. Detail of Plate 228

238. THE TOMB OF POPE JULIUS II. 1505–1545. (By Michelangelo: Moses, Rachel and Leah. By Montelupo: Madonna, Prophet and Sibyl. By Boscoli: The figure of the Pope.) Rome, San Pietro in Vincoli

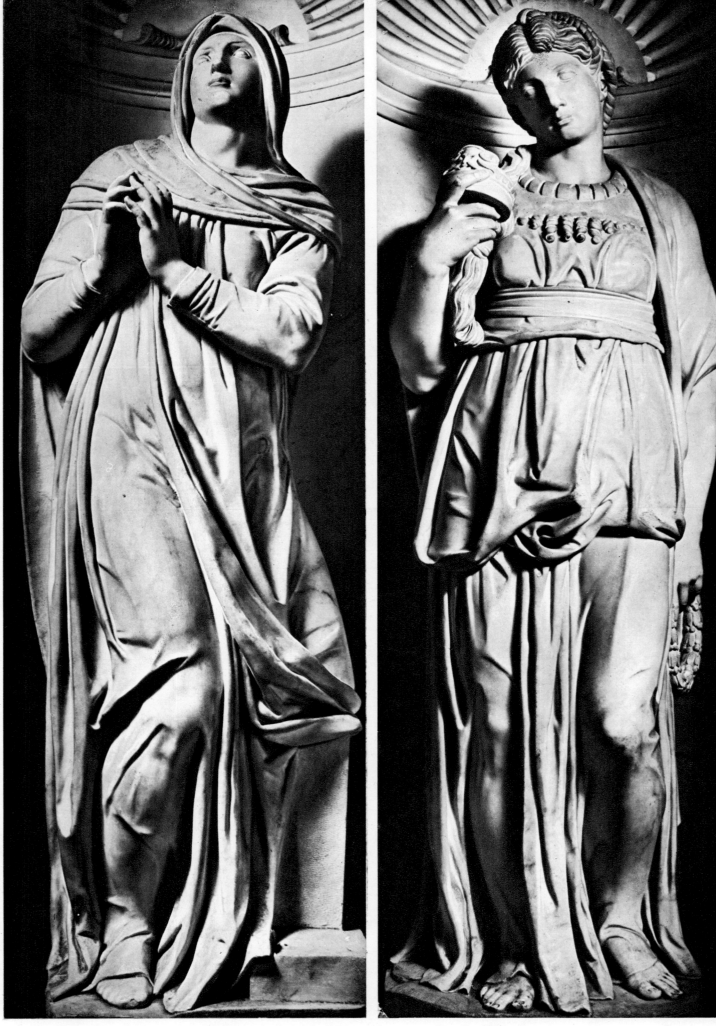

239-240. RACHEL AND LEAH: Vita contemplativa and Vita activa. 1542. Detail of Plate 238

241. BRUTUS. About 1542. Florence, Museo Nazionale del Bargello

242. BRUTUS. Detail of Plate 241

243. THE CONVERSION OF SAINT PAUL. Fresco, 1542–1545. Vatican, Cappella Paolina

244. THE CRUCIFIXION OF SAINT PETER. Fresco, 1546–1550. Vatican, Cappella Paolina

245. THE CONVERSION OF SAINT PAUL. Detail of Plate 243

246. LANDSCAPE FROM "THE CONVERSION OF SAINT PAUL". Detail of Plate 243

247. THE CONVERSION OF SAINT PAUL. Detail of Plate 243

248. THE CRUCIFIXION OF SAINT PETER. Detail of Plate 244

249. THE CRUCIFIXION OF SAINT PETER. Detail of Plate 244

250. THE CONVERSION OF SAINT PAUL. Detail of Plate 243

251. THE CRUCIFIXION OF SAINT PETER. Detail of Plate 244

252. MICHELANGELO'S PLAN FOR THE PIAZZA OF THE CAPITOL IN ROME. 1546.
Etching by Etienne du Pérac (1569)

253. THE OUTSIDE STEPS OF THE PALAZZO SENATORIO. Designed by Michelangelo, 1544–1552

254. PALAZZO DEI CONSERVATORI, ROME. Planned by Michelangelo in 1546, finished after his death

255. TWO VIEWS OF THE BASE FOR THE MARCUS AURELIUS STATUE. (Michelangelo designed this base for the antique equestrian statue about 1539)

256. PALAZZO FARNESE, ROME. Begun by Antonio da Sangallo the Younger, and continued after his death (1546) by Michelangelo, who designed the large window over the door, the windows of the upper storey and the cornice

257. THE COURTYARD OF THE PALAZZO FARNESE, from designs by Antonio da Sangallo the Younger. The upper storey designed by Michelangelo, about 1547–1550

258. CORNICE OF THE PALAZZO FARNESE. Designed by Michelangelo, 1547

259. PALAZZO FARNESE. The large coat-of-arms and the centre window designed by Michelangelo, about 1550

260. PALAZZO FARNESE. Window in the upper storey of the courtyard. About 1550

261. NICCHIONE DEL BELVEDERE. (The stairway designed 1550–1551)

262. PIETÀ. About 1548–1556. Florence, Duomo

263. MICHELANGELO'S SELF-PORTRAIT AT THE AGE OF ABOUT EIGHTY. Detail of Plate 262

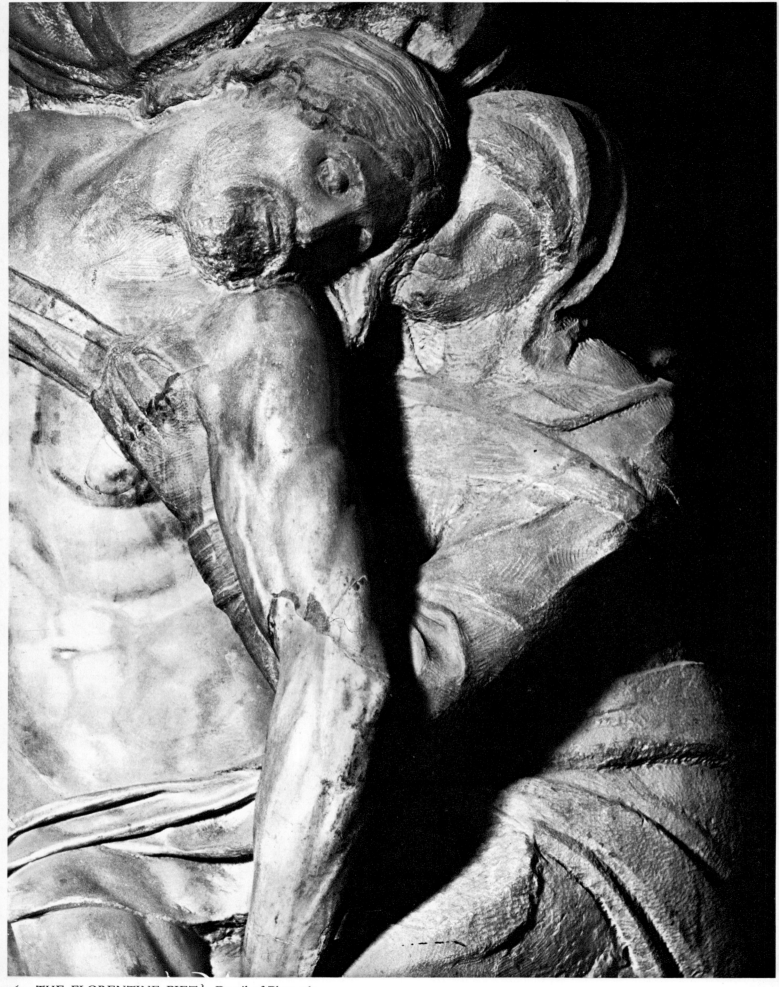

264. THE FLORENTINE PIETÀ. Detail of Plate 262

265. THE RONDANINI PIETÀ. 1556–1564. Detail of Plate 267

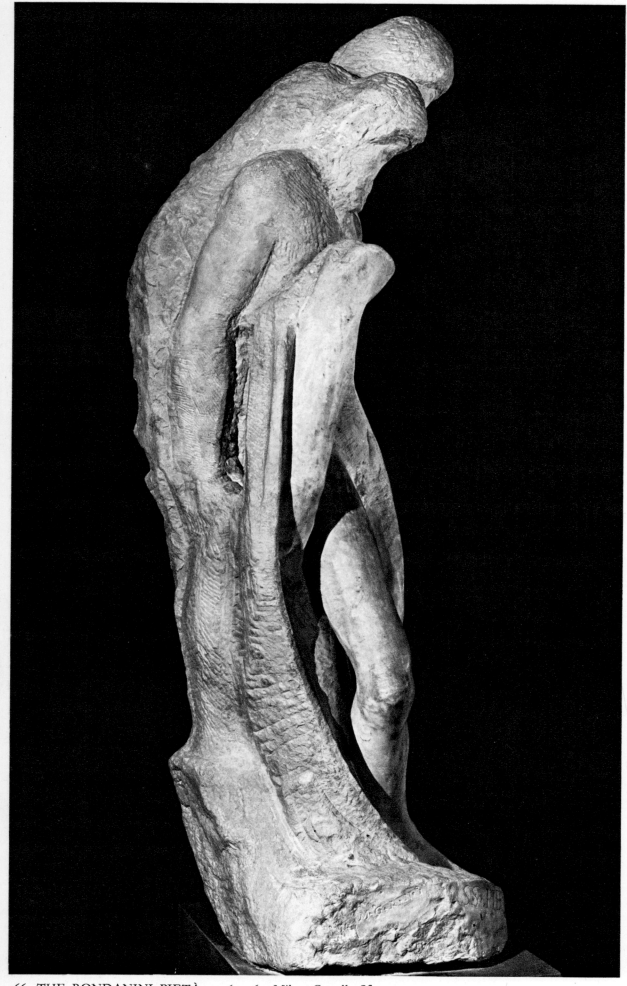

266. THE RONDANINI PIETÀ. 1556-1564. Milan, Castello Sforzesco

267. THE RONDANINI PIETÀ. 1556–1564. Milan, Castello Sforzesco

268. THE PALESTRINA PIETÀ. By Michelangelo and a follower. About 1556. Florence, Accademia

269. HEAD OF CHRIST. Detail of Plate 268

270. PORTA PIA, ROME. After Michelangelo's design, 1561–1564.
(The coat-of-arms of Pius IV by Jacomo del Duca, 1562; the centre top-piece added in 1853)

271. PORTA PIA, ROME. Detail of Plate 270

272. WOODEN MODEL FOR THE CUPOLA OF ST. PETER'S. 1558–1561. Rome, Museo Petriano (cf. Plate XIX)
(The hemispherical dome, planned by Michelangelo, was altered and elevated by Giacomo della Porta)

273. CUPOLA OF ST. PETER'S, ROME. (Planned by Michelangelo, built after the master's death by Giacomo della Porta and other architects)

274–275. ST. PETER'S, ROME. 1546–1564

276. ST. PETER'S, ROME. Detail of the southern apse

277. ST. PETER'S, ROME. One of the niches

278. ST. PETER'S, ROME. One of the capitals

279. THE PAPAL INSIGNIA. Detail of Plate 276

APPENDIX

MODELS: MICHELANGELO'S SKETCHES
IN WAX AND CLAY

LOST WORKS

ATTRIBUTIONS

APPENDIX OF PLATES

MODELS IN WAX AND CLAY

Only two models appear at present to be *generally* accepted as Michelangelo's own work, both of the same period and both in clay: the large *River God* (Plate 204), and the *Victory Group* (Plate 206). A. Gottschewski was the first to recognize the River God as an original model by Michelangelo.[1] Hildebrand, Fabriczy, Schottmüller, Wölfflin and Tolnay agreed with him, but neither Frey, nor Popp, who attributed this model to Ammanati. J. Wilde has proved[2] that it is now in an incorrect position and quoted old reproductions showing how it was originally placed; in the present volume two hitherto unknown examples are added (Plate III–e, f).

The small model of a *Victory Group* (Plate 206) was accepted as genuine[3] by Bode, Fabriczy, Thode, Grünwald, Brinckmann, Wilde, Panofsky and Tolnay. This attribution went uncontradicted and we can therefore take the *Victory Group* as a starting point for the consideration of other models.

First I shall count up those models which, though not generally accepted, are of very high quality and have the opinions of great critics in their favour. (1) Wax sketch for the *Young Giant* (Plate 218) in the Victoria and Albert Museum (Plate I–b). This very fine model was accepted by Berenson (*Italian Pictures*, 1932, p. 363); also by Thode, Fabriczy, Brinckmann, and by Laux (1943). (2) Clay sketch of a *Victoria*, Casa Buonarroti (Plate I–a). Accepted by Thode, Bode, Fabriczy and Wilde. Knapp (*Michelangelo*, Munich, 1923, p. 48) compares it rightly to the *Victory Group* (Plate 206); it is of (relatively) the same size and the same material, and the technique is identical. (3) Wax sketch for a *Giant* (Plate I–e), accepted by Laux and others. Three torsos, two in the Casa Buonarroti and the other in the British Museum, formerly also in the Casa Buonarroti (Plate I–f, 226, 227), are of equal quality as the sketch for a *Giant* and I can therefore see no reason why they should be rejected.

The two wax sketches of *Nude Youths* (Plate I–c, d) offer a more complicated problem. Both statuettes are modelled in wax (see note 3), but they are not of identical technique. Neither are they connected with the marble or the bronze David, as was thought before, and Fabriczy has already suggested that the one model (Plate I–d) should be regarded as possibly a sketch for a figure of the Julius monument; the same was suggested by Thode concerning the other model (Plate I–c). However, I feel doubtful about Plate I–c, and am inclined to consider only Plate I–d an original on the assumption that the surface of the wax has suffered and has been restored. All these models have been connected with the Julius monument, while the group below consists of models for the Medici tombs. Here we have only three statuettes which are, with some authority, ascribed to the master. One of them is a slight wax sketch for *Crepuscolo* (Plate III–d), published as authentic by Sir Charles Holmes.[4] This spirited little sketch was formerly in the Casa Buonarroti. From the Casa Piccolomini in Siena came two fine large terracotta models to the collection of Dr. Alejandro Pietri in Caracas, Venezuela (Plate V). Leo Planiscig, Evelyn Sandberg-Vavalà and Odoardo Giglioli have declared them to be genuine works of Michelangelo. I believe in the authenticity of these two models. They are in baked clay, and their hard surface is better preserved than that of the other models which are in air-dried clay. The two large models in the Pietri collection make a favourable impression, particularly as the position of the limbs of the terracotta figures is not exactly the same as that of the finished marble statues, and as the models contain richer detail. In fact, old drawings, certainly done from the models and not from the statues, show the same differences.

The study of drawings by artists of the sixteenth and seventeenth centuries reproducing Michelangelo models is indeed instructive. Tintoretto owned a large number of such models, some probably originals, others only copies, and used them for studies. One set of these models was of large size, and of 'gesso', as Vasari tells us (ed. Milanesi, VII, p. 63), whereas others, which we know only from his drawings, were apparently originals.[5] The 'model' of *Giuliano* in Edinburgh is no doubt an imitation inspired by the finished statue (Plate II–d); how Michelangelo's sketch for *Giuliano* looked we learn from a Tintoretto drawing (Plate II–c). His drawing after the *Giorno* (Oxford), on the other hand, is probably after Daniele da Volterra's gesso copy – the face is as coarse and unfinished as that of the statue. There were, however, also other copies after models and also after the marbles in the Medici Chapel available to the draughtsman of that period, and quite a number have come down to us, e.g. the *Four Allegories* by Vincenzo Danti (1573, stucco; now in the Accademia, Perugia, see Plate III–a), or another set by Tribolo (terracotta; one of the figures repr. Plate III–c). Out of this set Vasari owned the *Notte*, but this is now lost. Tribolo's copies are not very large, about one Florentine ell or 2 ft. long, and that is also the usual size of other early copies, some of which have been cast in bronze. The best of these bronze replicas is the Medici Madonna in the Louvre (Plate III–b; Thiers collection No. 65; 16¼ in. high), apparently not a copy after the statue, but cast from the original small model. Thode (VI, 285) mentions a tradition that Michelangelo presented this bronze statuette to the Archbishop of

---

[1] In 'Munich Yearbook', I, 1906, p. 43 f.; and in 'Rivista d'arte', IV, 1906, p. 73 f.
[2] In 'Belvedere,' Vienna, 1927, p. 143.
[3] In this case it can be shown how carelessly critics have on the whole dealt with the models. Knapp (*Michelangelo*, KdK VII, 5th ed., 1924) illustrates this model on p. 166 and calls it 'stucco'; on p. 185 he calls it 'wax' and 'doubtful'. Tolnay (I, fig. 286) calls a wax statuette (our Plate I–d) "terracotta".

[4] Sometimes described as a model for a river god. For references to the literature on this and the following pieces, see Bibliography, section X, p. 25 of this volume.
[5] Detlev Freiherr von Hadeln, *Zeichnungen des Giacomo Tintoretto*, Berlin, 1922. – Tietze, *The Drawings of the Venetian Painters*, New York, 1944, pp. 268–304. – W. Paesler, in 'Munich Yearbook', new series X, 1933. – Tolnay, III, 156, with references to Ridolfi and other old authors.

Florence, Giovanni Salviati, and adds that it remained in the collection of the family until 1830. A bronze of the *Thief on the Cross*, which I believe to have been cast from a wax model by Michelangelo (Plate II–b), can be compared to a related drawing by an imitator of Michelangelo (Plate II–a), almost certainly drawn from such a model.[6]

One could give a long list of lost Michelangelo models. There were, e.g., the clay models he made for the figures of *Cosmas* and *Damian* (Plate IV–c, d), parts of which were owned by Vasari; there was a model of *Hercules and Antaeus* (cf. Plate XXII–g) which Michelangelo gave to

Leone Leoni; there was a model for the left leg of *Giorno* which was in the possession of Alessandro Vittoria at Bologna (1563); there were the wax sketches Michelangelo made in 1517 for the figures on the wooden model for the Lorenzo façade; there was a small wax head, sent to Pietro Aretino in 1536, and a wax model for a bronze horse made a year later for Duke Francesco Maria of Urbino. There is mention of other models, such as two boxes full of them, which Michelangelo gave to Antonio Mini in 1531, or the four models which were stolen in 1529, when Michelangelo's Florentine studio was broken into. All those models are apparently lost, but I suspect that some of the clay models, which Mini took to France, re-appeared in Bologna and were bought by Paul von Praun (c. 1580), owned later by Prof. Haehnel in Dresden, and now in the Le Brooy collection, Montreal.

---

[6] Two other bronzes, wrongly attributed to Michelangelo by A. E. Popp, are not discussed any longer. The one is a life-size bronze Apollo in the Louvre, No. 681 (Popp, *Medici-Kapelle*, 1922, p. 171 f.; also J. Six, in *Gazette des Beaux-Arts*, 1921, p. 166 f.); the other a small torso in an unknown private collection (*Burlington Magazine*, vol. LXIX, November 1936, p. 202 f.).

LOST WORKS OF MICHELANGELO

I. SCULPTURE. The first work of Michelangelo's mentioned by Condivi is the *Head of a Faun*. The artist was fourteen years old when he made it. Attempts have been made to identify as this work a mask in the Museo Nazionale, Florence, but this has since been recognized as the work of a decadent seventeenth-century master. The *Faun* has disappeared, but there is perhaps a reproduction of it in a fresco in Palazzo Pitti (Plate XXII–d). The *Wooden Crucifix*, which Michelangelo made when he was about seventeen for the Prior of Santo Spirito in Florence, has also been lost; Thode believed that he had rediscovered it in a mediocre work there. Likewise lost is the *Statue of Hercules* which passed from the Palazzo Strozzi into the possession of the King of France; nothing has been heard of it since 1713. Michelangelo was seventeen when he made this statue, which was a little larger than the 'Dying Captive' in the Louvre. As regards the *Giovannino*, or youthful St John, which Michelangelo made when he was twenty (formerly in the possession of Botticelli's patron, Lorenzo di Pierfrancesco de' Medici), Bode believed that he had rediscovered it, and Thode, Justi and Frey supported Bode's claim. Wickhoff, Wölfflin, Knapp and Mackowsky rightly rejected it and Grünwald thought that this marble statue (now in the Berlin Museum) is the work of the manneristic Domenico Pieratti, though his grounds for this attribution are not convincing; Wölfflin suggested the Neapolitan artist Girolamo Santacroce, and Carlo Gamba thought of Silvio Cosini, one of Michelangelo's assistants. M. Gomez-Moreno (1931) found a statue in the Salvador chapel at Ubeda which he identified and published as Michelangelo's rediscovered Giovannino; Valentiner (1938) proclaimed however that an equally indifferent statue in the Morgan Library was the Giovannino. It has rightly been suggested that the St John of the Manchester Madonna might be a reproduction of this lost statue (Plate XXII–e). Condivi mentions two *Statues of Cupid* executed by Michelangelo between his return from Bologna and the time when he was working on the Bacchus (i.e.

about 1496). The first version represented a *Sleeping Cupid* and was sold by the Roman dealer Baldassare del Milanese to Cardinal Riario as a genuine antique (cf. Appendix Plate XXII–a). The statue came later into the possession of Cesare Borgia and then into that of Isabella d'Este, Margravine of Mantua. The Anonimo Morelliano mentions a sleeping Cupid in the house of Pietro Bembo at Padua, 'different from the statue belonging to the Duchess Isabella d'Este of Mantua'. Konrad Lange believed that he had rediscovered this early work of Michelangelo's in an indifferent exhibit in the Turin museum. A more likely supposition is that there is a reproduction of this lost work in a painting by Giulio Romano, who worked at the Mantuan court from 1525, and another in a painting by Tintoretto, of whom we know that he collected reproductions of Michelangelo's works (see Plate XXII–b and c; the Borghese Gallery Cupid has been lost, but there is a copy by A. Algardi in the same gallery). In 1631 the *Sleeping Cupid* is known to have passed to the collection of King Charles I of England, but all traces of it have since vanished. The other (lost) *Cupid*, sometimes also described as *Apollo*, a standing, lifesize marble figure, was made for Jacopo Galli. The lifesize *bronze statue of David*, commissioned in 1502 by Pierre de Rohan, was sent to France in 1508 via Leghorn, but nothing has been heard of it for the last three hundred years. Two wax models, one in the Casa Buonarroti (Plate I–c) and another in the Victoria & Albert Museum (Catalogue 1932, plate 89–c), and a bronze statuette in Amsterdam (Plate XXII–k), have been wrongly thought to be connected with the bronze David.[1] The only basis for the reconstruction of Michelangelo's lost *bronze David* would appear to be the drawing in the Louvre (Plate

---

[1] On the model in Florence, see Thode, III, 183; IV, 79; VI, 279; on the London model, Thode, IV, 89, VI, 283; Catalogue of Italian Sculpture in the Victoria & Albert Museum, 1932, p. 131; on the Paris statuette, Courajod, *Gazette archéologique*, X, 185, p. 77 f.; Thode, III, 180 f.; IV, 88; VI, 285; on the Amsterdam statuette, A. Pitt, *Revue d'art ancien et moderne*, 1897, 78 and 455; Thode III, 182; IV, 86 f.

XXII–j). From this drawing it is clear that Michelangelo followed Donatello (plate XXII-h), as was stipulated in the contract, but it is probable that he also borrowed certain features from Verrocchio and Bertoldo. From the end of November 1506 to the end of February 1508 Michelangelo was in Bologna, engaged in casting the over-lifesize *bronze statue of Pope Julius II*, who had just conquered the city. The first casting was a failure, as the bronze emerged from the furnace only as far as the girdle, but on 9 July 1507 the second casting was finished; on 21 February 1508 the statue was erected. It was nearly ten feet high and weighed about seventeen tons. The Pope was shown seated, with St Peter's keys in his left hand and his right raised in benediction. The statue stood above the main portal of San Petronio for only three years and nine months, after which the populace of Bologna rose in defence of its freedom, pulled the statue down and shattered it to pieces. From the fragments Duke Alfonso of Ferrara had a mighty cannon cast, which he ironically christened 'La Giulia'. The portrait head was preserved, as the only relic of this work of Michelangelo's, in the Duke's art gallery, but has since disappeared. The destruction of the Julius statue is the most notable loss which we have to deplore among the sculptures of Michelangelo.

It is impossible to say whether the small statue of *Christ bearing the Cross*, mentioned as 'non finita' in the inventory of Michelangelo's estate[2] dated 19 February 1564, was a design for the statue in Santa Maria sopra Minerva or perhaps a reduced replica. In any case it must have been another version, for in 1564 Daniele da Volterra described it as 'similar to the Christ in the Minerva, yet differing from it'.[3] (Cf. Thode, V, 272.)

II. PAINTING. It is impossible to determine whether Michelangelo's copy after Schongauer's engraving of the *Temptation of St Anthony* was a coloured pen-drawing (Vasari, 1550), a painting on a small wood panel (Condivi, 1553), or merely the over-painting of an original engraving (Max Lehrs, in 'Prussian Yearbook', XII, p. 130 f.; cf. Thode IV, 4). According to Varchi (1564) Michelangelo made a painting of *Ghirlandaio and his assistants at work in Santa Maria Novella* (1489); according to Vasari it was only a drawing. Vasari also mentions a tempera painting of *St Francis receiving the Stigmata*, which a dilettante is said to have executed after a cartoon by Michelangelo and which then hung in the first chapel on the left in the church of San Pietro in Montorio, Rome. This cartoon and the painting have since disappeared (Thode IV, p. 50).

The greatest loss we have suffered is that of the cartoon for the *Battle of Cascina*, which Michelangelo prepared in the winter of 1504–5. This work was executed in competition with Leonardo's 'Battle of Anghiari' and was intended for the left half of a wall of the council chamber in Florence (the other half of the wall was reserved for Leonardo's battle-piece); the execution in fresco was never begun. Fragments of this cartoon were preserved until 1635, and there are numerous copies of parts of it. The oil-painting in grisaille at Holkham Hall (Plate XXIV; 30 × 52 in.) is supposed to be the most comprehensive copy. The tempera painting of *Leda and the Swan*, which Michelangelo painted in 1530, was given by him to his pupil Antonio Mini, who took it with him to France. Mini's friend Benedetto del Bene established a regular 'Leda factory' in Lyons. The picture seems to have been very popular and numerous copies are extant. In London, the National Gallery and the Royal Academy own examples. (Both copies are by Rosso Fiorentino.)

On the wall opposite the 'Last Judgement', that is to say over the entrance to the Sistine Chapel, Michelangelo was to paint a *Fall of the Angels*, and he made several sketches for it. One of his colour-mixers afterwards executed a fresco, which was formerly in the no longer existing church of the Trinità dei Monti in Rome.

The Portal of the Sforza Chapel in Santa Maria Maggiore, Rome, designed by Michelangelo. Detail of an engraving, 1621.

---

[2] This Christ and a small Pietà were left to Michelangelo's servant, Antonio del Franzese. The inventory also mentions an unfinished statue of St Peter, which Thode (I, 487) is inclined to identify with the statue of Julius II for his monument, mentioned in a letter of 1508. (Cf. Jacob Hess, *Burlington Magazine* 1943, 55 f.; Tolnay IV, pp. 15 and 143.)

[3] Varchi, in his 'Funeral Oration for Michelangelo' (*Quellenschriften für Kunstgeschichte*, Vienna, 1874, VI, 119) mentions, in addition to the Minerva Christ (Plate 155), 'another Christ, completely nude, shown turning away, which he gave to the Marchesa di Pescara'.

III. ARCHITECTURE. All the models in clay and wood which Michelangelo made are lost, with the exception of the one for the cupola of St Peter's. To give two examples from the year 1559, there is no trace left of the model for the Church San Giovanni dei Fiorentini in Rome (although we know it quite well from old engravings), or of the model for the staircase of the Biblioteca Laurenziana. (See also Plate 159.)

The Church of Santa Maria degli Angeli alle Terme and the Sforza Chapel in Santa Maria Maggiore in Rome have been altered so much by later architects that they could be counted amongst Michelangelo's lost works.

The work on Santa Maria degli Angeli was started in 1563 and finished three years later. Pope Pius IV (1955–65) had commissioned Michelangelo to transform the best preserved part of the ancient Baths of Diocletian into a church. The *tepidarium* was strengthened and two large doors opened in the shorter side. Michelangelo had the help of Jacomo del Duca (who also assisted him in the work on the Porta Pia). The engraving (Plate XVII–a) shows the east side of the Thermae and the large Renaissance door, designed by Michelangelo as the main entrance to the Basilica. (This door is now walled up.) Plate XVII–b shows the transept of the church in the present state, as it was rebuilt by Clemente Orlandi and Luigi Vanvitelli from 1700 to 1749. Where the High Altar is now there was, in Michelangelo's time, the main entrance (see illustration). About other alterations see Thode V, 184. The Sforza Chapel (Plate XX–b, c) is also very much re-

The Thermae of Diocletian, Tepidarium. Drawing by Giov. Antonio Dosio, about 1563. Florence, Uffizi. (Cf. Plate XVII–b)

built. The commission to Michelangelo came from Cardinal Guido Ascanio Sforza. Most of the work was done by Michelangelo's assistant Tiberio Calcagni (who also worked on the Magdalen of the Florentine Pietà and finished the 'Brutus'); after Michelangelo's death, and the death of Calcagni (1565), Giacomo della Porta finished the Chapel in 1573. The Chapel had 'a façade within the church' with a portal designed by Michelangelo (see illustration on p. 224), but this was removed in 1748.

ATTRIBUTIONS

I. SCULPTURE. None of the many new attributions of the last forty years has had much success. There was first the 'Head of a Cyclops' in the Bargello,[1] a discovery of Adolfo Venturi (L'Arte, 1922, p. 177 f.); and then the 'Bozzetto of a Crouching Girl' in a private collection at Munich,[2] sponsored by Kieslinger ('Prussian Yearbook' 1928, p. 50 f.); but already doubted by Hekler in 'Wiener Jahrbuch für Kunstgeschichte', VII, 1930, p. 219). Tolnay has published twice (in 'Prussian Yearbook', 1933, p. 121 f.; and 'The Youth of Michelangelo', Princeton, 1947) a relief with the coat of arms of Pope Julius II in the Museo Civico, Bologna. He suggested that this relief was originally underneath the lost bronze statue of Julius II on the façade of San Petronio. Bertini ('Michelangelo fino alla Sistina', 1945, p. 25) has already protested against this attribution. A few more unsuccessful discoveries are mentioned in the foregoing note on the Lost Works. A marble group of Venus and Cupid in the Palazzo Vecchio at Florence was attributed to Michelangelo by Matteo Marangoni (1955). This sculpture is probably by the same hand as the *Cupid* (or *Narcissus*) in the Victoria and Albert Museum, formerly wrongly given to Michelangelo, now correctly to Vincenzo Danti. In Giovanni Papini's 'Vita di Michel-

agniolo nella vita del suo tempo', 6th edition, Milan, 1951, a new crop of finds is illustrated and discussed. One is the 'Head of Hercules', in the possession of a Polish sculptor in Paris; this head is supposed to be a fragment of Michelangelo's Hercules statue, which in the time of Henry IV was at Fontainebleau;[3] another find is a 'Bust of a Youth' in a private collection in Rome.[4]

II. PAINTING. Papini's third attribution concerns a painting in Santa Maria at Marcialla, near Florence, a 'Pietà'. This fresco was attributed to Michelangelo already by some scholars of the early eighteenth century, but since then it had been justly forgotten.[5]

---

[1] By some unknown sculptor of the Mannerist period.
[2] Perhaps by Vincenzo Danti.

[3] Papini, p. 54. To judge from the photograph, the poor work of a provincial Roman artist, or the copy after a Hellenistic sculpture without importance. Giovanni Antonio Gori, the Florentine archeologist, thought that he possessed the small model, about 4½ in. high, for the head of Michelangelo's 'Hercules' (Thode IV, 17).
[4] Papini, opp. p. 273. This bust is a copy from Michelangelo's 'Victory' in the Palazzo Vecchio. The technique of the copyist reminds one vaguely of Raffaelo da Montelupo's 'St Damian' in the Medici Chapel, and of his 'Prophet' on the Julius Monument, but this little bust shows even stronger relations with the work of Vincenzo Danti, who, as has been assumed, has done some work on Michelangelo's 'Victory'. (Plate 209).
[5] Papini, pp. 73–74, and opp. 53. Rather in the manner of Jacopo del Sellaio, but too weak to be by him. According to Stendhal (*Rome, Naples et Florence*; paragraph dated 25 October 1816), the Italians attributed at one time even the designs of their tarot cards to Michelangelo!

There is a group of paintings, not all of them by the same hand, which are at present by some writers considered as the earliest paintings by Michelangelo.[6] Here is a complete list (see Plates XXV–XXVII).

(1) *Pietà*. Rome, Galleria Nazionale, No. 948. (Zeri classes this painting in the same group as our Nos. 2–6, and attributes these seven pictures to Jacopo dell' Indaco. I agree with Zeri on the whole but believe that No. 7 is of a higher quality and probably by a different hand.)

(2) *Madonna with the Candelabrum*. Vienna, Academy, No. 1134. Ascribed to Michelangelo by Adolfo Venturi and Fiocco. Attributed to Antonio Mini by Anny Popp, and to Bugiardini by Berenson. (1932).

(3) *Madonna with Child and St John*. New York, private collection. (Formerly Florence, Conte Contini Bonacossi.) Fiocco's attribution.

(4) *Madonna and Child*. Private collection, Baden near Zurich. Fiocco's attribution.

(5) *Madonna and Child*. Florence, private collection. Fiocco's attribution ('Rivista d'arte', XXVI, 1950, p. 149).

(6) *The Manchester Madonna*. London, National Gallery, No. 809 (Plate XXV-a). Attributed to Michelangelo by Toesca (1934), Kenneth Clark (1938), Fiocco and Longhi (1941), Bertini (1945) and Johannes Wilde (1951). Not by Michelangelo according to Wölfflin, Frizzoni, Adolfo Venturi, Popp, Tolnay, and Dussler. Accepted by Berenson as a workshop production.

(7) *The Entombment*. London, National Gallery, No. 790 (Plate XXV–b). Attributed to Michelangelo by Fiocco, Longhi, Clark, Wilde, Gould, Berenson, Toesca, Bertini; but not by Wölfflin, Popp, Baumgart, Tolnay, Antal and Dussler.

(8) *St John the Evangelist*. Basle, private collection. Attributed to Michelangelo by Longhi, Fiocco, Nicodemi and Magugliani (1952).

(9) *Madonna with Child and St John in a Landscape*. Dublin. National Gallery of Ireland, No. 98. Attributed to Michelangelo by Fiocco. Correctly attributed to Francesco Granacci by Mary Logan, Gronau, Berenson and Zeri; this attribution is now almost generally accepted.

Nos. 1–8 are not all by the same hand. The pictures 6 and 7 are by far the best of the whole group. There is presently a pronounced tendency to attribute them to Michelangelo himself. This is, in my opinion, wrong. The 'Master of the Manchester Madonna' was apparently a Florentine painter influenced by Granacci and Bugiardini; between 1516 and 1534 he was inspired by Michelangelo, and probably worked in his studio at Florence, not necessarily as a painter.

[6] G. Fiocco, *La data di nascita di Francesco Granacci e un'ipotesi Michelangiolesca*, in 'Rivista d'arte', serie II, anno II, 1930, p. 193 f.; anno III, 1931, p. 109 f., 385 f. *Un'altra pittura giovanile di Michelangelo*, in 'Critica d'arte', anno II, 1937, fasc. X, p. 172 f. – *Sull'inizio pittorico di Michelangelo*, in 'Le Arti', anno IV, 1941, p. 5 f. – *Primizio di Michelangelo*, in 'Rivista d'arte', XXVI, 1950, p. 149 f. – R. Longhi, *A proposito dell'inizio pittorico di Michelangelo*, in 'Le Arti', anno IV, 1941, p. 136. – Cf. A. E. Popp, *Garzoni*, in 'Belvedere': VIII, 1925, p. 6f. – L. Magugliani in 'Annali', I, 1952, p. 20 f. – Federico Zeri, *Il Maestro della Madonna di Manchester*, in 'Paragone', 1953 July, pp. 15–27.

APPENDIX OF PLATES

b   c   d

e   f   g

PLATE I. *Models in clay and wax, all probably for the Julius monument.*
(*a*) Female statuette for a Victory group, clay. Casa Buonarroti. (*b*) Dark-red wax sketch for the 'Young Giant' (Plate 216). London, Victoria and Albert Museum. (*c*) Light wax sketch for a Captive. Casa Buonarroti. (*d*) Dark brown-red wax sketch for a Captive. Casa Buonarroti. (*e*) and (*g*) Front and back views of a wax sketch for a 'Giant'. Casa Buonarroti. (*f*) Clay sketch for a 'Giant'. Casa Buonarroti.

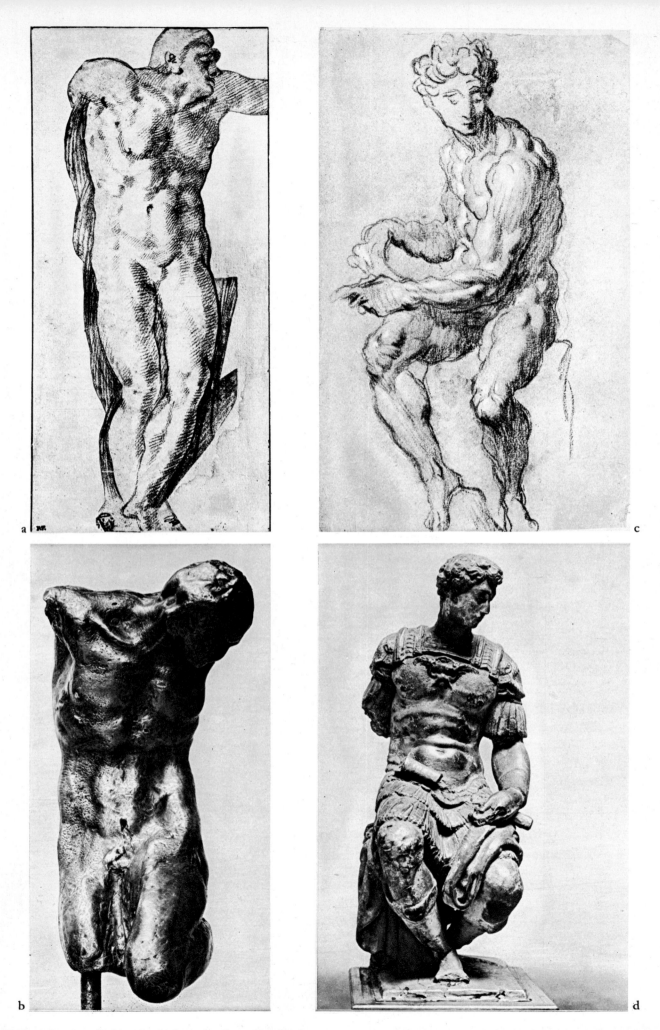

PLATE II. *After Lost Models*. (*a*) Thief on the Cross (drawing by Granacci after a Michelangelo model). Louvre. (*b*) Thief on the Cross, bronze cast from a wax model by Michelangelo. Berlin. (*c*) Drawing by Tintoretto after a lost model of Giuliano de' Medici by Michelangelo. Oxford, Christ Church. (*d*) Wax statuette of Giuliano de' Medici, by an imitator of Michelangelo, Edinburgh.

b

d

f

PLATE III. *The Problem of the Models for the Medici Chapel.* (*a*) Copy of Michelangelo's 'Notte', stucco, life size, by Vincenzo Danti, 1573. Perugia, Accademia. (*b*) Bronze copy of a model for the Madonna Medici. Louvre. (*c*) Terracotta copy by Tribolo of the 'Giorno'. Bargello. (*d*) Wax sketch for the 'Crepuscolo' by Michelangelo. British Museum.

(*e*) Detail of a drawing by Joseph Heintz, about 1592, after a model by Michelangelo for a 'River God'. Vienna, Albertina. (*f*) Detail of a drawing by Pierino da Vinci, about 1540, after a model for Michelangelo's 'River God'. London, Victor Koch Collection.

a

b

c

d

PLATE IV. *Designs and Models for the Medici Chapel*. (*a*) One of the sixteen marble reliefs with the Medici coat-of-arms. (*b*) Marble candelabrum
in the Medici Chapel. Designed by Michelangelo. (*c*) St. Cosmas, by
Giovanni Montorsoli; and (*d*) St. Damian, by Raffaello da Montelupo,
after models by Michelangelo. Florence, Medici Chapel. See Plate 169.

PLATE V. Terracotta models of 'Notte' and 'Aurora'. (Attributed to Michelangelo by L. Planiscig, E. Sandberg-Vavalà and O. H. Giglioli.)
Caracas, Venezuela, Dr. Alejandro Pietri Collection.

PLATE VI. The Medici Chapel, Florence.

PLATE VII. The Lantern on the Cupola of the Medici Chapel, 1524–1525, designed by Michelangelo.

a

b

PLATE VIII. (*a*) The Reading Room of the Biblioteça Laurenziana, Florence. (*b*) Desks in the Reading Room of the Biblioteca Laurenziana, carved by Battista del Cinque and Ciappino, 1534, after sketches by Michelangelo.

PLATE IX. *Ornamentation in the Reading Room of the Biblioteca Laurenziana.*
(*a*) Detail of the pavement, by Tribolo and Sante Buglioni.

(*b*) Detail from the carved ceiling, by Battista del Tasso and Antonio Carota, 1534.

PLATE IX. (*c*) One of the wooden reliefs on the desks (cf. Plate VIII–b).

PLATE X. *Ornamentation on the Tabernacle of the Julius Monument.* (*a*) to (*d*) The four reliefs on the front, by Antonio del Pontasieve, 1513, after drawings by Michelangelo. (*e*) and (*f*) The two lower reliefs inside the niche of Moses.

PLATE XI. *Ornamentation on the Tabernacle of the Julius Monument.* (*a*) and (*b*) Two halves of archivolts above the niches of Rachel and Leah. (*c*) and (*d*) The two upper reliefs inside the niche of Moses, by Antonio del Pontasieve, after sketches by Michelangelo.

a

e

b

c

d

f

PLATE XII. *Designs for pavements.* (*a*) Detail of a Roman floor mosaic, about A.D. 100. Rome, Museo Nazionale. (*b*) Detail of the floor of the Florence Baptistery, about 1225. (*c*) Detail of a marble intarsia, dated 1157. Faltona, S. Felicità. (*d*) Ornamental rosette for parquetry, woodcut by Dürer, published 1525. (*e*) and (*f*) Pavements, designed by Michelangelo. (*e*) The ornamental pavement of the Piazza del Campidoglio, Rome, designed 1546. (*f*) Detail of the pavement in the Biblioteca Laurenziana, designed in 1524.

PLATE XIII. (*a*) Partial view of the inside of the Cupola of the Pantheon, Roman, about A.D. 110. (Detail of a painting by Paolo Pannini in the National Gallery of Art, Washington.) (*b*) Inside of the Cupola of the Medici Chapel, built by Michelangelo, 1523–1524.

PLATE XIV. *Masks.* (*a*) Shouting head above the niche of Leah, from the tomb of Julius, about 1514 (cf. Plate 238). (*b*) Mask on the archivolt keystone of the Porta Pia, Rome, about 1562. Detail of Plate 270.

(*c*) A capital in the Medici Chapel, about 1524. Detail of Plate 169. (*d*) A capital on the Palazzo dei Conservatori, about 1546. Detail of Plate 254.

PLATE XV. *Details from the original frame of the Madonna Doni.* (*a*) and (*b*) Heads of Prophets. (*c*) and (*d*) Heads of Sibyls.

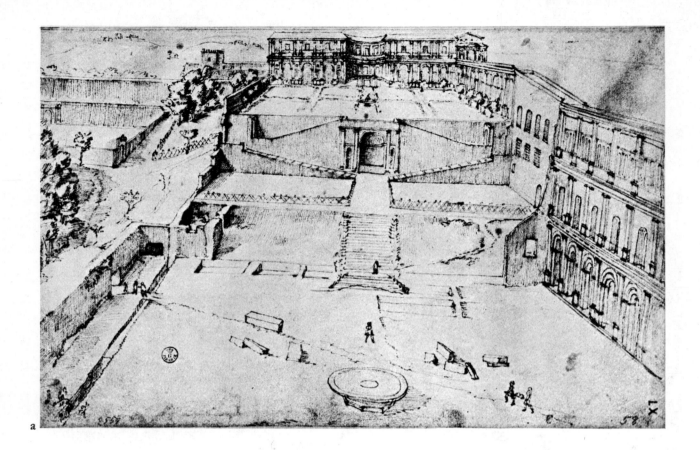

a

b

PLATE XVI. *Nicchione del Belvedere* (cf. Plate 261). (*a*) Pen and ink drawing, about 1560, by Giovanantonio Dosio. Florence, Uffizi. (*b*) Engraving by Ambrogio Brambilla, 1579. Rome, Print Room in the Palazzo Corsini.

PLATE XVII. (*a*) The Thermae of Diocletian, converted into the Church of Santa Maria degli Angeli. Begun by Michelangelo, 1563. Between the arches on the east side of the Thermae part of the portal of the Basilica, built by Michelangelo, can be seen. Detail of an engraving by Alò Giavannoli, about 1610. (*b*) The transept of Santa Maria degli Angeli, Rome, in the present state, rebuilt by Vanvitelli in 1749.

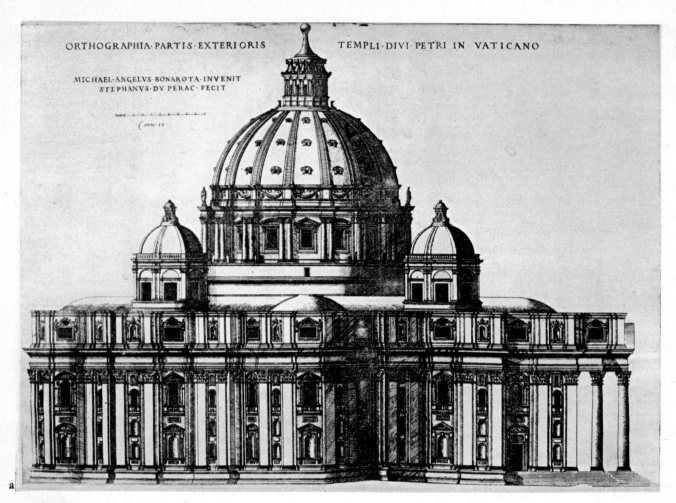

ORTHOGRAPHIA·PARTIS·EXTERIORIS   TEMPLI·DIVI·PETRI·IN·VATICANO

MICHAEL·ANGELVS·BONAROTA·INVENIT
STEPHANVS·DV·PERAC·FECIT

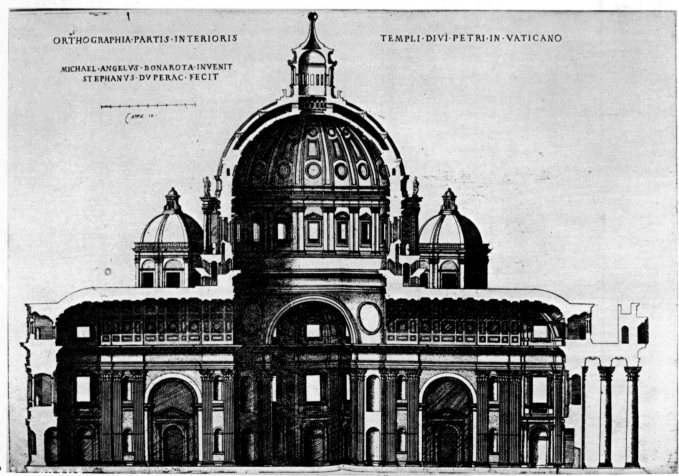

ORTHOGRAPHIA·PARTIS·INTERIORIS   TEMPLI·DIVI·PETRI·IN·VATICANO

MICHAEL·ANGELVS·BONAROTA·INVENIT
STEPHANVS·DV·PERAC·FECIT

PLATE XVIII. Michelangelo's designs for St. Peter's, engravings by Etienne du Pérac, 1569. (Vienna, Albertina)

PLATE XIX. Interior of the Model for the Cupola of St. Peter's. (cf. Plate 272.)
(This large wooden model, finished by Michelangelo in 1561, was altered by Giacomo della Porta about 1576–1578.)

a

b

c

PLATE XX. (*a*) The tomb of Cecchino Bracci, by Francesco Urbino, from a design by Michelangelo, 1545. Rome, Santa Maria in Araceli.
(*b*) and (*c*) The Sforza Chapel in Santa Maria Maggiore, Rome, by Tiberio Calcagni, about 1559–1565, finished by Giacomo della Porta, 1573.

a

c

b

d

PLATE XXI. (*a*) A capital on the Palazzo dei Conservatori, about 1546. Detail from Plate 254. (*b*) A window in the Medici Chapel, about 1520–1523. Detail from Plate 169. (*c*) and (*d*) Windows on the Porta Pia, about 1562. Details from Plate 270.

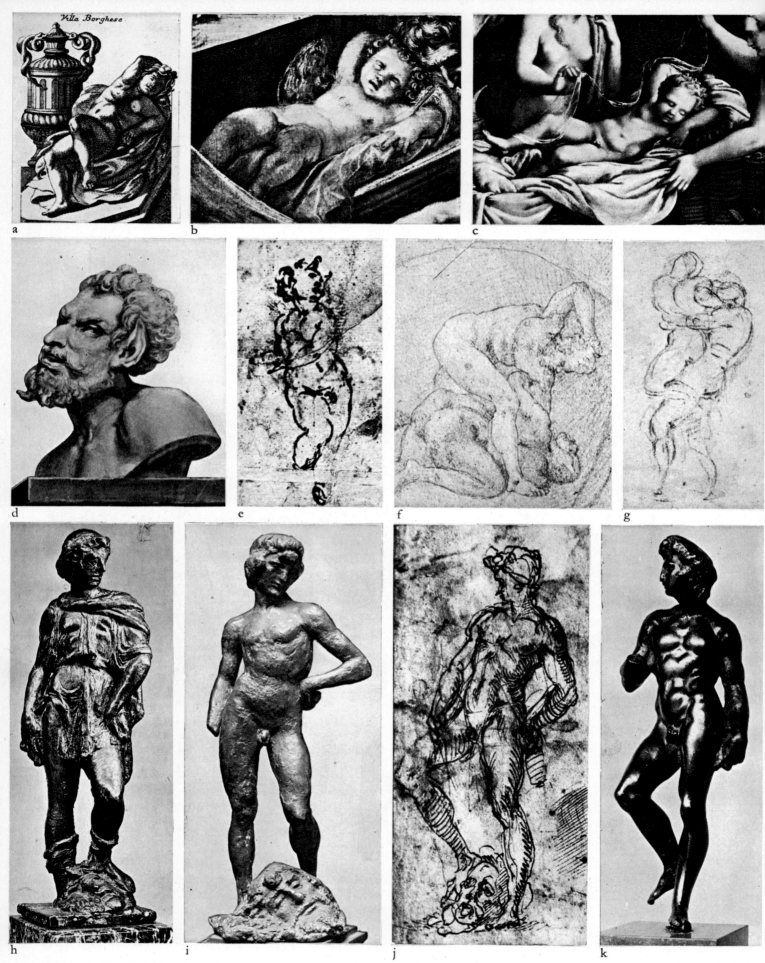

PLATE XXII. *Lost Sculptures.* (*a–c*) Michelangelo's 'Sleeping Cupid'. (*a*) The antique model, after an engraving in Montfaucon's 'L'Antiquité expliquée, 1720. (*b*) Detail from Tintoretto's 'Mars and Venus', about 1545, in the Pinakothek, Munich. (*c*) Detail from Giulio Romano's 'The Infancy of Jupiter', about 1535. London, National Gallery. (*d*) Michelangelo's 'Head of a Faun'. Detail from a fresco by Ottavio Vannini in the Palazzo Pitti, Florence, about 1640. (*e*) The 'Giovannino'. Detail of a drawing by Michel-angelo (about 1505, Louvre; cf. Plate XXV–a). (*f*) and (*g*) Sketches for lost models (Details of drawings from about 1525; British Museum, BB. 1688 and 1490), 'Hercules and Cacus' and 'Hercules and Antaeus'. (*h–k*) Michel-angelo's lost 'Bronze David'. (*h*) Donatello workshop, bronze statuette of David, Berlin. (*i*) Bronze statuette in the Louvre (cast from a wax by Michel-angelo?). (*j*) Detail of a Michelangelo drawing, 1502, Louvre. (*k*) Bronze statuette, about 1530, Amsterdam.

PLATE XXIII. *Samson fighting the Philistines; Hercules and Cacus.* (*a*) Bronze by Pierino da Vinci after a model by Michelangelo (about 1528). New York, Frick Collection. (*b*) A lost model by Michelangelo (in a Flemish replica perhaps by Adriaen de Vries). Detail from a Self-portrait by Gerard Dou, 1647. Dresden, Gallery. (*c*) A group similar to *b*, Flemish replica. Detail from *The Young Draughtsman*, by an unknown Dutch painter, about 1650. Brussels, Museum. (*d*) Terracotta model by Jean de Boulogne, about 1550. Tournai, Museum.

PLATE XXIV. Aristotile da Sangallo (1542): Copy after Michelangelo's cartoon for the 'Battle of Cascina'. Holkham Hall, Earl of Leicester.

PLATE XXV. 'The Master of the Manchester Madonna': Two paintings in the National Gallery, London. (*a*) Madonna and Child with St. John; (*b*) Entombment. (Attributed to Michelangelo by Fiocco, Longhi, Toesca, Kenneth Clark, Bertini, d'Ancona; but not by Wölfflin, A. Venturi, Popp, Antal, Baumgart and Tolnay.)

PLATE XXVI. *Four Madonnas.* (Attributed to Michelangelo by Fiocco and others.) (*a*) Vienna, Akademie. (*b*) New York, Private Collection.
(*c*) Baden near Zurich, Private Collection. (*d*) Florence, Private Collection.

PLATE XXVII. (*a*) Unknown assistant of Michelangelo: Painting based on Michelangelo's Pietà of St. Peter's. (*b*) The
Holy Family with St. John, by Granacci (wrongly attributed to Michelangelo), National Gallery of Ireland, Dublin.
(*c*) St. John the Evangelist in a Landscape, Basle, Private collection. (Attributed to Michelangelo by Longhi, Fiocco,
Nicodemi and Magugliani.)

PLATE XXVIII. The youthful Michelangelo collaborating on Ghirlandaio's frescoes in Santa Maria Novella, Florence, 1488. Four examples of attributions to Michelangelo: (a) Detail from 'The Visitation of the Virgin'. (b) Detail from 'The Virgin on her way to the Temple'. (c) Detail from 'The Assumption of the Virgin'. (d) Detail from 'The Baptism of Christ'.

PLATE XXIX. Two details from the Paolina Frescoes; photographed during the last restoration (1933) and showing the painting without any retouchings (cf. Plates 249–250, showing the present state).

PLATE XXX. Copy after Michelangelo's 'Last Judgement', by Marcello Venusti, executed in 1549 (before Daniele da Volterra had painted over the nudes). Naples, Capodimonte, Gallery.

PLATE XXXI. Descent from the Cross. Plaster cast from a lost wax relief by Michelangelo, about 1540–1542. Florence, Casa Buonarroti.

PLATE XXXII. (*a*) First version of Michelangelo's Pietà in the Florence Duomo. Wax. Florence, Gigli Collection. (*b*) Entombment, wax relief by an unknown pupil of Michelangelo (Pierino da Vinci?), about 1560, Berlin.

The models, Plates I–V, are discussed on pp. 222–223. Plate III–a is a stucco copy, in the same size as the marble statue; freely made, not a cast; one of a set of four.

Plate IV–c shows St Cosmas, the model for which, as Vasari relates, was made by Montorsoli himself, but Michelangelo reworked it extensively; clay sketches for the head and the arms of Cosmas were in Vasari's possession. The life-size model for St Damian was entirely by Michelangelo.

For Plates VI and VII see the notes on Plates 169–205 on p. 17.

Plate VI. According to Vasari, the New Sacristy was built from designs by Michelangelo. Johannes Wilde (*Michelangelo's Designs for the Medici Tombs*, in 'Journal of the Warburg and Courtauld Institutes', 1955, p. 54 f.) accepts this statement as correct; one of his proofs is a sketch by Leonardo which shows the north transept of the church without a sacristy (Manuscript L, folio 15 verso, datable 1502–03).

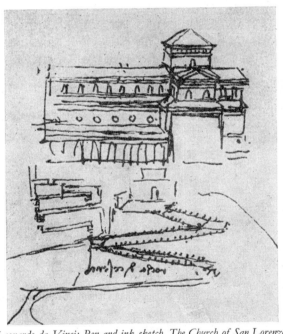

Leonardo da Vinci: Pen and ink sketch, The Church of San Lorenzo. Paris, Institut de France.

The reasons for and against Wilde's theory are analysed by James S. Ackerman (*The Architecture of Michelangelo*, London 1961, Catalogue, p. 23).

Plate VII. 'The lantern is Michelangelo's only important contribution to the exterior of the chapel' (Prof. Ackerman).

For Plates VIII and IX see the note on Plate 161 on p. 16 f. For Plates X and XI see the notes on the Tomb of Julius, p. 14.

Plate XII is a commentary, by means of illustrations, on Michelangelo's two designs for pavements, one for the floor of the Biblioteca Laurenziana, the other, twenty years later, for the Piazza del Campidoglio – two ornamental rosettes of similar design. This design was not invented by Michelangelo, but goes back to antiquity (Plate XII–a), was used in the Middle Ages (Plate XII–b and c) and later by Dürer, who gives such a rosette in woodcut No. 21 of his work 'Underweysung der messung mit dem zirckel und richtscheyt'. The rosette of the pavement of the Piazza del Campidoglio is not circular, but elliptical; it follows however the same pattern.

Plate XIII shows that the dome of the Medici Chapel has an ancient prototype.

Plate XIV shows, in four illustrations, a single strain of Michelangelo's inventiveness, the masks. See also Plates 11, 188, 190, 193.

Plate XV shows details from the original frame of the Doni Madonna (cf. note 11 on p. 11). The frame was, in my opinion, designed by Michelangelo himself, or at least the five heads. Elfried Bock (*Florentinische und venezianische Bilderrahmen*, Munich 1902, p. 78 f.) believes that the frame was executed in Siena. As Michelangelo worked on the statues for the Piccolomini altar in Siena from 1501 until 1504 – the period during which he also painted the Doni Madonna – he was in close touch with Sienese craftsmen and may have entrusted one of them with the carving of the frame.

For Plate XVI see text on p. 22.

Plate XVII is discussed on p. 225.

For Plates XVIII and XIX see text on p. 23.

Plate XX–a. Cecchino Bracci, the nephew of Michelangelo's friend Luigi del Riccio, died on 8 January 1545 at the age of fifteen. Michelangelo wrote fifty short epitaphs and, in a sonnet, promised a tomb with the boy's portrait. He made the design, which Urbino executed to the best of his ability.

For Plates XX–b and c see text on p. 225.

For Plate XXI see the notes on Plates 169, 253 and 270.

Plate XXII, which shows lost sculptures by Michelangelo, is discussed on p. 223 f.

Plate XXII–h. Leo Planiscig (*Piccoli Bronzi Italiani del Rinascimento*, Milan 1930, ill. No. 5) ascribed this statuette, a rough cast from a wax, to Donatello himself; but not the Martelli David in the Johnson collection, a life-size marble statue based on this small bronze ('Phoebus' II, 2, p. 55 f., Basle 1949).

Plate XXII–i. Thode (VI, p. 285, No. 606) accepted this bronze as a cast from a genuine Michelangelo model, 'the first sketch for the bronze David, based on Donatello'. Wilhelm Boeck (*Michelangelos Bronzedavid und die Pulszky-Statuette im Louvre* in 'Mitteilungen des Kunsthistorischen Instituts in Florenz', VIII, 1959, p. 131 f.) has given good reasons for this opinion. A slightly larger cast from the same model was formerly in the collection of Victor Koch, London, who sold it to a collector in South Africa.

Plate XXII–j. This famous Michelangelo drawing is the only trace left of the lost Bronze David.

Plate XXII–k. Thode (VI, p. 266, No. 557) called this statuette 'the final model for the Bronze David'. This opinion can hardly be defended any longer and the illustration is given here only for the reason that it cannot easily be found anywhere else.

XXIII–a. This bronze is connected with the clay sketch, Plate 206; several other bronzes of this group are extant, the two best known ones are in the Bargello, Florence; they are correctly ascribed to Pierino da Vinci (Vasari-Milanesi, VI, 128). Tintoretto apparently owned an original clay sketch of this group by Michelangelo and made numerous drawings from it (see Tietze, *The Drawings of the Venetian Painters*, 1944: Tintoretto drawings 1559, 1564, 1567, 1666, 1679, 1707, 1708, 1733, 1734 and 1741).

Plate XXIV is mentioned on p. 224.

Plates XXV–XXVII are discussed on p. 226.

Plate XXVIII: Since Michelangelo entered Ghirlandaio's workshop at the age of thirteen (and stayed for less than one year), most biographers have wondered on which of Ghirlandaio's frescoes he may have collaborated. Padre Fineschi (K. Frey, *Michelangniolo Buonarroti: Quellen und Forschungen*, vol. I, Berlin 1907, p. 18) thought he could recognize Michelangelo's hand in the boys leaning over the balustrade of the terrace of San Miniato (Plate XXVIII–a). Another attribution is mentioned by Raimond van Marle (*Italian Schools of Painting*, The Hague 1931, vol. XIII, p. 73), though he attributes this figure (XXVIII–b) to David Ghirlandaio. The question has been discussed by Giuseppe Marchini (*Burlington Magazine*, October 1953, pp. 320–331) after the recent cleaning of the frescoes of Santa Maria Novella. Two details reproduced here (XXVII–c and d) are examples of Marchini's attributions.

Plate XXIX contains two important illustrations. When they are compared with the colour plates 249 and 250, the true condition of the paintings can be recognized. The monochrome illustrations, made from photographs taken during the restorations of 1933 when the paintings were stripped of all retouches, leave no doubt about the bad state of preservation of the frescoes. The colour plates, made from photographs taken in 1953, show the present state, with the damage newly overpainted.

Plate XXX is mentioned on p. 20. According to Johannes Wilde (*Burlington Magazine*, Nov. 1959, p. 373) Venusti painted this copy 'obviously not from the fresco itself but from one of his own famous drawings after the fresco'; he took many liberties and gave St Peter the features of the Farnese Pope Paul III.

Plate XXXI. This relief ($12\frac{1}{4} \times 9\frac{1}{2}$ in.) is related to a drawing at Haarlem (Frey 330) and a number of reliefs. For a list of replicas see Thode V, p. 481 f., and Ulrich Middeldorf & Oswald Goetz, *Medals and Plaquettes from the Sigmund Morgenroth Collection (Santa Barbara, California)*, Chicago 1944, p. 43, No. 309.

For Plate XXXII–a: see Thode V, 276 and VI, 282. This wax sketch ($7\frac{5}{8}$ in. high) agrees with the engraving by Cherubino Alberti (B. XVII, 23, about 1580) and reproduces the Florentine *Pietà* (Plate 262) before it was reworked by Calcagni. Note the left leg of Christ.

Plate XXXII–b. With a faked signature; but the relief is probably based on a lost Michelangelo design. Frida Schottmüller (1933) attributed it, wrongly, to Vincenzo de' Rossi, but pointed out that (according to Gramberg) it is stylistically related to the Palestrina Pietà (Plate 268) and to the Pietà relief in the Vatican (Tolnay, *Michelangiolo*, Florence 1951, pl. 388). Middeldorf identified this assistant with Pierino da Vinci.

The fibula on the toga of Brutus (see plate 241).

INDEX TO THE PLATES

INDEX TO THE PLATES

I. ARCHITECTURE

II. PAINTINGS

III. SCULPTURES

IV. MODELS

Roman Figures refer to the Plates in the Appendix.

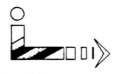

MICHELANGELO
COMPLETE EDITION

PHAIDON

TOMB OF GIULIANO DE' MEDICI · FLORENCE